DESIGNED TO BE LIKE HIM

Also by J. Dwight Pentecost

Design for Discipleship
Design for Living
The Divine Comforter
Faith That Endures
The Joy of Living
Life's Problems—God's Solutions
The Parables of Jesus
Things Which Become Sound Doctrine
Thy Kingdom Come
Your Adversary, the Devil

DESIGNED TO BE LIKE HIM

Understanding God's Plan for Fellowship, Conduct, Conflict, and Maturity

J. Dwight Pentecost

kregel
PUBLICATIONS

Grand Rapids, MI 49501

Designed to Be Like Him: Understanding God's Plan for Fellowship, Conduct, Conflict, and Maturity

© 1966 by J. Dwight Pentecost

Published by Kregel Publications, a division of Kregel, Inc., P.O. Box 2607, Grand Rapids, MI 49501. For more information about Kregel Publications, visit our web site: www.kregel.com.

Library of Congress Cataloging-in-Publication Data
Pentecost, J. Dwight.
    Designed to be like Him: understanding God's plan for fellowship, conduct, conflict, and maturity / J. Dwight Pentecost.
        p.   cm.
Originally published: [Chicago, Ill.]: Moody, 1966.
    1. Christian life–Biblical teaching. 2. Jesus Christ–Example–Biblical teacing. I. Title.
BS2545 .C48 P46   2001   248.4–dc21   2001029023
                                                                CIP

ISBN 0-8254-3465-3

Printed in the United States of America

1 2 3 4 5 / 05 04 03 02 01

Contents

III. DESIGN FOR CONFLICT

IV. DESIGN FOR MATURITY

INTRODUCTION

"Christ liveth in me." How great is the affirmation by Paul, yet how little understood and how much less appropriated by the average Christian today.

The Word of God has much to say about the "things which pertain unto godliness" (II Peter 1:3). It presents "doctrine which is according to godliness" (I Tim. 6:3) and exhorts us to "follow after righteousness, godliness, . . ." (I Tim. 6:11). It challenges us to "exercise . . . (ourselves) unto godliness" (I Tim. 4:7). Godliness is God's standard for His child.

The natural man is a complex individual. How much more complex is the child of God, to whom God has imparted a new divine nature (II Peter 1:4). Many believers fall short of God's standard in daily life because they have not been instructed in the principles of the Word of God. They do not understand themselves. They have no concept of the enormity of the conflict in which they are engaged. They have not learned the value of the death of Christ in its relation to deliverance from dominion by sin. They have never discovered the principles of the Word of God which govern Christian conduct. They have not seen the steps to maturity in Christian experience.

The truths in this book, prepared for the average reader, are gleaned from study of the Word of God and are designed to be truths unto godliness (Titus 1:1). They were prepared for my students at the Dallas Theological Seminary and for the congregation at Grace Bible Church in Dallas. The response has been so gratifying that the author felt encouraged to prepare them for a wider audience. The work of Mrs. Paul Allen and Mrs. Offie Bayless, who labored diligently in preparation of this manuscript, is gratefully acknowledged.

7

May the Lord Jesus Christ, who lives in believers, be pleased to speak through these pages to bring many to a knowledge of His indwelling presence and power, so that they might "war a good warfare" (I Tim. 1:18) and "put on the new man, which after God is created in righteousness and true holiness" (Eph. 4:24).

J. DWIGHT PENTECOST

Thou art calling me, Lord Jesus,
   As Thy living witness here.
Only by Thy life within me
   Can I any witness bear.

Thou art calling me, Lord Jesus,
   To be working one with Thee.
Only by Thy life within me
   Can there any service be.

Thou art calling me, Lord Jesus,
   To prevailing power in prayer.
Only by Thy life within me
   Can I intercession share.

Thou art calling me, Lord Jesus,
   To a victor's holy life.
Only by Thy life within me
   Is there conquest in the strife.

Fill me, Holy Spirit, fill me,
   All Thy filling would I know.
I am smallest of Thy vessels,
   Yet I much can overflow.

—LEWIS SPERRY CHAFER

PART
I

DESIGN FOR FELLOWSHIP

1

GOD'S PURPOSE FOR HIS CHILD

I Corinthians 6:19-20

THE GREATEST THEME with which the mind and the heart of the child of God can be occupied is the theme of the glory of God. Our Father, who has imparted Himself to us in the Person of Jesus Christ and revealed Himself in His Son, has revealed Himself as a God of glory. The glory of God occupies the attention of heaven, and the earth was created for the manifestation and the revelation of the glory of God. And created intelligences who recognize the perfection of God's Person, His attributes, and His character give Him glory when they serve, honor, worship, adore, and praise Him. And we should take special note that "the chief end of man is to glorify God, and to enjoy Him forever."

The theme of the glory of God runs throughout the Word of God. God's method of revealing His glory is to take lowly things, things that have no glory in themselves, and to transform them and use them as instruments to reveal His glory so that He may be glorified. God may use material things, God may use created beings, God may use His own Son for the purpose of glorifying His name.

CREATION

When we consider creation, we find that it was designed to be an instrument to bring honor and glory to God. Psalm 19:1 extols God and proclaims that "the heavens declare the glory of God; and the firmament sheweth his handiwork." The Apostle Paul, writing to the Colossians, reminds us in 1:16: "By him were all things created, that are in heaven, that are in earth, visible

and invisible, whether they be thrones, or dominions, or principalities, or powers: all things were created by him, and for him."

Note the last words of that verse, that "all things were created
for him." Creation was brought into existence not only for the
benefit of the creatures who one day would walk upon the face
of the earth but for God's glory. This universe was created that
it should bear testimony to, and reflect the glory of, an all-glori-
ous God. Men can learn much of the power and the wisdom of
God from creation.

IN THE GARDEN

Yet as we go back to the first chapters of Genesis, we find not
only that creation was designed to bring glory to God but that
God personally manifested Himself to Adam in the Garden of
Eden. In Genesis 3:8 we read: "They heard the voice of the LORD
God walking in the garden in the cool of the day: and Adam and
his wife hid themselves from the presence of the LORD God
amongst the trees of the Garden." If we understand Genesis 3:8
aright, Adam and Eve knew of the personal presence of God in
their midst not only by the sound of His voice but by the sight
of a manifestation of His glory. Throughout the Word, when
God would reveal Himself to men, He demonstrated His presence by the manifestation of His Shekinah glory, that resplendent
shining of the light of His own Person. It seems to have been
God's purpose to come into the garden to manifest Himself to
Adam and Eve in order that they might recognize Him as the
glorious God, and as a result they would adore and glorify Him,
thus bringing satisfaction to His heart.

But this mode of manifesting His glory, this manner of get-
ting glory to Himself, was of temporary duration. Adam and Eve
rebelled against the command of God and were expelled from
the Garden of Eden. They were no longer fit for the presence of
God; they were unfit even for the place where God's glory had
been manifested. We read in Genesis 3:23-24: "The LORD God sent
him forth from the garden of Eden, to till the ground from
whence he was taken. So he drove out the man; and he placed at
the east of the garden of Eden Cherubims, and a flaming sword
which turned every way, to keep the way of the tree of life."

It seems as though God established a place of sacrifice outside the garden. As cherubim were later to overshadow the mercy seat, so here cherubim watched over this meeting place between God and man. But at this place of sacrifice was seen the flaming sword, a visible manifestation of the glory of God in whose brilliance they had walked before they fell, and a reminder that they were separated from the glory of God by an instrument of death and judgment.

MOSES

In Exodus 33 we read how God took that humble man Moses and so transformed him by the manifestation of His glory that he became an instrument to reveal the glory of God. We read in Exodus 33:18 that Moses, after receiving the greatest revelation of the holiness of God given since the fall, presented this petition to God: "I beseech thee, show me thy glory." And God said, "I will make all my goodness pass before thee." The manifestation of the very goodness of God would be the manifestation of His glory and bring glory to God. God said, "I will proclaim the name of the LORD before thee, and will be gracious to whom I will be gracious, and will shew mercy on whom I will shew mercy." That which would bring glory to God was the manifestation of His grace and mercy as it was revealed to Moses and to a sinning guilty people.

"And he said, Thou canst not see my face: for there shall no man see me, and live. And the LORD said, Behold, there is a place by me, and thou shalt stand upon a rock: and it shall come to pass, while my glory passeth by, that I will put thee in a clift of the rock, and will cover thee with my hand while I pass by: and I will take away mine hand, and thou shalt see my back parts: but my face shall not be seen" (Exodus 33:20-23). You will get the force of what God said if you read the last verse this way: "I will take away my hand, and thou shalt see my afterglow." Or the verse might be rendered: "Thou shalt see my radiance, my effulgence, but my face shall not be seen."

When Moses asked God for a manifestation of His glory, God said He would secrete His servant in the cleft of the rock and would cover him so that he could not see the face of God, but would open His fingers so that the light of the glory of God could shine through. Continuing in Exodus 34:5, we read: "And the Lord descended in the cloud, and stood with him there, and proclaimed the name of the Lord." The name of the Lord was manifested to Moses as he beheld the goodness, mercy, and grace of God. Moses' response would bring glory to God.

The result of this revelation was a transformation, which we read about in Exodus 34:29-30: "And it came to pass, when Moses came down from mount Sinai with the two tables of testimony in Moses' hand, when he came down from the mount, that Moses wist not that the skin of his face shone while he talked with him. And when Aaron and all the children of Israel saw Moses, behold, the skin of his face shone; and they were afraid to come nigh him." This was not an inherent glory that belonged to Moses but the manifestation of the glory of God which permeated the person of Moses. He reflected the glory which he had beheld when God opened His fingers and revealed His effulgence or His afterglow.

And yet as Moses was speaking, "he put a vail on his face. But when Moses went in before the Lord to speak with him, he took the vail off, until he came out. And he came out, and spake unto the children of Israel that which he was commanded. And the children of Israel saw the face of Moses, that the skin of Moses' face shone: and Moses put the vail upon his face again, until he went in to speak with him" (vv. 33-35). There was open-faced communion between God and Moses, but Moses put the veil between himself and those to whom he spoke.

The Apostle Paul speaks of this in II Corinthians 3:13: "Not as Moses, which put a vail over his face, that the children of Israel could not stedfastly look to the end of that which is abolished." Paul tells why Moses veiled his face. It was not that Israel could not behold the glory of God, but that this glory given to the face of Moses was a passing, transitory, temporary manifestation of the glory of God. Moses realized that the glory would pass away, and he veiled his face so that Israel should not see the passing of that glory.

THE TABERNACLE

After a time the face of Moses no longer reflected the glory of

God. God was no longer using this transformed individual as a vehicle for the manifestation of His glory. Next He used the Tabernacle, which was built according to His directions, as the instrument to manifest His glory. When the construction was completed, "a cloud covered the tent of the congregation, and the glory of the LORD filled the tabernacle. And Moses was not able to enter into the tent of the congregation, because the cloud abode thereon, and the glory of the LORD filled the tabernacle" (Exodus 40:34-35). The Tabernacle had no external beauty. It had animal skin coverings on the outside which soon became weather-beaten, dull in color, and unattractive to the human eye. But God used that which was unattractive and which had no glory of itself as the instrument through which He would reveal His glory to the nation Israel.

When God manifested His glory, there was an outshining of His glory in a radiance that could not be hidden. When the priest walked into the Holy Place and passed beyond the veil into the Holy of Holies, his attention was not arrested by the blood-encrusted mercy seat, which could hardly be attractive to the natural eye. That which would attract his attention was the manifestation of the Shekinah glory of God between the Cherubim. Because he was standing in the place where the glory of God was being manifested, all else would become insignificant as he went about the ritual of offering the blood.

When the children of Israel looked at the Tabernacle, it must have been transformed by the Shekinah glory that dwelt within it. The beauty and the attractiveness were not in the animal-skin coverings but in the manifested glory of God.

THE TEMPLE

When the Tabernacle no longer served the needs of God's people, after they had become settled inhabitants in the land of promise, David was minded to build a temple for the Lord. However, God did not permit David to construct the Temple, because he had been a man of war. But the Lord told David that a Temple was to be built by a son to be born unto him who was to be named Solomon, who would be a man of peace. David collected materials for building the Temple and gave instructions concerning "the house that is to be builded for the LORD." He said it "must be exceeding magnifical, of fame and glory throughout all countries" (I Chron. 22:5).

The record of the dedication of the Temple is found in I Kings 8. Here we read, in verse 10, "It came to pass, when the priests were come out of the holy place, that the cloud filled the house of the LORD, so that the priests could not stand to minister because of the cloud: for the glory of the LORD had filled the house of the LORD." God, in His condescending grace, had moved into this building made with human hands that He might use it as a place in which to manifest His glory. The Temple must have been one of the most spectacular of all buildings ever erected, for Solomon used multiplied millions of dollars of·gold to adorn the Temple. However, it was not the architecture nor the abundant use of gold and silver and costly stones that brought glory to God but it was the manifestation of the presence of God in the Shekinah glory.

The reaction of the Queen of Sheba to the beauty of the Temple is recorded in II Chronicles 9:3-6: "When the queen of Sheba had seen the wisdom of Solomon, and the house that he had built, . . . and his ascent by which he went up into the house of the LORD; there was no more spirit in her. And she said to the king, It was a true report which I heard in mine own land of thine acts, and of thy wisdom: howbeit I believed not their words, until I came and mine eyes had seen it: and, behold, the one half of the greatness of thy wisdom was not told me: for thou exceedest the fame that I heard." The Temple, erected to be a place where God's glory would be manifested, had degenerated to a place which manifested only the wisdom and the honor of Solomon. Therefore it became necessary for God to judge this place designed for His use but now prostituted to bring glory to the builder rather than to God who manifested His glory there.

When we come to the prophecy of Ezekiel, we find the record of the departure of the glory of God from the nation Israel. The prophet is taken into the Temple, and in the place that was to have been occupied by the altar of sacrifice, the meeting place between God and man, there had been erected what the prophet calls an "image of jealousy." Next Ezekiel is told to look inside

the Temple, into the sanctuary. There he finds the walls deco-
rated with all the heathen idols of the nations round about. As
the prophet listens, he hears women weeping from Tammuz.
They are following the practices of worshipers of the Babylonian,
Assyrian, Phoenician, and Egyptian gods. The Temple, which
had been set apart to bring glory to God, had now been set apart
to the glory of Belial.

In Ezekiel 10:3-4 we read, "Now the cherubims stood on the
right side of the house, when the man went in; and the cloud
filled the inner court. Then the glory of the LORD went up from
the cherub, and stood over the threshold of the house; and the
house was filled with the cloud, and the court was full of the
brightness of the LORD's glory." The Shekinah glory which
came to occupy the sanctuary of the Temple, had departed from
the sanctuary and was seen over the threshold of the door of
the Temple itself. Next the glory departed from the threshold
and stood over the east gate, as described in verses 18 and 19:
"The glory of the LORD departed from off the threshold of the
house, and stood over the cherubims. And the cherubims lifted
up their wings, and mounted up from the earth in my sight:
when they went out, the wheels also were beside them, and everyone stood at the door of the east gate of the LORD's house."

A further step in the departure of the glory is seen in Ezekiel
11:22-23, where we read that Ezekiel saw "the cherubims lift
up their wings, and the wheels beside them; and the glory of the
God of Israel was over them above. And the glory of the LORD
went up from the midst of the city, and stood upon the mountain
which is on the east side of the city." Now the glory has gone to
the Mount of Olives, outside the city and away from the sanctuary area entirely.

The prophet next sees the glory leave the land entirely and
depart into Chaldea (v. 24). Over the city and the sanctuary
could be written Ichabod, meaning, "the glory has departed."

After God's people went into exile, a remnant returned to their
land and built another temple—a humble edifice compared to
the one Solomon had built. But God spoke to His people through
the mouth of the prophet Haggai, saying, "Yet once, it is a little
while, and I will shake the heavens, and the earth, and the sea,

and the dry land; and I will shake all nations, and the desire of all nations shall come: and I will fill this house with glory, saith the LORD of hosts. The silver is mine, and the gold is mine, saith the LORD of hosts. The glory of this latter house shall be greater than the former, saith the LORD of hosts: and in this place will I give peace, saith the LORD of hosts" (Hag. 2:6-9). God thus promised that the glory of God which had departed from Solomon's Temple, would come to the Temple they had erected, and they would again see the manifestation of the Shekinah glory of God in their midst.

THE PERSON OF CHRIST

It is not until we turn to the New Testament that we read of the coming of this glory to the people of God. In John 1:14 John testifies that "the Word was made flesh, and dwelt among us, (and we beheld his glory, the glory as of the only begotten of the Father,) full of grace and truth." Of what is John speaking when he says, "We beheld his glory"? You will get your answer by turning to Luke 9:28-36, where you read that Peter and James and John went up into a mountain with the Lord to pray. "As he prayed, the fashion of his countenance was altered, and his raiment was white and glistering. And, behold, there talked with him two men, which were Moses and Elias: who appeared in glory, and spake of his decease which he should accomplish at Jerusalem. But Peter and they that were with him were heavy with sleep; and when they were awake, they saw his glory." Peter bore testimony in his second epistle (1:16-18) that he beheld the glory of God as it was manifested in the Person of Christ Jesus. The glory that the Old Testament had spoken of and that the prophets had anticipated would be seen again, was manifested through the *Person* of Jesus Christ.

Yet this was to be a temporary mode of manifestation, for in Luke 9:31 we read that Moses and Elias "spake of his decease," the death which Jesus Christ should accomplish in Jerusalem when He would become the sacrifice for the sins of the world. Eiljah did not speak of the glories of prophecy, nor did Moses speak of the triumphs or failures of the law. They talked with the Lord about "the decease which he should accomplish at Jerusalem." Just as creation and Eden were temporary in their manifestation of glory; just as Moses was a temporary instrument to manifest God's glory; and just as the Tabernacle and later the Temple were temporary manifestations of God's glory, so Jesus Christ's life in the flesh among men was a temporary manifestation of the glory of God.

THE CHURCH

But after the death, resurrection, and ascension of Christ, God did not leave Himself without a means of manifesting His glory. When we turn to Ephesians 2:21-22 we are reminded by the Apostle Paul, "In whom all the building fitly framed together groweth unto an holy temple in the Lord: in whom ye also are builded together for an habitation of God through the Spirit." The function the Temple and the Tabernacle performed in manifesting the glory of God, has now been assigned to believers who are incorporated into the Church. God's purpose in bringing the Church into existence was that He might manifest through the Church the manifold wisdom and grace and power of God; that believers should be instruments to bring praise and honor and glory to Him.

This was what the apostle had in mind in II Corinthians 4:6-7: "God, who commanded the light to shine out of darkness, hath shined in our hearts, to give the light of the knowledge of the glory of God in the face of Jesus Christ. But we have this treasure in earthen vessels, that the excellency of the power may be of God, and not of us." God has chosen those who had nothing in themselves to bring glory to God, and through them—by a transforming work, by the power of the Holy Spirit—He will bring glory to His own name and to the name of His Son, Jesus Christ.

The apostle brings this out in Ephesians 1 as he speaks of the work of the Father in our redemption, in verses 1-5, and says all that the Father has done, He has done "to the praise of the glory of his grace" (v. 6). In verses 7-11 he speaks of the work of the Father through the Son in our redemption. Why has He redeemed us? "That we should be to the praise of his glory" (v. 12). In verses 13 and 14 the apostle speaks of the work of the Father through the Spirit in our redemption. To what end? "Unto the praise of his glory."

That is why Paul says in Colossians 1:27 that "Christ in you" is "the hope of glory." It is not the individual who will manifest the glory of God; it is the transforming presence of God the Father, God the Son, and God the Holy Spirit who take up residence within the child of God that will manifest the glory of God.

Yet even this form of manifestation is temporary, for our Lord will call to Himself through the glorious experience of resurrection and transformation every believer in the Lord Jesus Christ, and the Church will no longer be on the earth as a temple to manifest the glory of God. (See John 14:3; I Thessalonians 4:13-17.)

THE PERSONAL PRESENCE OF CHRIST

After all believers have been taken into Heaven, then those on earth will see the fulfillment of our Lord's words in Matthew 24:30: "Then shall appear the sign of the Son of man in heaven: . . . and they shall see the Son of man coming in the clouds of heaven with power and great glory." This manifestation of Christ's glory will be a sign of such significance that the nations of the earth gathered together at the conclusion of the campaign of Armageddon will forget their natural animosity one against the other and will join together in a great federation of nations to prevent the appearance of the Son of God in this earth to reign. But they will be unsuccessful, and He will subjugate all His enemies. The Son of God will reign as King of kings and Lord of lords, sitting upon a throne of glory, as we read in Matthew 25:31: "When the Son of man shall come in his glory, and all the holy angels with him, then shall he sit upon *the throne of his glory*." God will manifest His glory to this earth when the Son of God, who is also the Son of Man, will receive the scepter to David's throne, and reign in power and great glory. God will be glorified in the personal presence of His Son on this earth as King of kings and Lord of lords.

The Apostle Paul tells us in Colossians 3:4 that "when Christ, who is our life, shall appear, then shall ye also appear with him in glory." The phrase "in glory" has been interpreted by many to be synonymous with *heaven* as though the apostle wrote "When Christ, who is our life, shall appear, ye also shall appear with him in heaven." That is not what Paul is saying. The phrase "in glory" describes the condition of the child of God when Jesus Christ comes. Let me read it this way: "When Christ, who is our life, shall appear, then shall ye also appear with him as glorious ones, or glorified ones." We shall be so transformed by the Son of God that we shall be instruments of praise to bring glory to God while the Son of God is manifesting the glory of God throughout His millennial reign on the earth and throughout the unending ages of eternity.

In Revelation 7:9-12 we have a picture given to us of the praise and the glory that will be given to the Son of God when He shall have put down every enemy and this earth is subject to His authority. "After this I beheld, and, lo, a great multitude, which no man could number, of all nations, and kindreds, and people, and tongues, stood before the throne, and before the Lamb, clothed with white robes, and palms in their hands; and cried with a loud voice, saying, Salvation to our God which sitteth upon the throne, and unto the Lamb. And all the angels stood around about the throne, and about the elders and the four beasts, and fell before the throne on their faces, and worshipped God, saying, Amen: Blessing, and glory, and wisdom, and thanksgiving, and honour and power, and might, be unto our God forever and ever, Amen." And why will the white-robed multitudes ascribe glory to God and to the Lamb? Because they "have washed their robes, and made them white in the blood of the lamb" (v. 14).

Revelation 21:10-11, 23-24 describes the habitation which the redeemed will occupy when they come to this earth with Christ to reign with Him, and which they will occupy from then on throughout the unending ages of eternity. John wrote: "He carried me away in the spirit to a great and high mountain, and shewed me that great city, the holy Jerusalem, descending out of heaven from God, having the glory of God: and her light was like unto a stone most precious, even like a jasper stone [or a diamond], clear as crystal; . . . the city had no need of the sun, neither of the moon, to shine in it: for the glory of God did lighten it, and the Lamb is the light thereof. And the nations of them which are saved shall walk in the light of it: and the kings of the earth do bring their glory and honour into it."

This habitation which will be prepared by the Bridegroom for His Bride is a place which will be characterized by the glory of God. In that place those redeemed by the blood of the Lamb manifest the glory of God, and both the inhabitants and the habitation will become that by which God brings glory to Himself throughout the ages of our Lord's reign and the unending ages of eternity. As much as the Scripture has to say concerning our glorification in Christ, the Word of God puts primary emphasis on that glory which will come to Him when we are translated into His presence. The hymn writer has put it this way:

> The Bride eyes not her garment,
>   But her dear Bridegroom's face;
> I will not gaze at glory,
>   But on my King of grace;
> Not at the crown He giveth,
>   But on His pierced hand,
> The Lamb is all the glory
>   Of Immanuel's land.

God has chosen believers today to do that for which this earth was created, for which Moses was transformed, for which the Tabernacle was erected and for which the Temple was built, that for which Jesus Christ came into the world the first time. He has chosen us that we might be instruments to bring glory to God. That is why the Apostle Paul could say, "I want Christ to be manifested in my body, whether it be by life, or by death." The compelling motive in the life of the child of God must be to glorify God.

WHAT IS FELLOWSHIP?

I John 1:1-10

MAN'S CHIEF END is to glorify God and to enjoy Him forever. God has revealed His glory to men, and men are to respond to that revelation by ascribing glory, majesty, dominion, and power unto a glorious God. The truth contained in Colossians 1:16 ("For by Him were all things created, that are in heaven, and that are in earth, visible and invisible, whether they be thrones, or dominions, or principalities, or powers: all things were created by him, and FOR HIM") gives us reason for believing that creation is no accident. All created things were brought into existence in order that they should glorify God.

This question arises: How can we glorify God? By fellowship with God. We were created in order that we might have fellowship with God. And we were made a new creation in Christ Jesus in order that we might have fellowship with God, so that through our fellowship with Him we might bring glory to God. The Apostle John, in his first epistle, told why he wrote the epistle: "that ye . . . may have fellowship with us: and truly our fellowship is with the Father, and with His Son Jesus Christ."

Because the scriptural concept of fellowship has been ambiguous to many believers, let us consider portions of the Word which will help us to understand what constitutes fellowship.

MAN MADE IN GOD'S IMAGE

In the first chapter of the book of Genesis, God's purpose in creating man is stated in verses 26 and 27: "And God said, Let us make man in our image, after our likeness; and let them have dominion over the fish of the sea, and over the fowl of the air, and over the cattle, and over every creeping thing that creepeth upon the earth. So God created man in his own image, in the image of God created he him; male and female created he them." And four times in these two verses you read expressions of God's purpose to make man in His image. In order to understand the scriptural concept of fellowship, we must examine these expressions and consider what constitutes the image of God which was reflected in Adam.

As we trace these words translated "image" and "likeness" through the Scriptures, we find that they are used, first of all, to show the essential relationship which existed between God the Father and God the Son. In II Corinthians 4:4 the Apostle Paul says that "the god of this world hath blinded the minds of them which believe not, lest the light of the glorious gospel of Christ, who is the image of God, should shine unto them." There the apostle affirms the fact that Jesus Christ in His essential being is the image of God. Again, we find the same truth affirmed in Colossians 1:15 where, speaking of Jesus Christ, the apostle says that Christ is the image of the invisible God. This same word, used of the relationship between the Father and the Son, is used of the relationship existing between God and man at the time of creation in Genesis 1:26-27, where we read that God made man in His image and in His likeness. The same truth is affirmed in the New Testament, for in I Corinthians 11:7 Paul stated that a man ought not to cover his head, "forasmuch as he is the image and glory of God." The Apostle Paul could say that humanity bears the image of God.

The word "image" or "likeness" emphasizes resemblance, the correspondence between one thing and another. The word translated "likeness" gives us the interesting picture of a coin that has been stamped in a die, so that what was in the die reappears in the coin. One who examines the coin can tell what was engraved in the die, because the coin bears the image of the die that pressed it. Now, when Scriptures assert that man is made in the likeness of God, it does not say that man is a little god. Rather, it says that by representation and manifestation, there is in man that which was in God, and that which was in God was manifested in Adam as he was created, and in Jesus Christ in His humanity.

In what way does man bear the image or likeness of God? Several explanations have been given. One common explanation is that Adam bore a physical likeness to God, that Adam's body was fashioned in the likeness of God so that Adam, in his physical structure and makeup, bore a likeness to God. That hardly seems an adequate explanation. The Apostle Paul, writing concerning this physical body in I Corinthians 15:49, contrasts the body which we have now with the body which we shall have by resurrection and glorification. Paul says, "As we have borne the image of the earthly, we shall also bear the image of the heavenly." He tells us that the image which man bears in his body is not an image of the heavenly but of the earthy. It will not be until the resurrection that our body will bear likeness or image to the spiritual body. In I Corinthians 15, Paul tells us that there are different kinds of bodies. There is a celestial body, and there is a terrestrial body. There is a body suited to heavenly existence, there is a body suited to an earthly existence. Then he contrasts the two. Thus we conclude that the likeness and image which Adam bore was not a physical resemblance, and we cannot know what God looks like by looking at ourselves or by trying to imagine what Adam looked like in his unfallen state.

The second explanation, which is frequently given, is that Adam was made in the moral, or ethical, likeness of God. That would make the image in Adam not a physical likeness but a spiritual likeness. Adam in his inner being bore a likeness to the God who had created him. Again, while this is an improvement on the first explanation, we do not believe that it is scriptural nor a satisfactory explanation. Adam was not created holy. Holiness is an unchangeable, inviolable, unalterable, incorruptible quality of God's being. God could not sin. God, who was holy, could not become unholy. If Adam had been created holy, it would have been impossible for Adam to sin. Adam was created with an untried innocence. Adam was given the capacity of choice, and Adam could choose to sin, or choose to obey God. But to say that Adam's likeness to God was a moral or ethical likeness would be to say that God could sin, that God had been kept from sin only by a choice, but that He might have chosen otherwise and thus have become a sinner. Impossible! For God is a holy God.

MAN GIVEN PERSONALITY

What, then, will explain the likeness, or image in man which reflects what God is, and yet satisfy the requirements of Scripture? When we examine the creation record that is given to us in the opening chapters of the book of Genesis, we discover that God did for Adam that which He did not do for any other part of His creation. God did not breathe spirit into any animal. Adam was endowed with capacities which differentiated Adam from all the animal creation. God gave to Adam a personality, so that Adam, as a person, might have fellowship with God, who is a person. God created matter, but material substance did not possess personality, and God could not communicate Himself to material substance. God created the vegetable kingdom, but the vegetable kingdom did not possess capacity for fellowship with God. God created the animal kingdom, but the animals could not glorify God by entering into fellowship with God because they did not possess personality. But when God created Adam, God made Adam in the image and likeness of Himself, a person with all the essential components of personality so that Adam might enter into fellowship with God and glorify God.

What were these capacities which were given by God to Adam, and to the human race, so that the race might enjoy fellowship with the Creator? We know that God has a mind, and a part of God's personality is His intellectual capacity. God knows! God is possessed of infinite wisdom. We refer to this, theologically, as omniscience. God possesses the capacity of love. God loves. And God possesses the capacity of will; God can choose, God can act. Scripture shows us that God is a person in the richest and fullest sense of the word because Scripture reveals how God has manifested His personality. God knows; God loves; and God acts, or decides, or chooses. When God made Adam in His likeness, God endowed Adam with the same component parts of personality which He Himself possessed. When Adam was made in the likeness and image of God, he was given a mind so that he might know; he was given a heart so that he might love; he was given a will so that he might choose to obey God. Now, Adam possessed these capacities only to a limited degree, for Adam was not God. But Adam could exercise these capacities Godward. In the garden of Eden provision was made for the exercise of these capacities.

Adam was given an opportunity to exercise his mind when he was given the responsibility of naming all of the animals. He examined each animal in order to give it a suitable name. Every time Adam discovered some new thing about God's creation, whether fauna or flora, he was exercising his mind and he understood something more of God, for God revealed Himself to Adam through creation.

When God gave Adam a wife, Adam's heart was centered upon the gift that God had given to him and he exercised his capacity to love in a new relationship. Adam's capacity to love was to be exercised as a responsibility, under the authority of God, toward his wife and toward the God who had revealed Himself as the God of love.

When God placed the tree of knowledge of good and evil in the garden, He said, "Thou shalt not eat of it, for in the day that thou eatest thereof, thou shalt surely die." The tree of knowledge of good and evil was placed in the garden as a test of the fellowship between the will of Adam and the will of God. If there had been no test of Adam's obedience, there could have been no fellowship between the will of Adam and the will of God. Thus we see that when God created Adam and made him a person and endowed him with all of the capacities of personality, God made fellowship possible between the mind of Adam and the mind of God, the heart of Adam and the heart of God, and the will of Adam and the will of God. For Adam, fellowship was the exercise of these three capacities of his personality Godward. Adam could not enjoy full fellowship if he exercised his mind and his heart Godward but not his will. There would be no full fellowship if he exercised his mind and his will Godward but not his heart. Nor, could he enjoy full fellowship if he exercised his heart and his will Godward but did not exercise his mind Godward. Fellowship between God and Adam in the garden of Eden consisted of the mind of Adam in harmony with the mind of God, the heart of Adam in harmony with the heart of God, and the will of Adam in harmony with the will of God.

THE EFFECTS OF THE FALL

We do not know how long it was before Adam exercised his will contrary to the will of God, thus breaking, immediately and completely, the fellowship which had existed between Adam and God. Sin severed the creature from fellowship with the Creator! And the effects of Adam's sin are far-reaching. In the first chapter of the book of Romans, the Apostle Paul shows the effects of Adam's sin. First of all, the apostle shows that the intellect of man was darkened by the fall, so that man in his intellect could not know God. Romans 1:19-20 states, "That which may be known of God is manifest in them [that is, among them]; for God hath shewed it unto them. For the invisible things of him [that is, about God] from the creation of the world are clearly seen, being understood by the things that are made, even his eternal power and Godhead; so that they are without excuse." From these verses we learn that creation is a revelation of the wisdom of God, and that nature is an open book in which all men may see two things: God's eternal power, and His Godhood or deity. But even though men were able, through that revelation, to know something of God, how did they respond? "When they knew God, they glorified him not as God, neither were thankful; but became vain in their imaginations [that is, their thought processes], and their foolish heart [that is, their seat of perception], was darkened" (Rom. 1:21). In Ephesians 4:17 the same truth is affirmed: "This I say therefore, and testify in the Lord, that ye henceforth walk not as other Gentiles walk, in the vanity [or, emptiness] of their mind, having the understanding darkened, being alienated from the life of God through the ignorance that is in them, because of the blindness of their heart." There, the apostle affirms again what he taught in Romans 1, that the heart of the natural man is darkened because of sin. The apostle did not say that the mind is blindfolded, but rather, blinded. If one has been blindfolded, all he needs to do is to remove the blindfold and he will see. But Paul says that men have been blinded by sin. They no longer have the capacity to see. The first great result then of Adam's sin is that man's intellect was darkened.

Not only was man's intellect darkened but his emotional capacity was degraded. "God . . . gave them up to uncleanness through the lusts of their own hearts, to dishonour their own bodies between themselves: who changed the truth of God into a lie, and worshipped and served the creature more than the Creator, who is blessed for ever, Amen. For this cause, God gave them up to vile affections" (Rom. 1:24-26a). In Ephesians 4:19 we read: "Who being past feeling have given themselves over unto lasciviousness, to work all uncleanness with greediness." It is not that man lost his emotional capacity, but his emotional capacity was so perverted and prostituted that it cannot be directed Godward. Thus the natural man cannot experience fellowship between his heart and the heart of God.

Romans 1 closes by showing us another result of Adam's fall: the will of man was deadened Godward. In verse 32 we learn that men, "knowing the judgment of God, that they which commit such things are worthy of death, not only do the same [notice it, *do* the same], but have pleasure in them that do them." In Romans 7:18 Paul says, "I know that in me (that is, in my flesh) dwelleth no good thing: for to will is present with me; but how to perform that which is good I find not." Natural man is marked by the deadness of his will toward God. In Romans 8:7, the apostle says, "The carnal mind is enmity against God: for it is not subject to the law of God, neither indeed can be." In Galatians 5:17 the apostle again adds his testimony, "The flesh lusteth against the Spirit, and the Spirit against the flesh: and these are contrary the one to the other: so that ye cannot do the things that ye would." When you put these passages together, you find that Paul consistently teaches that while a man still has a will, and can choose, his will is a will that is enslaved to sin, a will that cannot and will not exercise itself Godward, a will that wills only that which is iniquitous.

Because of the fall of Adam, man has been brought under judgment and under a curse, but he still continues to be a man. He did not lose his personality; he has not been degraded to the level of an animal. But it is impossible for man to exercise his God-given capacities Godward. The unsaved man has an intellect, but it has been darkened and he cannot know God; he has an emotional capacity, but it has been degraded, and he cannot love God; he has a will that has been deadened toward God and he cannot and will not obey God. Even though God created us for fellowship with Himself, so that He might be glorified through our fellowship with Him, that purpose is unattainable in the natural man. Man still bears the image of God and possesses the component parts of personality, yet he has been so bound and enslaved that he cannot exercise these parts of His personality Godward to the glory of God.

THE NEW CREATION

In order that God's purpose in man might be attained, God planned a new creation—in Christ Jesus. In II Corinthians 5:17, the Apostle Paul says, "If any man be in Christ, he is a new creation." By this miracle of new creation, God has so enlarged the capacity of one who believes in Christ and thus becomes a child of God that he now can enter into fellowship with God and glorify God again. Several passages will show that God's purpose in the new creation is that we might again manifest the image of God. In II Corinthians 3:18, the Apostle Paul says: "We all, with open face beholding as in a glass the glory of the Lord, are changed into the same image from glory to glory, even as by the Spirit of the Lord." Notice it! We are being changed into *His* image. Again, in Colossians 3:10, the apostle says that we "have put on the new man, which is renewed in knowledge after the image of him that created him." God is working in the new creation in order that the new creature might manifest the image of Him that created him. In Romans 8:29 the apostle says that "whom he did foreknow, he also did predestinate to be conformed to the image of his Son."

What has God done for us in order that we who are re-created in the image of God might glorify God through the intimacy of fellowship with Him?

First of all, God has given us a new mind. In I Corinthians 2:16 the apostle tells us that "we have the mind of Christ." This is not a renovation of the old mind; this is the implantation of a new capacity in the area of mind of the regenerate child of God, so that he might enjoy fellowship with God. You will notice in I Corinthians 1:30 that "Christ Jesus is made unto us wisdom, and righteousness, and sanctification, and redemption." Jesus Christ is made unto us, first of all, wisdom. God has given us a new mind so that we might appropriate the truth that in Christ there is righteousness, and sanctification and redemption. God's program for us, according to I Corinthians 1:30, begins with the impartation of a new mind, so that we might know Him.

In the second place, we were given a new capacity of heart. God has not tried to renovate or purify the old capacity that is under judgment, but God has given us a new and enlarged capacity, that through that capacity we might love Him. In speaking to the disciples in the upper room in John 15, Christ presented this crucial test of discipleship: "By this shall all men know that ye are my disciples, if you have love one to another" (John 13:35). In writing to his spiritual children, the Apostle John said, "We know that we have passed from death unto life, because we love the brethren" (I John 3:14). In chapter 4 of the same epistle, verses 7-10, he said, "Let us love one another: for love is of God; and every one that loveth is born of God, and knoweth God. He that loveth not knoweth not God; for God is love. . . . Herein is love, not that we loved God, but that he loved us, and sent his Son to be the propitiation for our sins." We have been given a new capacity of heart in order that the new heart might exercise itself Godward.

Third, we have been given a new will in order that we might obey God. Peter says, in II Peter 1:4, that believers are partakers of the divine nature. Now the child of God has a new relationship to the will of God because of the new nature given to him by the new birth. In Ephesians 6:6, Paul told those to whom he wrote that they were to do the will of God from the heart, something that is utterly impossible for a man who is an alien from God's grace. Again, in Colossians 1:9, Paul prayed that the believers "might be filled with the knowledge of his [God's] will in all wisdom and spiritual understanding." And in chapter 4, verse 12, he speaks of Epaphras, who prayed for the Christians at Colosse that they might stand "perfect and complete in all the will of God." The apostle, writing to the Hebrews, closes that great epistle by praying, "Now the God of peace, . . . make you perfect in every good work to do his will."

What we have endeavored to make clear is that when man was made in the image of God he was endowed with the capacities of personality so that he might have fellowship with God, who is a person. God gave him a mind that he might know God, and a heart that he might love God, and a will that he might obey God. Adam disobeyed, and Adam's race was cursed and cut off from fellowship with God. Adam's sons still possessed personality, but the intellect was darkened, their emotions degraded, and their will deadened. As a result, there was no fellowship between the sinner and God. But God has made believers in Christ members of a new creation. He has given us a new mind, that we might know Him, and a new heart that we might love Him, and a new will that we might obey Him. When you, child of God, exercise your mind Godward to know Him, and you exercise your heart Godward to love Him, and you exercise your will Godward to obey Him, then you are in fellowship with God. But if any area of your personality is not in harmony with the Person of God, then you are not enjoying the fellowship which is the purpose for which you were created and for which you were re-created in His image. You cannot glorify God apart from that fellowship.

In this fellowship with God there must be growth. Believers must grow in the area of knowledge. That is why Peter said in II Peter 3:18, "Grow in grace, and in the knowledge of our Lord and Saviour, Jesus Christ. . . ." They must grow, or increase, in love. That is why Paul's prayer for the believers at Philippi included this request: "that your love may abound yet more and more." Believers must choose the way of complete obedience to God's will. In John 14, verses 21 and 23, the Lord emphasized the necessity of obedience when He said, "He that hath my commandments, and keepeth them, he it is that loveth me . . . If a man love me he will keep my words: and my Father will love him, and we will come unto him, and make our abode with him." Believers glorify God by their growth and fruitfulness as they abide in Christ, as their mind, heart, and will are in harmony and fellowship with the mind and the heart and the will of the Redeemer. This is God's purpose in creation and in your re-creation in Christ.

THE OLD MIND

I Corinthians 1:18-31

GOD, AS A PERSON, possesses a mind. With that mind He knows and thinks. As a person, He possesses a heart and with that heart He loves. And, as a person, He possesses a will, and with that will He moves and decides and acts. When God created man in His own image, God gave man a mind so that he could know, a heart so that he could love, and a will so that he could obey. And it was God's design that with his mind man should receive truth from God and know God, that man should receive the love of God and love God in return, that man should receive a revelation of the will of God and obey God. The fellowship which Adam enjoyed with God in the garden of Eden was fellowship between his mind and the mind of God, his heart and the heart of God, and his will and the will of God.

This intimacy of fellowship was enjoyed for only a limited period of time, according to Genesis 3, for Adam rebelled against God, chose to disobey God, and translated his choice into an overt act of disobedience. Because of Adam's sin, his mind was darkened so that he did not know God; his emotions were degraded so that he did not love God; and his will was deadened so that he did not obey God. All of Adam's children have been born with an incapacity for person-to-person fellowship with God. It is our purpose to discuss with you, in the next studies, the effect of Adam's sin upon these three great areas of man's personality and to follow that with a study of God's work in re-creating us and thus providing us with a new capacity so that we might again enter into fellowship with God.

We direct your attention to the subject of the "old mind," and consider the capacities of the intellect with which all men are born as the result of Adam's sin. We recognize that the thought is father to the word and deed. We cannot speak without first thinking of what we will say. We cannot act without first conceiving that act in the mind. The words men speak, and their actions, have their origin in the mind of the speaker or the doer. We are considering, then, that which is basic to all conduct as we examine the scriptural teaching on "the old mind" or the mind after the fall.

THE MIND OF ADAM

Let me begin by reminding you that Adam's mind, before the fall, could enjoy fellowship with the mind of God. And God gave certain responsibilities to Adam which would cause him to exercise the capacity of mind which God had given to him. In Genesis 2:19 we read: "Out of the ground the LORD God formed every beast of the field, and every fowl of the air; and brought them unto Adam to see what he would call them: and whatsoever Adam called every living creature, that was the name thereof. And Adam gave names to all of the cattle, and to the fowl of the air, and to every beast of the field." Now, the only way Adam could give a suitable name to each created thing was to exercise his God-given capacity of mind and discover the characteristic of each creature, and then give it a name that was in keeping with its character. God could have affixed a name to each animal, to each of the fowl, which Adam could have memorized. Instead, God said to Adam, "You give names to all created things." Indirectly, as Adam studied each creature to discern its peculiar characteristics, Adam was learning more of God, and created things were revealing to Adam God's power, wisdom, and glory. Adam's fellowship with God in the garden of Eden was an expanding fellowship because his mental faculties were being enlarged, and he was understanding more and more of the Person of the Creator.

We also discover in the second chapter of Genesis that Adam's mind was exercised not only in respect to naming the animals but in giving his wife a name after God formed her from one of Adam's ribs. In verse 22 we read: "The rib, which the LORD God had taken from man, made he a woman, and brought her unto the man. And Adam said, This is now bone of my bones, and flesh of my flesh: she shall be called Woman, because she was taken out of Man." In calling his wife "woman" Adam emphasized her origin. He had discerned the fact that, since she had been taken from man and her physical body had been formed from the body of man, it was fitting to call her "woman," as a reminder of her origin, for she had come from Adam. And in chapter 3, verse 20, we read, "Adam called his wife's name Eve, because she was the mother of all living." He called her Eve because of her destiny; she was destined to be the mother of all living men and women. Again, this was an exercise of the mind, and the name Eve is the result of Adam's using the capacity which was his because God created him in His own likeness.

In the first chapter of Romans, the Apostle Paul affirmed that originally the mind of man was exercised Godward. He said in verse 19: "That which may be known of God is manifest in [or among] them; for God hath shewed it unto them." But this knowledge they had, this truth about God, was held down (or suppressed, or stifled). In their ungodliness and unrighteousness they refused the truth. They did not want to know God. For this reason "the wrath of God is revealed from heaven against all ungodliness and unrighteousness of men, who hold the truth in unrighteousness" (Rom. 1:18). What justification is there for God's revealing His wrath against all ungodliness and unrighteousness of men, even those who have never heard the Gospel and have never heard of salvation through Jesus Christ? The apostle showed that God is just in His wrath because a revelation had been made to all men. There is universality of judgment because there was universality of revelation. Now what was the revelation which was the basis of universal condemnation? We find out by reading verse 20: ". . . the invisible things of him [or, concerning him] from the creation of the world are clearly seen, being understood by the things that are made, even his eternal power and Godhead; so that they are without excuse." What Paul says is this: There are two discernible facts which all men could know, which render them subject to divine judgment. Those two facts are God's power and His Godhood. All that has been created by the hand of God is an evidence to rational creatures that God is a God of power, a God who must be obeyed. His power and His Godhood were clearly seen from the things that were made. God's revelation to Adam through creation was designed to bring Adam into fellowship with Himself in the area of the mind. The garden of Eden with all that God had placed in it, was designed to bring Adam's mind into fellowship with the mind of God, and as Adam enlarged his knowledge as he studied creation, he would be brought into deeper fellowship with God in this area.

CHARACTERISTICS OF THE NATURAL MIND

We discover from Scripture that there was a radical change in the mind of man because of the fall. Let us consider a number of passages of Scripture that show the characteristics of the mind of the natural man. First of all, in Romans 1, verse 21 and following, we discover that the mind of the natural man is marked by *darkness*: "When they knew God, they glorified him not as God, neither were they thankful; but became vain [that is, empty] in their imaginations [that is, their thought processes], and their foolish heart [that is, their power of perception] was darkened." Their powers of perception were darkened! This same truth is revealed in Ephesians 4:17, where the Apostle Paul refers to the Gentiles who walk "in the vanity [or, the emptiness] of their mind, having the understanding darkened." By the use of this word "darkened" the apostle is emphasizing the fact that the mind of the natural man, of itself, has no power to receive light. It cannot receive divine revelations. Just as a fish born in the Mammoth Cave in Kentucky without the capacity of sight cannot respond to light—no matter how bright—focused upon it because it has no sensory perception, so the men born into this world cannot, of themselves, respond to light from God because the intellect has been darkened in respect to divine truth.

Again, a passage such as Genesis 6:5 shows us that not only is man's mind darkened but his mind is *evil*. "God saw the wickedness of man was great in the earth, and that every imagination of the thought of his heart was only evil continually." "Heart," as used in that passage, represents the seat of the

thought process, or the intellect. Will you notice the universality
of the darkness of mind? *Every* imagination of the thoughts of
man's heart was *only* evil *continually*. The intellect is not only
darkened in respect to divine truth but what it produces is always evil in the sight of God.

Turning again to Romans 1, we discover that the natural
mind is marked by a *distorted worship*. The natural mind recognizes a responsibility to worship *some* God. The darkness of
his mind has not obliterated responsibility. But when the natural
mind was darkened and became evil, and could not exercise itself Godward, the natural mind devised gods of its own making.
The Apostle Paul says in Romans 1:22, "Professing themselves
to be wise, they became fools, and changed the glory of the uncorruptible God into an image made like corruptible man, and to
birds, and fourfooted beasts, and creeping things." They made
gods for themselves. They deemed this an act of wisdom, but
God says it is an act of absolute foolishness. This is well illustrated in the eleventh chapter of the book of Genesis, where we
find the first false organized religious system that existed upon
the face of the earth. It seemed an act of wisdom to erect a temple as a gathering place for the human race that was in rebellion
against God. They called that temple Bab-el, the gate of God.
God, in divine wisdom, called it Babel, or confusion. The
natural mind is characterized by distorted worship.

Furthermore, the natural mind is *at war with God*. In Romans
8:6-7 the Apostle Paul writes: "To be carnally minded is death;
but to be spiritually minded is life and peace. Because the carnal
mind is enmity against God: for it is not subject to the law of
God, neither can be." Notice again that the natural mind is
marked not only by rebellion but by incapacity. It *cannot* be
subject to the law of God! Why? Because of "the ignorance that
is in them" (Eph. 4:18). The apostle says when the carnal mind
is enmity against God, he pictures men who, having had a revelation of God, of His infinite power and Godhood, have refused
to submit to Him. They have declared war upon God. They
exist in a perpetual state of enmity and warfare against God and
in their blindness and ignorance, have made for themselves gods
to suit themselves.

Further, we find that the natural mind is marked by *incapacity to receive God's truth*. In I Corinthians 2:14 we read: "The natural man receiveth not the things of the Spirit of God: for they are foolishness unto him: neither can he know them, because they are spiritually discerned." Spiritual truth can only be discovered and appropriated by a spiritual nature. But the natural man does not have a spiritual mind, and therefore does not have the capacity to receive divine truth. Since the natural mind does not have the capacity to receive divine revelation, that natural mind is marked by ignorance and can never be educated into divine truth. It takes an entirely new capacity to receive divine truth.

The mind of the natural man is called by God a *reprobate* mind in Romans 1:28: "As they did not like to retain God in their knowledge [that is, in the intellectual capacity which God gave], God gave them over to a reprobate mind." A reprobate mind is a mind that not only wanders into evil but it gravitates to evil as a body which has mass is pulled toward the center of the earth. The reprobate mind is given over totally to evil.

In Ephesians 4:17 the apostle says that the mind of the natural man is an *empty* mind. They are walking "in the vanity [or the emptiness] of their mind." Paul does not mean that the mind is not full. The mind is never a vacuum. Something is always going through the mind. But when God looks at the mind of the natural man He says that it is devoid of any content Godward; that it does not retain God in its thoughts. Because God is left out of all that passes through that mind it has no spiritual content. In that sense it is empty and is characterized by vanity.

"The *carnal* mind" is a phrase used by the Apostle Paul in Romans 8:7: "The carnal mind is enmity against God." This same thought is given to us in Colossians 2:18, where the apostle says, "Let no man beguile you of your reward in a voluntary humility and worshipping of angels, intruding into those things which he hath not seen, vainly puffed up by his fleshly mind." Now the carnal mind, or the fleshly mind, is a mind that is focused only upon sensual things, things that have to do with this life and this existence. When the natural mind exercises itself, it never exercises itself toward things of God, things that shall be here-

after, things concerning eternal destiny. It is always occupied
with things that have to do with this body, the gratification of its
desires and appetites, the satisfaction of its wants.

In this same verse the apostle says that the mind is "vainly
puffed up." That is, it is a *conceited* mind, a mind that thinks
well of itself. It is this characteristic that the apostle is referring
to in Romans 12:3: "I say, through the grace given unto me, to
every man that is among you, not to think of himself more highly
than he ought to think." There Paul was warning his Christian
brothers lest their thinking be like that of a natural man, who is
puffed up within himself, and concerning himself. The conceited
man loves to elevate himself above all those with whom he has
to do. He sees himself in a superior position. In so thinking he
is reflecting the sin of the first sinner, Satan, who was puffed up
in his mind and rebelled against God and refused to remain in
his place of submission to rightful authority. All those who are
in Satan's kingdom are characterized by that same vain mind,
that same puffed-up mind, thinking of themselves more highly
than they ought to.

The *defiled* mind is mentioned by the Apostle Paul in Titus
1:15, where he says, "Unto the pure all things are pure: but unto
them that are defiled and unbelieving is nothing pure; but even
their mind and conscience is defiled." The defiled mind refers
to the mind that is so under the blight of sin that it can think
nothing clean, can think nothing pure, and is driven to think the
worst in every situation. Closely related to the defiled mind is
the *corrupt* mind which the apostle speaks about in I Timothy
6:5, where he refers to "perverse disputings of men of corrupt
minds, and destitute of the truth." The corrupt mind has been
perverted so that it cannot exercise the function for which the
mind was originally given to man. The natural man may be
imaginative in sin, but he cannot be imaginative in the things
of God and cannot think himself Godward.

We read of an *earthly* mind in Philippians 3:19. There the
apostle speaks of certain sinners "whose end is destruction, whose
god is their belly, and whose glory is in their shame, who mind
earthly things." You talk to a natural man about material wealth
and he can understand you; in fact, he is two steps ahead of you.

But when you begin to talk to him about spiritual things, about the things of heaven, about the things of eternity, you might as well be talking to a man who is stone deaf, because he has no comprehension of them whatsoever. Scientists frequently justify their rejection of God because they say they cannot accept anything that they cannot see, feel, taste, touch, or measure. They mind earthly things, but have no capacity for heavenly things.

In II Corinthians 4:4, the apostle says that the minds of natural men have been *blinded*. "In whom the god of this world hath blinded the minds of them which believe not, lest the light of the glorious Gospel of Christ, who is the image of God, should shine unto them." The natural man has not been blindfolded by sin, for then, in order to see, all he would need to do is remove the blindfold. But he is marked by blindness, an inability to see.

Finally, the natural mind is characterized by *death*. In Romans 8:6 the apostle says that " to be carnally minded is death; but to be spiritually minded is life and peace." A man is physically dead when he can no longer perform physical functions. A man is spiritually dead when he cannot function toward God. The mind of man is dead when he cannot perform the function for which the mind was given to man by his Creator—to receive truth from God, to appropriate and assimilate that truth, to know the God who revealed Himself in truth, and then glorify God because of the revelation which God has made.

Since the mind of man is marked and designated as a reprobate, carnal, empty, puffed up, fleshly, defiled, corrupt, earthly, blinded, and dead mind, do you begin to understand, child of God, why it is difficult for you to control your thoughts? Do not be deceived into thinking that your mind has been changed because you have been born into God's family. What we have seen from the Scripture is that which describes the mind you have, which you received by physical birth from Adam. You possess, within yourself, the same capacity for carnality, vanity, fleshly defilement, ·corruption, enmity, and attention to earthly material things that characterized you before you were born into God's family. And if that old mind is allowed to exercise itself, that mind will father words and actions that are in keeping with the corruption and the defilement and the blindness and the dead-

ness that God says characterizes the mind of the unsaved man.
I thank God that this old mind was brought under judgment at
the cross. God did not try to improve it, to clean it up, to change
its distortion and its perversion. He judged it at the cross. And
He imparts to those who believe in Christ the new mind of Christ
in order that it might manifest itself Godward in fellowship with
God.

THE NEW MIND

I Corinthians 2:7-16

A NEW CAPACITY OF MIND has been given to the man who has experienced the new birth, the man who is a new creation in Christ Jesus. To the one who believes in Christ God gives new life through what is called the new birth in John 3 and the new creation in II Corinthians 5:17. In making a man a new creation in Christ Jesus, God does not remake the capacities of the natural man, nor does He change the basic characteristics of his personality. But God, by the new creation, gives the person a new capacity of mind, of heart, and of will. With the new mind the man can know God, with the new heart the man can love God, and with a new will the man can obey God.

It is our purpose in this study to examine Scripture concerning the capacity of the new mind. In our previous study we surveyed the teaching of the Word of God concerning the mind after the fall, the mind that we call "the old mind."

God does not try to use this old mind. By a new creation, He imparts a new mind to man, with a capacity to receive divine truth, to exercise itself Godward, to enjoy fellowship with God in the realm of spiritual truth. The apostle emphasizes this fact in I Corinthians 2:16 as he says, "We have the mind of Christ." The apostle has been reminding his readers that God had revealed a body of truth through the Holy Spirit. But, according to verse 9, the natural eye has not seen, the natural ear has not heard, nor has there entered into the thought processes of the natural man the things God has prepared for them that love Him. In verse 14 he explains the ignorance of the natural mind when he says, "The natural man receiveth not the things of the Spirit of God: for they are foolishness unto him, neither can he know them, because they are spiritually discerned." The natural man does not have a spiritual capacity in the realm of the mind. The natural man has only what we call "the old mind," and the old mind cannot receive and perceive divine truth. But the apostle says that this revelation which natural minds cannot receive can be received by those who have the mind of Christ. A new capacity is given to the person who has received Jesus Christ as Saviour so that, as he exercises the new mind, he can grasp of the truth of God, and appropriate the revelation which God has made of Himself and, as a result, enjoy fellowship with God—the mind of the believer in harmony with the mind of God.

In Romans 12:1-2 we learn more about God's work in the area of mind. The apostle says, "Be not conformed to this world: but be ye transformed by the renewing of your mind." That word translated "renewing" is the word that is used in Titus 3:5 where we read, "Not by works of righteousness which we have done, but according to his mercy he saved us, by the washing of regeneration, and the *renewing* [that is, the making new] by the Holy Ghost." To us the word *renew* means to rejuvenate, to modernize, or to bring up to date. We speak of renewing furniture when we refinish an antique, when we patch up a chair that is falling apart, give it a coat of gloss varnish that will hide its defects, or give it a coat of paint that will cover up the mars and blemishes. That is not the scriptural meaning of the word *renew*. The Greek word translated "renew" means "to make new from above." That is what God does when He makes a man a new creature in Christ Jesus. He looks at the natural mind and sees it as it is, defiled and evil and lawless and reprobate and dead. Instead of remaking the old mind, God imparts an entirely new capacity—a new mind.

When the Holy Spirit seeks to do His work of teaching and instructing us in the things of Christ, He never appeals to the old mind. He never addresses truth to the natural man, with his natural capacity. It is the new mind in Christ that is the vehicle through which divine truth is learned and appropriated. Our Lord said to His disciples, "The Comforter, which is the Holy

Ghost, whom the Father will send in my name, he shall teach you all things, and bring all things to your remembrance, whatsoever I have said unto you" (John 14:26). Again, in John 16:12-15, our Lord said, "I have yet many things to say unto you, but ye cannot bear them now. Howbeit when he, the Spirit of truth, is come, he will guide you into all truth: for he shall not speak of himself; but whatsoever he shall hear, that shall he speak: and he will shew you things to come. . . . All things that the Father hath are mine: therefore said I, that he shall take of mine, and shall shew it unto you." Until Christ died and the Holy Spirit came on the day of Pentecost to indwell the body of believers, and to do His work of teaching, there was no new mind in believers which could be the vehicle to receive divine truth, nor was there a Teacher to impart that truth. But since then all who are new creatures in Christ Jesus have new minds, and God, through the Holy Spirit, can teach us the things concerning Christ.

CONFLICT

Because of this new mind, with its capacity to receive divine truth and to respond to that revelation of God by fellowship with God and by glorifying God, the believer is engaged in a constant warfare. There is a continuous, perpetual warfare between the new mind in Christ and the mind of the natural man. Often we refer to the two natures in the child of God. When we do that, we do not mean to suggest that the child of God is two persons, that he possesses two distinct personalities. This concept is not taught in the Word of God. However, man, in the area of mind, has two capacities: the capacity for divine things through the NEW mind and the capacity for the carnal, fleshly, sinful, dead things through the OLD mind. There will be constant, ceaseless, incessant, unrelenting opposition from the old mind as the new mind seeks to manifest itself in glorifying God.

We see this conflict in Romans 8:5-8, where the Apostle Paul says: "They that are after the flesh do mind [or, literally, have a mind for] the things of the flesh; but they that are after the Spirit [have a mind for] the things of the Spirit. For to be carnally minded is death; but to be spiritually minded is life and peace. Because the carnal mind is enmity against God: for it [the carnal mind] is not subject to the law of God, neither indeed can be. So then they that are in the flesh cannot please God." Do you notice what the apostle is saying here? They that are after the flesh have a mind for the things of the flesh, but they that are after the Spirit, those who exercise the new mind, have a mind for the things of the Spirit. He says that the carnal mind is at war with God, but the spiritual mind pursues those things that are characterized by life and peace.

We also see this conflict in Romans 7, where the apostle said, "I am carnal, sold under sin" (v. 14). Now the apostle did not say, "I am doing carnal, worldly things." He says, "This is my essential makeup." He says, "In the area of my mind I am carnal. That is, although I have the new mind of Christ, I still have the old capacity, the old, natural mind. Therefore I have to be characterized in the realm of mind as one who is carnal because the old mind has not been eliminated; it has not been changed." After the apostle speaks of his essential makeup in the fourteenth verse, he tells us, "I see another law in my members, warring against the law of my mind, and bringing me into captivity to the law of sin, which is in my members. . . . So then with the mind I serve the law of God; but with the flesh the law of sin" (vv. 23, 25). May I paraphrase the last part of verse 25 in order to make it plain? The apostle says, "With the new mind I serve the law of God, but with the fleshly mind I serve the law of sin." Now this is the principle that Paul is laying down for us: Every child of God, in the area of the mind, would have to be classified as carnal; that is, he has the old capacity which can manifest itself in sin, lawlessness, ignorance, corruption, defilement, and death. He experiences a constant battle in the area of mind—the new against the old, the old against the new. Never will the old mind and the new mind agree on anything in the believer's life. There is never a time when these two capacities agree on any thought, on any word, on any action in your life. Constant, incessant, unrelenting warfare goes on in the area of your mind.

TRANSFORMATION

Because of this conflict in the area of the mind, the apostle addresses a number of exhortations to believers. Briefly, we may direct your attention to some of these.

First of all, in Ephesians 4:23 Paul enjoins believers: "Be renewed in the spirit of your mind." Paul is not commanding believers to GET the new mind. As believers they already had the new mind. But they are to allow the new mind to do its renewing work in transforming their lives. When the old mind is allowed to dominate the child of God, the result will be sin, defilement, and corruption. But when the new mind dominates or controls the child of God, his life will manifest that which comes from a holy, a righteous, and a just God.

In Romans 12:2, we read a second exhortation. "Be not conformed to this world, but be ye transformed." The apostle is speaking of a changed life, and the changed life of the child of God comes from the renewing of the mind. The old mind will produce its corrupt fruit, but the new mind will manifest itself in righteousness and true holiness. In Colossians 3:5-7 Paul has cataloged a list of heinous sins. Every one is a manifestation of the natural mind. The apostle includes "fornication, uncleanness, inordinate affection, evil concupiscense, and covetousness, which is idolatry: . . . anger, wrath, malice, blasphemy, and filthy communication." Now don't think such sins are impossible for the child of God. The new mind will never produce these sins, but if the old mind is permitted to control the child of God, this is exactly the fruit it will produce every time. After having cataloged these sins that the old mind will produce, the apostle says, in verse 9, "Lie not one to another, seeing that ye have put off the old man with his deeds; and have put on the new man, which is RENEWED IN KNOWLEDGE after the image of him that created him." When God made man, He made him in His image and gave him a mind with the capacity to know Him. Since the fall of Adam the minds of all men born into this world were darkened by sin. In order for us to know God we had to become new creatures. We were "renewed in knowledge after the image of him that created him." So the new creature in Christ Jesus is a person who has been re-created in the image of God and endowed with the capacity to enter into fellowship with God. The child of God, then, is to put off the fruit of the old mind, and to put on the fruit of the new mind because he has been renewed in knowledge, that is, in the area of mind.

In Philippians 2:5 the Apostle Paul gave a further command concerning the new mind: "Let this mind be in you, which was also in Christ Jesus." Or more literally, "Have this mind in you." Paul did not say, "Get this mind in you." Had the apostle said that, we would have known immediately that he was writing to unbelievers. But since he said, "Let this mind be in you [or, 'Have this mind in you'], which was also in Christ Jesus," we know that he wrote to believers, exhorting them to manifest the fruits of the new mind instead of the fruits of the carnal mind.

Now what characterized the mind of Jesus Christ? In this glorious passage, the apostle speaks of the humiliation of Christ, who, "being in the form of God, thought it not robbery [something to be grasped and held onto at any cost] to be equal to God: but made himself of no reputation, and took upon him the form of a servant, and was made in the likeness of men: and being found in fashion as a man, he humbled himself, and became obedient unto death, even the death of the cross." The mind of Christ was characterized by submission to the will of God. You see, the mind of Christ knew God, and perceived the will of God, and willingly submitted to the will of God.

The apostle, in Philippians 4:8, speaks of the exercise of the new mind, and he exhorts believers, "Finally, brethren, whatsoever things are true, whatsoever things are honest, whatsoever things are just, whatsoever things are pure, whatsoever things are lovely, whatsoever things are of good report; if there be any virtue, and if there be any praise, think on these things." The new mind is to be centered on those things which can be characterized as true, just, lovely, and of good report.

RESPONSIBILITY

Now, what does the Word of God have to say about the believer's responsibility in the use of this new capacity which has been given to him since he has been renewed in the area of the mind, after the image of Him that created him in Christ Jesus?

First, the mind of the child of God is to be *occupied with Christ*. I think of being occupied with Christ in connection with the verse we have just referred to (Phil. 4:8), for Jesus Christ is the One in whom all of these lovelinesses have been fully displayed. "Whatsoever things are true" refers to Christ, for Jesus Christ was the One who could say of Himself, "I am the way, the *truth*, and the life." "Whatsoever things are honest" refers to Him, for it was said of Him that in His lips was no guile. "Whatsoever things are just" refers to Him. Remember what the centurion who stood at the cross said when he looked at Him: "Truly this was a righteous man! Truly this was the Son of God!" "Whatsoever things are pure" refers to Christ, for in Him was no sin. "Whatsoever things are lovely" refers to Him, for He is the altogether lovely One. "Whatsoever things are of good report" points to Him, for this phrase means "Whatsoever is praiseworthy," and certainly the Lord Jesus Christ is worthy of all praise and honor. If we would exercise the new mind so as to enjoy fellowship with God, this new mind must be centered upon the Person of the Lord Jesus Christ. As soon as our mind turns from Him, then the old mind takes over and manifests what a cesspool it is. The new mind was given to the child of God in order that with that mind the child of God might know the Father. God did not have to make a man a new creation so that the man could understand history, or mathematics, or languages, or physics, or medicine. The old mind was sufficient for that. The new mind was given because of man's one great deficiency in the area of mental activity, his inability to exercise his mind Godward. If the child of God is not exercising his mind Godward, then he cannot know fellowship with God, and he cannot fulfill the purpose for which he was re-created in Christ Jesus.

The Apostle Paul is an outstanding example of this exercise of mind for, in Philippians 3:10, he shows us the great impelling, compelling, propelling force in his life. ". . . that I may KNOW him." How? With the old mind? God forbid! But he had the new mind, which was occupied with Christ. The child of God will never fulfill the purpose for which he was made a new creation in Christ Jesus until he exercises his mind Godward.

Second, we find that the Word of God reveals that which will *sustain* the new mind. In I Peter 2:2 the Apostle Peter says, "As newborn babes, desire the sincere milk of the word, that ye may grow thereby." The Word of God is spiritual food to promote growth. This same truth is presented to us by the Prophet Jeremiah. He said, "Thy words were found, and I did eat them; and thy word was unto me the joy and rejoicing of mine heart: for I am called by thy name, O LORD of hosts" (Jer. 15:16). The child of God who saturates his mind with the Word of God will be strengthened from within in such a way that the old mind will be kept from controlling his thoughts and his actions. That is why the Psalmist said, "Thy word have I hid in my heart, that I might not sin against thee." It is not the word you have bound in a nice black cover that is going to keep you; it is not the words that you have underlined in that Bible that will sustain you and protect you, but it is the Word of God that you have stored in your mind that will sustain you in a day of temptation. The mind must be sustained by the Word of God.

Third, we find that the Apostle Paul speaks of the *defense* of the mind. He says, "Be careful for nothing; but in everything by prayer and supplication with thanksgiving let your requests be made known unto God. And the peace of God, which passeth all understanding, shall keep your hearts and minds through Christ Jesus" (Phil. 4:6-7). The peace of God will keep your MINDS! What does this mean? As a child of God sustains his mind by the Word of God, the knowledge that he has gained through the Word will defend him in a time of temptation, in a time of discouragement, in a time of testing, or in a time of doubt. We see the relationship between knowledge and faith in Romans 10:17, where the Apostle Paul said, "Faith cometh by hearing, and hearing by the word of God." We cannot believe something we do not know, nor can we believe a fact of which we are ignorant. We cannot trust God in a time of testing unless we know Him. When the child of God is brought into some trying experience, the truth of God that has been revealed through the Word of God to his new mind will sustain him, defend him, protect him, and uphold him. Many a child of God has walked confidently into a valley of dark shadows with the Word of God upon his lips. Why? The Word of God sustains and defends the new mind of the child of God.

Fourth, we find that the new mind has been *set free from the dominion of the old mind.* In II Timothy 1:7 we read: "God hath not given us the spirit of fear; but of power, and of love, and of a sound mind." God has given to us a *sound mind.* The "sound mind" which God has given us is the new mind, for the new mind is characterized by soundness. Soundness means the new mind can perform that function for which mind was given to man at creation, that is, knowing God and having fellowship with Him. Paul illustrates this in Romans 7:25, "With the mind [that is, the new mind of Christ] I myself serve the law of God." Fellowship with God, the reception of divine truth, the enjoyment of God because we have come to know Him are the grand possibilities presented to everyone who is a new creature in Christ Jesus.

Finally, we find in II Corinthians 10:3-5 some very practical words concerning the use of the new mind: "Though we walk in the flesh, we do not war after the flesh: . . . Casting down imaginations [that is, thought processes that would emanate from the old mind], and every high thing [that is, every manifestation of the old mind] that exalteth itself against the knowledge of God, and bringing into captivity every thought to the obedience of Christ." We are to bring into subjection every manifestation of the old mind with its sin, licentiousness, greed, enmity, and corruption. We are to bring every thought into subjection to the obedience of Christ. We recognize that man, of himself, cannot do this. It is only the Spirit of God who can restrain the outbreakings of the evil nature that is within every one of us. But God has charged us with the responsibility of bringing our thoughts into captivity, and bringing them into subjection to Jesus Christ. Our minds dart so rapidly from one thing to another, and we are surrounded today with many stimuli to the old mind from billboards, newspapers, magazines, television, and conversation overheard as we pass along the street. All of us experience countless appeals to the old mind. God says that those thoughts are not to be retained, or harbored, but that every thought is to be subjected to the authority of Christ in order that we might manifest Jesus Christ through the mind.

It is of utmost importance to realize that it is not the heart that is the primary receptacle and repository of divine truth but the mind. If our minds are so cluttered with manifestations of the old mind that the new mind cannot manifest itself, we will continue in carnality, we will be ignorant of divine truth and, even though born into the family of God, we will continue to stumble and totter. We will be babes in Christ until we let the mind of Christ control us.

CHAPTER

5

THE OLD HEART

Romans 1:18-32

IN OUR PREVIOUS STUDIES, we have considered the old mind and the work which God has done to give us a new mind in Christ so that we might enjoy fellowship with Him. Now we want to direct your attention to the second area of the new creation, heart.

The term "heart," as it is used in the Word of God, is a very broad term. It may be used of any part of the total personality. In the first place, the heart is referred to in Scripture as the seat of the *intellectual capacity,* or the mind. In II Corinthians 4:6 the apostle says, "God who commanded the light to shine out of darkness, hath shined in our hearts, to give the light of the knowledge of the glory of God in the face of Jesus Christ." While the light has shined in the heart, this shining has brought us knowledge of the glory of God. Now the reception of knowledge is the function of the mind. Yet in this passage it is the heart that is said to have received this revelation of the knowledge of God. This shows us that the terms "heart" and "mind" may be interchangeable. And this is true in I Corinthians 2:9-11, where the apostle writes: "Eye hath not seen, nor ear heard, neither have entered into *the heart* of man, the things which God hath prepared for them that love him. . . . Now we have received, not the spirit of the world, but the spirit which is of God; that we might KNOW the things that are freely given to us of God." "The heart of man" referred to in this Scripture is that part of the personality that receives knowledge, for with the heart we know the things that are freely given to us of God. So we see that "heart," in its broad sense, is used first of all as the mind of the personality.

In the second place, the term "heart" is used of the seat of the *affections* in the personality. In II Thessalonians 3:5, Paul writes: "The Lord direct your heart into the love of God, and into the patient waiting for Christ." In I Peter 1:22, Peter says, "Seeing ye have purified your souls in obeying the truth through the Spirit unto unfeigned love of the brethren, see that ye love one another with a pure heart, fervently." In both of these passages the heart is seen to be that part of the personality that feels emotion and love.

In the third place, we discover in II Corinthians 9:7 that the term "heart" is used of the seat of the will. "Every man according as he purposeth in his heart, so let him give; not grudgingly or of necessity: for God loveth a cheerful giver." The term "heart" may be used, therefore, of the seat of the mind; of the seat of the affections; or of the seat of the will. Thus, when the apostle speaks of the heart of man, he is speaking of the whole personality. The thought seems to be this: The affections control the whole man in his actions. What a man knows, he loves or hates; and what he loves or hates results in an action of the will. Therefore, the seat of the affection may be used of the total person. When we discuss the old capacity of heart, while we are speaking particularly of the realm of the emotions, let us understand that the word cannot be restricted to that, but encompasses the whole being.

We know from the Word of God that God loves. In I John 4:8, the Apostle John wrote a simple statement, "God is love," which gives to us a great categorical affirmation about the Person of our God. He is not only infinite in His intellect but He is also infinite in His compassion. God is love.

One outreach of God's love about which we read in Scripture is God's love for His Son. At the time of the baptism of Christ by John the Baptist, the heavens opened and the voice of God was heard saying, "This is my BELOVED Son, in whom I am well pleased." God's voice again came from heaven saying, "This is my BELOVED Son: hear him," at the time of Christ's transfiguration. From all eternity past God the Father had loved His Son. God did not begin to love the Son at the time of His incarnation, His baptism, His transfiguration, or His crucifixion. The Eternal Father eternally loved the Son.

Not only did God love the Son, who was worthy to be loved, but He loved sinful men, who were *not* worthy of His love. Jesus Himself bore witness to this love when He said, "God so loved the world that he gave his only begotten Son, that whosoever believeth in him should not perish, but have everlasting life."

THE HEART OF ADAM

When God created man in His own image, He gave to man not only a mind so that he could think and know but a heart so that he could love. In Genesis 2:21-24 we read of the creation of Eve. "The LORD God caused a deep sleep to fall upon Adam, and he slept: and he took one of his ribs, and closed up the flesh instead thereof; and the rib, which the LORD God had taken from man, made he a woman, and brought her unto the man. And Adam said, This is now bone of my bones, and flesh of my flesh: She shall be called Woman, because she was taken out of Man. Therefore shall a man leave his father and mother, and shall cleave unto his wife: and they shall be one flesh." In that last statement, which gives us God's divine principle in marriage, we find that Adam's heart was responding to Eve, and Eve in turn, responded to his affection. Man was able to use the capacity to love which God had given to him when God gave Eve to Adam to love.

As we go through the Word of God we discover that Adam's sin not only darkened his mind but had its effect in his heart, and the emotional capacity in Adam was degraded by his sin. A glaringly clear description of the degradation of the emotional capacity in the sinner is given to us in the first chapter of Romans. Here we have God's description of the old heart. As you read through this passage carefully with understanding, and discern the truth God has given here, you will feel defiled. One cannot look at this portrait of the heart of the natural man without drawing back from the revelation it makes of the capacity for evil that is within the human heart. But you will not understand some of the thoughts, some of the desires, some of the affections that grip your heart until you see the effect of Adam's sin in the area of the emotions by looking at God's picture of the human heart.

THE EFFECT OF THE FALL

In verse 21, the apostle says, "When they [that is, those who had received revelation concerning God] knew God [with the mind], they glorified him not as God, neither were thankful." In other words, natural men received revelation from God, but they were blinded in the area of the mind and could not receive, appropriate, and respond to the revelation that was given to them. Instead, they "became vain [or empty] in their imaginations [that is, their thought processes], and their foolish heart was darkened" (v. 21). Now "heart" in verse 21 may refer to the capacity of the mind to receive truth, or it may refer to the emotional capacity of the mind to receive truth, or it may refer to the emotional capacity which was to respond to the truth that had been revealed. In either case, the first description of the natural heart in this verse is that it is *foolish*. A fool is not necessarily one who is marked by a low IQ but one who leaves God out of his consciousness. (See Psalm 14:1: "The fool hath said in his heart, there is no God.") The fool is the man who does not take God into consideration in every area of his life. Thus when the Apostle Paul speaks of "their foolish heart," he is referring to a heart that leaves God out. The man with such is perfectly willing to continue without God's presence, without feeling God's love.

Going on in Romans 1 we read, "Professing themselves to be wise they became fools, and changed the glory of the uncorruptible God into an image made like to corruptible man, and to birds, and fourfooted beasts, and creeping things" (vv. 22-23). You will notice that man did not become demented as a result of the fall. He was not deprived of his reasoning processes. He could reason, and he reasoned that he was responsible to some deity. He refused to worship and serve the God who had revealed Himself, and so he made for himself gods. By manufacturing deities made like unto corruptible man, and birds, and fourfooted beasts, and creeping things, he showed that his reasoning processes were functioning but could not function properly.

Next, the apostle shows the result of this corrupted thinking upon the emotions: "Wherefore God also gave them up to uncleanness through the lusts of their own hearts." We see a double characterization of the heart in the first part of verse 24: It is a *lustful* heart and an *unclean* heart. The insatiable desires of this lustful heart do not include a desire for God, a desire for godliness. Rather, this degraded heart has insatiable debauched lusts.

In verse 25 we read that "men changed the truth [or literally, exchanged the truth] of God for a lie." And in verse 26 we read, "For this cause God gave them up unto vile affections." The old heart is the seat of *vile affections*. Now God intended that in the relationship existing between a husband and wife they should express the God-given capacity to love, but in verses 26 and 27 the apostle shows that, as a result of the fall and because of the degradation of the natural heart, men and women did not exercise the capacity of affection as God had ordained. Instead they invented perverted ways of manifesting the capacity of emotion in the most degraded forms and practices. And from what the Apostle Paul says, it is very clear that the sodomy, the homosexuality, and the perversion so rampant today is the direct result of the degradation of the emotional capacity. In verse 29 the apostle lists some specific things which are manifestations of this degraded emotional capacity. Men are filled with all unrighteousness, fornication, wickedness, covetousness (or lust), and maliciousness, and are disobedient to parents and without natural affections. Public complacency concerning the open manifestation of such forms of degradation is further evidence of the filthiness of the human heart.

CHARACTERISTICS OF THE NATURAL HEART

Other aspects of the natural heart are described elsewhere in the New Testament.

In Romans 2:5, the apostle says: "After thy hardness and impenitent heart treasurest up unto thyself wrath against the day of wrath and revelation of the righteous judgment of God." The heart is *hard* and *impenitent*. The word *hardness*, when used in reference to the heart, is a translation of the word which means "calloused." Perhaps you have seen someone with a calloused hand who could take a needle and put it through the skin of his hand with no feeling whatsoever. Why? Because that which is calloused is not sensitive to external stimulation. And the heart of the natural man has become hardened and is not subject to any stimulation concerning righteousness, with the result that it is impenitent. The Word of God may be declared, the righteousness of God may be revealed, the judgment of God that will be poured out upon sinners is preached, and the sinner is not affected the least bit. He is not convicted of the enormity of his sin, and he can complacently go on in his degradation, perversion, and immorality. Why? Because his heart is characterized by hardness, which explains his impenitence. Why is it so hard to reach some people with the Gospel of Jesus Christ? You have lived before them, you have testified to them, you have given them the Word of God, and they brush it aside. Why? Because they are insensitive to external stimulation, and their resisting the truth of God simply builds up the callous and makes the heart harder and more impenitent. Do not be surprised that men reject the Gospel when they have a heart that is characterized by hardness and impenitence.

In Ephesians 4:18, the apostle says that the Gentiles have "the understanding darkened, being alienated from the life of God through the ignorance that is in them, because of the blindness of their heart." The heart is *blinded*, not blindfolded. One who has been blindfolded simply needs to have the blindfold taken away and he can see. But one who has been blinded has lost the capacity to see. The apostle does not speak of the heart of the natural man as a blindfolded heart, but as a blinded heart. As ambassadors of Jesus Christ we do not seek to take blindfolds off men. We are presenting the Gospel to men who cannot see the truth of the Gospel because of the blindness of their hearts. We are brought face to face with the fact that we cannot make men see. We cannot convince men of Christ's power to save. It is only Christ who can perform the miracle that causes blinded hearts to perceive who Christ is and thus receive life eternal.

In Hebrews 3:10-12 we have two further descriptions of the heart of the natural man. The writer is quoting from the Old Testament. He is telling what God said about the children of Israel when they were in the wilderness: "I was grieved with that generation, and said, They do always err in their heart; and they have not known my ways." The natural heart is an *erring* heart.

When men follow the natural propensity of their hearts, they err and follow ways which are far from God's ways. Then the writer warns in verse 12, "Take heed, brethren, lest there be in any of you an evil heart of unbelief."

The natural heart is an *evil* heart. Our Lord characterized the heart of man as evil when He was brought into question by the Pharisees because some of His disciples had not followed the traditional procedure of washing the hands. The Pharisaic philosophy was that man was basically clean within, and that defilement is external. A man was defiled by what was outside. Christ corrected their erroneous thinking when He said that defilement is not external but internal. Very clearly He delineatd what proceeds from within an evil heart. He said, "From within, out of the heart of men, proceed evil thoughts, adulteries, fornications, murders, thefts, covetousness, wickedness, deceit, lasciviousness, an evil eye, blasphemy, pride, foolishness: all these evil things come from within and defile the man." Remember, Christ did not need that any should testify to Him about what was in man, for He knew what was in man. What He said is a divine revelation of what God sees in the human heart. The natural heart is an evil heart, and it is about this kind of heart that the apostle wrote in Hebrews 3:12.

Then the Apostle James referred to a deceived heart when he said, "If any man among you seem to be religious, and bridleth not his tongue, but deceiveth his own heart, this man's religion is vain" (James 1:26). A *deceived* heart sets a false standard, and then convinces itself that it measures up to the standard that it has adopted. Can you conceive of a man's daring to think he has attained to the righteousness of God? Or a sinner persuading himself that he is holy as God is holy? But the sinner can deceive himself into believing that in his sinful state he can be acceptable to God by the works of his own hands. This is an act of self-deception. "The heart is deceitful above all things, and desperately [or, incurably] wicked: who can know it?" (Jer. 17:9).

Finally, in Romans 1:31 Paul said that the heart is without natural affection. He uses the same expression in II Timothy 3:2, where he says, "Men shall be lovers of their own selves, covetous, boasters, proud, blasphemers, disobedient to parents, un-

thankful, unholy, without natural affection. This, perhaps, will
create a problem for you, for you know unsaved men who deeply,
devotedly love their wives. They adore their children. They love
their country. You say, "What does this Scripture mean when it
says men are without natural affections, when natural men do
manifest affection?" What the apostle is referring to in these passages is that the heart of man, because of the degradation by the
fall, cannot perform the function for which the capacity of emotion was given to man at creation. Remember that the primary
function of emotion was not to love wife; not to love children;
not to love home; not to love country. The primary purpose of
the emotional capacity was to love God. And men are without
natural affection, that is, the capacity to exercise the capacity of
love Godward.

Now when we synthesize all of these passages dealing with the
human heart, we recoil and rebel against the revelation which
God has given us. May I remind you that even though you have
been made a new creation in Christ Jesus, and have been given
a new capacity of heart, this old capacity has not changed one
bit. All that we have had to say about the heart of the natural
man characterizes you, even though you have been made a new
creature in Christ Jesus. Your natural heart is still lustful, vile,
foolish, hard, impenitent, blind, erring, evil, deceived, and without natural affection. Do not feel, because you have been made a
new creature in Christ Jesus that you no longer have the capacity
to manifest the old lusts, the old desires, the old immorality, for
those capacities are still there. But you have been given a new
capacity of emotion and you can submit yourself to the control
of the Spirit of God. Unless your new capacity is energized by
the Spirit of God, the old capacity will manifest itself. We cannot have victory over the old heart until we understand its capacities, and until we appropriate God's provision for victory.

6

THE NEW HEART

I John 4:7-21

A NEW HEART has been given to the child of God. A new emotional capacity has been given to the believer by new creation that makes it possible for him to fulfill that for which he was created.

In I John 4:19 the Apostle John says, "We love him because he first loved us." Until this new capacity was given, man was without natural affection. He could neither know the love of God, nor respond to that love, and yet the apostle can affirm in I John 4:19, "We love him." This is because of the work of new creation. But the fact that we love Him demonstrates that we have received a new heart, or a new capacity. This truth is affirmed in a number of other passages. In Romans 5:5, the Apostle Paul writes, "Hope maketh not ashamed; because the love of God is shed abroad in our hearts by the Holy Ghost which is given unto us." The love of God is shed abroad *in our hearts*. The apostle is not so much affirming that the love of God manifests itself *through* us as that the love of God has been manifested *to* us by the Holy Ghost who is God's gift to us.

In II Corinthians 4:6, the apostle asserts the same truth as he says, "For God, who commanded the light to shine out of darkness, hath shined in our hearts, to give the light of the knowledge of the glory of God in the face of Jesus Christ." Frequently in Scripture, the thought is presented that God makes His entrance through the mind, and then from the mind into the heart, from the heart into the will. But in verse 6 the apostle suggests that God makes His entrance into the individual through the heart. The heart receives the love of God, and then through the heart enlightenment is given to the mind of the child of God. Note that the apostle says that God commanded the light to shine out of darkness and shine *in our hearts to give the light* of the knowledge of the glory of God in the face of Jesus Christ.

In the first chapter of this same epistle Paul writes that God "hath also sealed us, and given the earnest of the Spirit in our hearts" (v. 22). The seal is the Spirit of God, and He comes to dwell in the believer's heart, the seat of his emotions. As a result, the person who formerly had only a vile, lustful, foolish, hard, and impenitent heart, now has a new heart.

Again, in II Corinthians 3:2-3, the apostle says, "Ye are our epistle written in our hearts, known and read of all men: forasmuch as ye are manifestly declared to be the epistle of Christ ministered by us, written not with ink, but with the Spirit of the living God: not in tables of stone, but in fleshly tables of the heart." There the apostle affirms that the truth that came to them through the Gospel penetrated to the heart. Evidence that they have received the truth that has been given to them by the apostles was seen in transformed lives.

A NEW CAPACITY TO LOVE

Our Lord, speaking to the disciples in the upper room, anticipated a new capacity to love as a result of the new creation, for He said, "This is my commandment, That ye love one another, as I have loved you. Greater love hath no man than this, that a man lay down his life for his friends. Ye are my friends, if ye do whatsoever I command you. Henceforth I call you not servants; for the servant knoweth not what his lord doeth: but I have called you friends" (John 15:12-15). When our Lord used the word *friend*, He was emphasizing a heart-to-heart relationship which had been established. They had been His servants, and He had been their master. But now that servant-master relationship has been superseded by this intimate relationship based on affection.

Now this love enjoined in the Word of God is not the purification of the old heart; it is not the remodeling, the remaking, or the refurbishing of the old capacity. But within the area of the emotions, God, by new creation, has given a new capacity with which we may love God, receive God's love, and love others. We find in the Word of God two different Greek words which are translated by the one English word *love*. The first word is the word *phileo*. *Phileo* is love which responds to that which is attractive. A natural man, with his old heart, may respond to that which is attractive. He may love his wife, his children, his home, his country, his luxuries, and so on. He responds to that which is attractive. Now, when *God's* love is referred to in the Word of God, it is referred to, almost without exception, by a second Greek word, *agapao*. *Agapao* is not love that responds to what is attractive but love that manifests itself because the lover wills to love. God loved the world. Why? Because the world was attractive to Him? Never! A sin-cursed people could not be attractive in His sight. But God loved them because He willed to love them. The major emphasis in the first word is on *receiving*; in the second on *giving*. Now it is with these words in mind that we discover why love demonstrates that one has been born into God's family. A natural man may manifest *phileo* love, responding to that which is attractive, but only the child of God, in whom the Holy Spirit reproduces the love of God, can manifest God's love, *agapao* love. The proof that one has been born into God's family is to love as God loves—not responding to that which is attractive but loving that which may be unattractive, because one wills to love. Such love manifests the new capacity to love which God gives the believer in Christ.

A NEW CONFLICT

Because of the presence of both the old and a new capacity within the believer, there is a constant conflict going on within the child of God. This conflict is absent in the unbeliever because the unbeliever does not have a second, or new, capacity to war against the first. The unbeliever may have conflicts *within* this one area, but he cannot have conflicts *between* the old capacity and the new. Because you and I, as new creatures in Christ Jesus have been given this new capacity, we are engaged in a constant warfare within this emotional realm to determine whether the old heart will manifest its fruit or the new heart will manifest its fruit. In I John 2:9-11 we see this conflict spelled out for us:

"He that saith he is in the light, and hateth his brother, is in darkness even until now. He that loveth his brother abideth in the light, and there is none occasion of stumbling in him. But he that hateth his brother is in darkness, and walketh in darkness, and knoweth not whither he goeth, because that darkness hath blinded his eyes." Again, in chapter 4, verse 20, we read, "If a man say, I love God, and hateth his brother, he is a liar: for he that loveth not his brother whom he hath seen, how can he love God whom he hath not seen?" Now you will notice that these verses mention two manifestations of the capacity of affection. The apostle refers in I John 2:9 to the man who says "he is in the light and hateth his brother." Now, this hatred comes from the old capacity. Hatred will never, under any circumstances, come from the new capacity given by new creation. The apostle says he that hateth his brother is in darkness. Such a man is manifesting the fruits of the old capacity. But he that loveth his brother abideth in the light. This loving does not come from the old capacity; it comes from the new capacity. So, the apostle says we have within us two potentialities: love and hate. Both come from within the same realm of the heart. The old heart manifests itself in hatred, rancor, bitterness, and maliciousness; the new heart manifests itself as the love of God is manifested through the individual. Constant warfare therefore exists between the old heart and the new heart within the child of God.

It will help us in the problems we face in the realm of our affections if we understand our conduct, our thinking, our feelings. We must examine every manifestation of the affections to trace it to its source. If this manifestation springs from the old heart, then we know immediately that it is wrong. If it can be traced to the new capacity, then the Holy Spirit of God is manifesting His fruit through us. But we should never feel that this old heart will somehow be changed, so that it no longer manifests its corrupt fruit. We will live with daily conflict not only in the area of the mind, as the old mind battles against the new and the new against the old, but also in the area of the heart, with the old against the new and the new against the old. And then, as we shall see in further studies, this same conflict goes on in the area of the will, the old against the new and the new against the old.

The person who is a new creation in Christ will experience continuous, unrelenting, incessant warfare in every area of his person.

NEW AFFECTIONS

Since the Word of God has a good deal to say concerning the child of God and his affections, let us examine some passages of Scripture that give exhortations in the realm of the heart. However, we cannot be exhaustive for the Word of God has so much to say. We must be selective.

First of all, we will notice that there are certain negative commandments, things that we are to leave off; and then there are certain positive exhortations to which we, as believers, are to respond. Let us look, first of all, at the negative commandments.

In I John 2:15, the Apostle John gives a command concerning the believer's relationship to the world. "Love not the world, neither the things that are in the world. If any man love the world, the love of the Father is not in him." The apostle is saying in the last part of the verse that if any man loves the world, it will be because he manifests the old capacity, for it is not the love of the Father loving the world through him. So the apostle says if any man love the world it is not the new heart which is doing the loving. Thus we have the prohibition, "Love not the world."

This same truth is brought out in James 4:4, "Ye adulterers and adulteresses, know ye not that the friendship of the world is enmity with God? whosoever therefore will be a friend of the world is the enemy of God."

What James and John are bringing to us in these two passages quoted is the truth that this God-given capacity of love may be prostituted. The child of God, through his old capacity, may focus his affections on that which is displeasing and distasteful to God and he may love the world. The believer is commanded to abstain from such spiritual prostitution, which is evidence of a perverted affection.

When we turn to the fifth chapter of Ephesians, beginning with verse 3, we are reminded of a second great area in the realm of the affections concerning which commandment is given to the child of God. "But fornication, and all uncleanness, or covetousness, let it not be once named among you, as becometh saints; neither filthiness, nor foolish talking, nor jesting, which are not convenient: but rather giving of thanks. For this ye know, that no whoremonger, nor unclean person, nor covetous man, who is an idolater, hath any inheritance in the kingdom of Christ and of God. Let no man deceive you with vain words: for because of these things cometh the wrath of God upon the children of disobedience." And in these very clear words the apostle says that no child of God has any right to manifest the capacity of affection in any immoral act, word, or thought. He has the potentiality in his old heart to practice all of these things. But the child of God is not to give place to the devil and to manifest his capacity of affection in these directions. In I Thessalonians 4:3-7, the apostle says, "This is the will of God, even your sanctification, that you should abstain from fornication: that every one of you should know how to possess his vessel in sanctification and honor; not in the lust of concupiscence, even as the Gentiles which know not God: that no man go beyond and defraud his brother in any matter: because that the Lord is the avenger of all such, as we have also forewarned you and testified. For God hath not called us unto uncleanness, but unto holiness." In very plain words, the apostle commands these believers that they should abstain from fornication. They had practiced such in the name of religion before they met Jesus Christ as Saviour. They still had the potentiality to manifest the old affection in all kinds of immorality. But for the child of God that is unthinkable, because God has called us to holiness.

What does the Word of God say about the manifestation of a new heart in Christ Jesus? In Colossians 3:2 the Apostle Paul said, "Set your affection on things above, not on things on earth. For ye are dead, and your life is hid with Christ in God." Then, in Romans 12:9, Paul wrote, "Let love be without dissimulation [or literally, without hypocrisy]. Abhor that which is evil; cleave to that which is good. Be kindly affectioned one to another with brotherly love; in honour preferring one another." Here we see that the genuine manifestation of the new capacity will be a love that is without hypocrisy. No empty profession of affection, no empty endearing words such as salespeople are wont to use to establish rapport with a customer, but rather a genuine manifestation of the love of Christ toward those whom Christ loves. This is love without hypocrisy, true brotherly love.

Again, in Romans 13:8, the apostle puts every child of God in debt: "Owe no man anything, but to love one another." This is one obligation that cannot be discharged by a monthly payment. It takes weekly, daily, hourly, and momentary payments to discharge the debt which God has put upon us. He commands us to constantly manifest the new capacity which has been given to us by constantly loving one another.

In I Thessalonians 4:9-10, the apostle, after forbidding all manifestations of uncleanness, says, "But as touching brotherly love ye need not that I write unto you: for ye yourselves are taught of God to love one another. And indeed ye do it toward all the brethren which are in Macedonia: but we beseech you, brethren, that ye increase more and more." The apostle's desire for those who had walked in uncleanness, licentiousness, and lust, who had manifested the fruits of the old heart, was that they should now manifest the fruits of the new creation, the new capacity, by their love for one another.

The Apostle Peter writes in the same vein when he says, "Seeing you have purified your souls in obeying the truth through the Spirit unto unfeigned love of the brethren, see that ye love one another with a pure heart fervently" (I Peter 1:22). Here again God commands His children to love one another. How? To love with a pure heart, and to love fervently. Here is a flaming love, a love that purifies the person by his very affection for those that are bound to him in the ties of the Gospel. Peter also writes in chapter 2, verse 17, "Love the brotherhood."

The Apostle John is known as the apostle of love, and John has devoted much of his epistles to this subject. In I John 2:10 he says, "He that loveth his brother abideth in the light, and there is none occasion of stumbling in him." And then, in chapter 3, verse 11, he says, "For this is the message that ye heard from the beginning, that we should love one another. Not as Cain, who was of that wicked one, and slew his brother. And wherefore slew he him? Because his own works were evil, and his brother's righteous." And in verse 14 he says, "We know that we have passed from death into life, because we love the brethren." You will notice that the first public crime committed after the fall, as far as we have any record in the Word of God, was a crime against love. Cain slew his brother, Abel, and in so doing he sinned against love. And the apostle, conscious of that first manifestation of the old heart, says that you who have been born into God's family must be very careful lest you repeat in some form or another the sin of Cain, a sin against love. The evidence that you have passed from death unto life is that you love the brethren.

Five of the New Testament epistles close with an exhortation to the believers to greet or salute one another with a holy kiss. Why? The brethren greeted the brethren with a kiss, as an evidence of a pure, burning love, and the sisters greeted the sisters with a kiss as an evidence that they loved out of a pure heart fervently. It was not enough to say to an individual, "I love you." That love was to be manifested, to be expressed. Often Christians fail to express their affection one for another in Christ. And they may be reticent about expressing their affection to God, who has loved them with an everlasting love. Somehow it is deemed unmanly today to show emotion. But God has given the child of God a new capacity to love so that that capacity might manifest itself toward God and toward the brethren. The Word of God assumes that the child of God will love God "first" (I John 4:19), and it also gives a commandment "that he who loveth God love his brother also."

But since we are engaged in a warfare every moment of every day, the old heart seeks to manifest all of which it is capable. The old heart wants to focus its affection on that which God hates. But the Holy Spirit has been given to us to energize us as new creatures in Christ and to produce His fruit of love so that God's purpose in giving us the capacity of affection might be realized as we enter into fellowship with the heart of God and then manifest that love one toward another.

THE OLD WILL

John 6:35-45, 60-65

IT SEEMS as though every teacher has some idiosyncrasies. Some teachers have more than others. I am sure that one class at the seminary where I teach thought that I had gone beyond all bounds when they read one of the questions on a final examination. The question was, "Wherein do you differ from a horse?" I was not trying to be facetious. I wanted the students to recall that when God created man He did a work for man that set him apart from all animal creation. God endowed man with all of the capacities of personality so that he could enter into fellowship with God. To none of the animal creation did God give a mind to respond to the mind of God. To none of the animal creation did God give a heart so that an animal could respond to the love of God. Nor did He give to any of the animal creation a will so that an animal could decide to obey God. But to man God gave a mind, a heart, and a will, and when Adam fell, man suffered the effects of the fall in each of these aspects of his total personality.

It is our purpose now to direct your attention to the area of the will. We will consider the will at the time of creation, and then the results of the fall in the area of the will, so that we may understand what characterizes the will of the natural man. Such a study will reveal the characteristics of man's will apart from the new creation in Christ Jesus.

THE WILL OF ADAM

We have looked frequently into the record of creation given in the first two chapters of Genesis, where God said, "Let us make man in our image, after our likeness: . . . So God created man in his own image, in the image of God created he him, male and female created he them" (Gen. 1:26-27) . In the second chapter, verses 15-17, we read, "The LORD God took the man, and put him into the garden of Eden to dress it and to keep it. And the LORD God commanded the man, saying, Of every tree of the garden thou mayest freely eat: but of the tree of the knowledge of good and evil, thou shalt not eat of it: for in the day that thou eatest thereof thou shalt surely die." In our previous studies we have seen that in the garden of Eden Adam was given the capability of exercising each part of his capacity Godward so that Adam could enjoy full fellowship with God. To Adam was given the responsibility of naming all of the animals. This was an exercise of his mind. Through that mind Adam entered more and more deeply into the greatness of God's power and wisdom and, as a result, into fellowship with God. It was God's custom to come to the garden in the cool of the day, thus giving Adam an opportunity to exercise his heart Godward as God and Adam enjoyed fellowship heart to heart as well as mind to mind. If Adam, in his total person were to have fellowship with God, there must be something in the realm of the will through which Adam would subject himself to the will of God so that the will of God and the will of Adam might enjoy fellowship together. That is the reason we read in Genesis 2:15-17 that God set apart one particular tree and forbade Adam to partake of the fruit of that tree.

God's creation was a perfect creation. There was nothing poisonous in the fruit of that tree which could harm Adam physically. There was nothing in it which of itself could defile Adam. Rather, God forbade Adam to take of the fruit of that tree to test Adam's obedience to the will of God, so that through the exercise of his will God and Adam could have fellowship in the area of the will. If Adam's *mind* was in fellowship with the mind of God, and Adam's *heart* was in fellowship with the heart of God, but Adam could not exercise his *will* Godward, there could not have been full fellowship between the creature and the Creator. Therefore, in order that Adam and God might enjoy the fullest fellowship together, God set apart this tree of the knowledge of good and evil and forbade Adam to partake of it. When God prohibited Adam's partaking of the fruit of the tree of the knowledge of good and evil, He did not do this to withhold from Adam something that would have been a blessing or benefit to him but to bring the greatest blessing possible to him, to bring Adam into complete fellowship with God.

In Genesis 3 we have the record of how Adam was dissuaded from the path of perfect obedience to the will of God and, as a consequence, lost all fellowship with God. In Genesis 3:1 we find that this temptation appealed, first of all, to the mind of Adam. Satan began by raising a question in the mind of Eve. Then the serpent came and said to the woman, "Yea, hath God said, Ye shall not eat of every tree of the garden?" This raised a question of fact. This was a challenge in the area of mind. Next Satan moved from the mind to the heart, for he said, "God doth know that in the day ye eat thereof, then your eyes shall be opened, and ye shall be as gods [or literally, ye shall be as Elohim], knowing good and evil." This was a subtle temptation to doubt the love of God, to doubt the goodness of God. Satan's subtle seed, planted in the mind of Eve through his original question, was that God was not the loving, good God that He set Himself forth to be, for if He really loved Eve He would not have withheld from Adam and Eve that which would make them like Himself. When one is jealous, he reserves for himself something which he claims exclusively. Jealousy is a sin against love, and Satan said to Eve that God was jealous; God was selfish. Satan implied that in being jealous and selfish God had withheld from them something that would be for their greater good. Thus he led Eve to doubt the love of God.

Now when one entertains a thought in the mind, and then lets that thought penetrate to the heart so that one loves that thing, or that idea, that love soon moves upon the will. So "when the woman saw that the tree was good for food, and that it was pleasant to the eyes, and a tree to be desired to make one wise, she took of the fruit thereof, and did eat, and gave also unto her husband with her; and he did eat" (Gen. 3:6). You will notice that the fall did not come when the woman exercised her mind and saw and recognized that the tree was good for food. The fall did not take place when Eve's emotions were stirred and she saw that it was pleasant to the eye. The fall did not take place when the woman entertained the suggestion of Satan that she eat of the fruit of the tree in order to become wise. But the fall took place when Eve took of the fruit and ate it. The sin was not in Eve's looking, evaluating, and considering, but in exercising her will to stretch out her hand, pluck the fruit, and then eat it in disobedience to the commandment of God.

EFFECTS OF THE FALL

Because of this act of the will in which both Adam and Eve were involved there were far-reaching effects. We have already discovered that because of this sin the mind was darkened and, while men did not lose the ability to think, they could not *know* God. In the realm of the heart, the emotions were degraded, and while man did not lose the capacity to love, his emotional capacity was degraded and he could not love God. Great as were the effects in the realm of the mind and the heart, the greatest effect of Adam's sin, in the light of the revelation of the Word of God, was in the realm of the will. The will of man, because of Adam's sin, is a will that is enslaved to sin, a will that lives for sin and loves sin; in other words, a will that is under the dominion of sin. In Romans 6:14, Paul says, "Sin shall not have dominion over you." The word *dominion* is the word for a master or sovereign who exercises authority and control over the individual. Paul, in this verse, is writing to believers to tell them that sin should no longer have dominion over them as it formerly had, for now they were "not under the law, but under grace." In this statement, addressed to believers, we discover the relationship of the unbeliever to sin in the realm of the will. Sin has dominion over the unbeliever. Sin is the overlord of unbelievers. Sin is their taskmaster. They are in bondage to sin. Again in Romans 6:16-20, Paul writes, "Know ye not, that to whom ye yield yourselves servants to obey, his servants ye are to whom ye obey; whether of sin unto death, or of obedience unto righteousness? But God be thanked, that ye were the servants of sin, but ye have obeyed from the heart that form of doctrine which was delivered you. . . . For when ye were the servants of sin, ye were free from righteousness." These verses describe the relationship of the individual to sin as a principle. The individual is a servant; he is not free to do as he pleases; he is a bondslave of sin.

A true servant sets his own will aside; he is expected to do the will of his master implicitly and immediately. He has no right to question an order given to him by his master. The Apostle Paul says that we, before we met Jesus Christ as Saviour, were in bondage as servants to sin, without any will of our own, without any choice in the matter. We followed the dictates of sin; sin was our sovereign.

FREEDOM OF THE WILL

We frequently hear the question of the freedom of the will debated. We need to understand the scriptural teaching on this doctrine. First of all, we must define what is meant by *freedom of the will*. With our lawless natures, we like to consider freedom as the right to do as we please, with no restraint on us from without, no obligation to anyone other than ourselves. That concept of freedom is not found anywhere in the Word of God. That is the philosophy and practice of Satan. In the scriptural sense of the word, a creature is free when it can move in its native element, when it can fulfill the function for which it was created. The fish is free when it can move in the sea, but if the fisherman removes that fish from the sea, it has lost its freedom. The bird is free when it can move in the air, for it is the native element of the bird. The animal is free when it can roam in the forest, or across the prairie, because the forest or the prairie is its native element. A man is free when he can move in his native element. God created man for Himself, for fellowship with God. By the fall man was expelled from his native element and consequently was no longer free. We sometimes say man has a free will. But fallen man is not free. Fallen man is free in the same way a bird in a cage is free. The bird is free to move within that cage, but his life is bounded by that cage. What a mockery it would be to take a free-flying bird out of the air, confine that bird in a cage, and then say to the bird, "You are free." No, it is only free to move within certain bounds, certain restrictions, certain limitations; it is not free to move in its native element. Likewise natu-

ral man is free to move in the element of sin. His life is circumscribed by sin. Sin is the foundation under him, and the canopy
over him. A man's total life apart from Jesus Christ is lived in the
element of sin and in the sphere of sin. Since man is not free to
live in his native element, we cannot say he is free. And man is
not free until he can move in that area for which he was created,
and that is the area of pleasing God because all things, including
man, were created for God. This is indicated by the Apostle Paul
in Colossians 1:16: "By him were all things created, that are in
heaven, and that are in earth, visible and invisible, whether they
be thrones, or dominions, or principalities, or powers; all things
were created by him and for him."

Every individual enjoys a certain amount of freedom. When
you got dressed today you could choose whether to put on a blue
tie, a black tie, or a red tie. You are free to choose the color of
the car that you buy, but that is not freedom in the scriptural
sense of the word. Dr. Donald Grey Barnhouse used to say that
a man is free to jump from the fifteenth floor of a building, but
he does not have the freedom to jump back up again. This is a
graphic illustration of the limitations upon our freedom. Various
passages in the Word of God show us restrictions upon man's
freedom. In Galatians 5:17 it is recorded, "The flesh lusteth
against the Spirit, and the Spirit against the flesh: and these are
contrary the one to the other: so that ye cannot [or, so that ye may
not] do the things that ye would." Notice the last part of verse
17: "Ye cannot [or may not] do the things that ye would." Here
we see that there are some things the will cannot do. And then
in verse 19 we read, "The works of the flesh are manifest, which
are these." The works listed are a manifestation of the will of
the natural man. When the natural man wills, acts, chooses, or
decides, he chooses in the realm of sin, for all of the works of
the flesh listed in verses 19-21 are sins.

In Romans 7:23 the Apostle Paul says, "I see another law in
my members, warring against the law of my mind, and bringing
me into captivity to the law of sin which is in my members." The
phrase "bringing me into captivity to the law of sin" shows that
a man is a captive, a slave, to sin. Sin is his lord. In Romans 5:12
the apostle reminds us that "by one man [that is, Adam] sin en-

tered into the world, and death by sin; and so death passed upon all men, for that all have sinned." We are dead in that we cannot fulfill that for which we were created by God, that is, to enjoy fellowship with God. Then in verse 17, Paul says, "by one man's offence death reigned by one." And in verses 20-21, he says, "Where sin abounded, grace did much more abound: that as sin hath reigned unto death, even so might grace reign through righteousness unto eternal life by Jesus Christ our Lord." Note the word *reigned* in verses 17 and 21. Here sin is viewed as a mighty potentate, a dictator, if you please, who manifests an exorable will in giving commands to all the serfs who are under him. Sin has dominion over unsaved men in the same way that a monarch reigns over his subjects.

Again, in Ephesians 2:2 we read, "In time past ye walked according to the course of this world, according to the prince of the power of the air, the spirit that now worketh in the children of disobedience: among whom also we all had our conversation in times past in the lusts of our flesh, fulfilling the desires of the flesh and of the mind; and were by nature the children of wrath." Observe the expressions "ye walked" and "we had our conversation," or, more literally, "we had our manner of life." Now, the walk and the manner of life were the external manifestations of acts of the will and when the will acted within the individual, it produced the lust of the flesh, and the desires of the flesh and of the mind which were contrary to the nature and character of God.

From these passages, it is very clear that because of Adam's sin the will of the creature was deadened toward God. The natural man cannot obey God. The natural man has no desire to obey God. He is by nature a rebel. He is lawless, and he manifests his lawlessness and rebellion against God by living under the dominion of sin, serving as a vassal under sin.

This is our Lord's view of the will of man as it is revealed to us in the sixth chapter of John's Gospel. Our Lord had presented evidence that He was the Son of God, the Messiah. By His words and His works He had sought to convince an unbelieving nation that He had come to bring light and life to the world. But those to whom He came rejected Him; they did not believe

Him. Christ points out that the unbelief of Israel was not because Jesus Christ had not authenticated His Person and had not validated His words. There was another explanation for the unbelief of the nation. The Lord said, in verse 38, "I came down from heaven, not to do mine own will, but the will of him that sent me." In this verse our Lord is contrasting His will to the will of those unbelievers. They desired to do their own will. Their will was in rebellion against the will of God. But Jesus' will was not like the will of fallen men, for He came to do the will of Him that sent Him. Then, in verse 44, our Lord said, "No man can come to me, except the Father which hath sent me draw him." He also said, "Therefore said I unto you, that no man can come unto me, except it were given unto him of my Father" (v. 65). Now why does our Lord speak of the utter impossibility of a man's coming to Him unless God the Father brings him? It is because Christ knew that the will of the natural man is deadened toward God, that natural man is bound and enslaved by sin, that natural man lives under dominion of sin, takes his orders from sin, and serves sin. Sin will never point a man toward Jesus Christ, and sin will never relax its reign over the individual. It is only as Jesus Christ breaks the shackles of sin and sets the captive free that an individual will respond to Christ's invitation to come to Him for light and for life. And Christ explained the unbelief of the nation Israel in terms of a will that was in bondage to sin and enslaved to sin.

A man, in the deadness of his will toward God, may do things that morally or ethically are acceptable and approved by society. But he can never do anything that is pleasing to God because all that he does, he does in response to the commands issued by sin, which is his master. And God cannot and will not accept obedience to sin as acceptable to Himself. This portion of our study strikes a very dark and somber note. There is no joy in proclaiming to you the truth of the Word of God that men are the bondslaves of sin, but we rejoice in the message of the gospel that men who believe in Christ will be made a new creation and will be given a new will in order that they might obey the Word of God.

THE NEW WILL

Colossians 3:1-15

NATURAL MAN is a bondslave to sin. According to Romans 6:14 the natural man is under the dominion of sin. Sin is his lord and master. This emphasizes the relationship of sin to the individual. In Romans 6:16-17, the apostle says that we were enslaved to sin. This was the relationship of the individual to sin. Now, by the work of new creation (II Cor. 5:17), the believer in the Lord Jesus Christ is brought to a glorious freedom. The chains of sin which bound him as a slave have been broken. The door that confined him within certain prescribed limitations has been opened, and he has been liberated from sin as the master he was obligated to obey. It is this truth which we want to examine with you now.

LIBERTY IN CHRIST

In the sixth chapter of the Epistle to the Romans the Apostle Paul is dealing with the glorious liberty that belongs to the children of God. We discover in verses 12 and 13 that God has given the believer freedom from bondage to sin as his master. The apostle says, "Let not sin therefore reign in your mortal body [that is, as it used to], that ye should obey it in the lust thereof. Neither yield ye your members as instruments of unrighteousness unto sin [as you used to have to do]: but yield yourselves unto God, as those that are alive from the dead, and your members as instruments of righteousness unto God."

The apostle can make such appeals as "Let not sin therefore reign" and "neither yield ye your members as instruments of unrighteousness," only because of the freedom from bondage that has been given to us through our becoming a new creation in Christ Jesus. The appeal "do not let sin continue to reign in your mortal bodies, as it used to" is based upon a liberation which has been accomplished. It is based upon the impartation of a new capacity in the area of the will, for whenever an appeal is made to the believer to do something that will be pleasing to God, it is never an appeal to this old will. God never makes an appeal to the old mind, to the old heart, to the old will. God never asks the old mind to receive spiritual truths or divine revelations. He never appeals to the old heart to receive and respond to the love of God. He never makes an appeal to the old will to do something that will be acceptable to God, or to obey God. God knows the limitations of the old personality and never makes an appeal to it. So when the apostle makes an appeal to the child of God, as he does in verses 12 and 13, he appeals to a new capacity imparted by the miracle of new creation which makes it possible for the child of God to respond to that which is enjoined.

In verse 18 the apostle says, "Being then made free from sin, . . ." You must be very careful here. The apostle did not say, "You have been made free from any possibility of committing sin again." He did not say, "You have been made free of the possibility of the old will obeying sin further." But he says, "You have been made free from the obligation to obey the sin nature and to obey the dictates of the old will."

How is one made free from sin? Only as he is given freedom by the new creation in Christ Jesus. Then he is made free from enslavement to the old will because a new capacity has been imparted to the child of God. The same thing is affirmed in verse 22 of this passage, where the apostle says, "But now, being made free from sin, . . . [ye became] servants to God." You were the servants or bondslaves of sin; you served it voluntarily. But now you have been made free from sin and you have become servants, or slaves, to God. There is now a choice within the capacity of will. A choice pleasing to the old capacity will result in sin; a choice conforming to the new capacity will result in obedience and righteousness and holiness.

The apostle teaches us this same truth in Romans 8:2, where

he says, "The law of the Spirit of life in Christ Jesus hath made me free from the law of sin and death." A principle operated within me as an unsaved man which is referred to here as the principle of sin and death. It is called the principle of sin and death because sin is its character and death is its result. Whereas I once served this principle as a master and lord because I had no other possibility, yet now by the Holy Spirit, which Paul calls the law of the Spirit of life in Christ Jesus, I have been made free from the law of sin and death. Again, we affirm the fact that the apostle is not saying that the possibility of sinning has been removed from us. That would mean that the old mind, the old heart, and the old will were eradicated. No, the apostle says that there is an emancipation from servitude to the old capacity because a new capacity has been imparted through the new birth. "What the law could not do, in that it was weak through the flesh, God sending his own Son in the likeness of sinful flesh, and for sin, condemned [or judged] sin in the flesh: that the righteousness of the law might be fulfilled in us, who walk not after the flesh, but after the Spirit." God's purpose is to produce righteousness in His child. But righteousness never comes from the operation of the old mind, the old heart, and the old will. Rather, righteousness comes as the Holy Spirit energizes the new mind, the new heart, and the new will.

The principle that the apostle affirms in Galatians 5:1 concerning the law is a valid principle related to the old capacities which the child of God had. In the fourth chapter of Galatians, the apostle dealt with the relationship of the individual to the law of Moses. The law cannot save, neither can it sanctify. Paul has shown that faith in the Lord Jesus Christ liberates from bondage to the law. Now he gives this appeal: "Stand fast therefore in the liberty wherewith Christ has made us free, and be not entangled again with the yoke of bondage." To those who were considering the idea of submitting to the law of Moses as a guiding principle for the fulfillment of God's requirements for the Christian life, the apostle addresses the question, "Why will those who have been liberated from the bondage of the law seek to put themselves back into bondage again?" And he affirms the glorious truth of liberation from any obligation to serve the law of Moses or the law of sin (the old nature) that dwells within us.

CONTINUAL CONFLICT

Because of the impartation of a new capacity to the will, the child of God is in constant conflict. There is an unrelenting and ceaseless warfare going on within him all the time. This warfare is described for us very clearly in Galatians 5:17 where the apostle says, "The flesh lusteth against the Spirit, and the Spirit against the flesh: and these are contrary the one to the other: so that ye cannot [or, may not] do the things that ye would." The word *flesh* in Galatians 5:17 refers to the sum total of the individual's personality: his mind, his heart, his will—all corrupted by the fall. The word *Spirit* in Galatians 5:17 refers to the Holy Spirit living in the child of God and expressing Himself in the new creation—the new capacity of mind, the new capacity of heart, the new capacity of will. In the area of the mind there is a constant warfare. What the old mind loves, the new hates; and what the new desires, the old despises. That same warfare is true in the realm of the heart. What the old heart desires and lusts after, the new capacity hates and despises; what the new seeks, the old utterly repudiates. That same warfare is true also in the area of the will. What the old will delights to serve, the new will draws back from obeying; what the new desires to do, the old utterly hates. So in every area of the total personality there is constant warfare. The old capacity and the new will never, under any circumstances, agree on a thought or a word or a deed. Never will the old mind agree with the new mind. Never will the old heart agree with the new heart. Never will the old will agree with the new will. If the old purposes one thing, the new contradicts it, and if the new would set something into operation, the old immediately seeks to countermand it. You, therefore, as a child of God, are facing constant, ceaseless, unrelenting warfare in the areas of mind, heart, and will every moment that you live.

The seventh chapter of Romans gives us Paul's testimony concerning this warfare within himself. In verses 22 and 23 he says,

"I delight in the law of God after the inward man: but I see another law in my members, warring against the law of my mind, and bringing me into captivity to the law of sin which is in my members." There the apostle again emphasizes this fact of constant warfare. When he says, "I delight in the law of God after the inward man," he is referring to the sum total of the capacities given to him in the new creation. And Paul says that his new mind revels in the truth of God, and his new heart loves the Person of God, and his new will delights to obey the will of God. But when with his new mind he knows, loves, and serves God, immediately war is declared by the old against the new so that the old mind fights against the truth of God, and the old heart against the love of God, and the old will against obedience to God. We will never understand the conflict that we believers in Jesus Christ face day by day and moment by moment until we grasp this truth concerning the warfare that goes on within the total person in every area. Again and again we face discouragement, defeat, and frustration, just as the Apostle Paul did. He writes concerning his experience in conflict in Romans 7:15, "That which I [the old] do I [the new] allow not: for what I [the new] would, that I [the old] do not; but what I [the new] hate, that do I [the old]. If then I do that which I [the new] would not, I consent unto the law that it is good [for it condemns me]. Now it is no more I [the new] that do it [this wicked thought, this false affection, this disobedient act] but sin [the old capacity] that dwelleth in me. For I know that in me [that is in my flesh, my old mind and heart and will] dwelleth no good thing: for to will is present with me [because I have a new capacity of will], but how to perform that which is good I find not. For the good that I [the new] would I [the old] do not: but the evil which I [the new] would not, that I [the old] do. Now if I do that which I [the new] would not, it is no more I [the new capacity] that do it, but sin [the old capacity] that dwelleth in me." Thus Paul explains the origin of this conflict. It is not a conflict from without, but it is a conflict from within. And Paul explains it by continuing, "I see another law in my members, warring against the law of my mind [the new mind] and bringing me into captivity to the law of sin [that is, the old capacity] which is in my members."

According to human reasoning, it would have been wonderful if at the moment we were saved this old capacity had been eradicated immediately or if when we reached a certain state of maturity or sanctification this old capacity would become eradicated, leaving us with only a new heart, will, and mind. But the Word of God says that until the time of our translation into His presence and our glorification we will continue with both the old capacity and the new capacity. Consequently we face a lifelong conflict. We can be grateful for the teaching of the Word of God that gives very, very clearly the principles upon which one may have victory over the old capacity. The Word of God makes it very clear that we can walk in the train of His triumph.

APPEALS TO THE WILL

It is our purpose in succeeding studies to examine those portions in the Word of God which give instruction concerning the power provided by the Holy Spirit in order that we who are children of God might live so as to please Him. But, as we conclude this study on the new will, we would direct you to several passages where the apostle makes a specific appeal to the individual. I emphasize this in order that you might see that the Christian life is not a passive life but an active one. It is true that the Christian life is a life of rest, a life of trust, and we shall examine the teachings of the Word of God concerning the faith-rest life. But God has given to us a new will, a new will that He expects us to exercise. We are commanded to exercise the new will Godward. In Romans 6:13 the apostle says, "Yield yourselves unto God, as those that are alive from the dead, and your members as instruments of righteousness unto God." Now the word *yield* is the word which means "to present." When you yield, you turn yourself over completely to control by another. The believer is commanded to turn himself over to the Lord Jesus Christ, to be controlled by the Holy Spirit, so that righteousness might be reproduced in him by the Spirit's power. Now when Paul gives the command "Yield yourselves as instruments unto

God," and exhorts the believer, "Yield yourselves unto God," he is making an appeal to the new capacity of will. This is something which the child of God can do which he could not do before he was saved, for he has this new capacity, and he can exercise that capacity in a Spirit-directed choice. So when the apostle commands believers not to let sin continue to reign, and not to continue yielding their members to sin's control but to yield themselves unto God and to present their members as instruments of righteousness, he is calling for an act of the new will. In verse 16, the apostle affirms the same truth when he asks, "Know ye not that to whom ye yield yourselves servants to obey, his servants ye are to whom ye obey; whether of sin unto death, or of obedience unto righteousness." Paul shows us the capacity which the child of God has, the capacity to present himself as an obedient servant unto God so that the fruits of righteousness may be reproduced in him.

In Ephesians 4:24, the apostle has another word to say concerning righteousness as God's objective in the new creation: "Put on the new man, which after God is created in righteousness and true holiness." He has exhorted the child of God (v. 22) to put off the former manner of life. That putting off is an act of the will. But he is not to be left naked. He is to put on the new man so that instead of lying he will speak the truth; he can be angry and not sin; he will stop stealing; he will stop gossiping, and so on. Now this act of putting off and of putting on is an act of the new will. The old will can never put off the things of the flesh, but the new will may obey God in this.

In Colossians 3:9-10 the apostle brings us this same truth. He tells us of the divine work that has been done for us through the new birth: "Ye have put off the old man with his deeds; and have put on the new man." Now the old man that you have put off is the old mind, heart, and will. The new man that you have put on is that which has been imparted as the result of new creation. What are you to do because you have become a new creature in Christ Jesus? Paul says to believers, "Put off all these" (v. 8), and then he mentions some of the sins of the flesh which they are to put off. In verse 12 he says, "Put on therefore, as the elect of God," and then he mentions the fruit that the Spirit will produce through the new creature. Now when Paul says, "Put off" (v. 8) and "put on" (v. 12), he is making an appeal to the new will, which can be in subjection to the Spirit of God. By Him the righteousness of Christ will be reproduced in the believer.

In mentioning these verses in which an appeal is made to the will, we do not mean to imply that the Christian life is lived because a man, by determination, by his own strength, manifests the new mind, the new heart, and the new will. Not at all! Apart from the power of the Spirit of God the child of God cannot do this putting off and this putting on. But when either a command or an exhortation is given to the child of God, it is given because sin's bondage has been broken, because we have been freed from servitude to sin, and because we have been given a new capacity, a new will, that we may fulfill that which God commands. Those who once were bondservants and slaves have been liberated. Sin's chains have been broken! Not only has the condemnation of sin been removed through the death of Christ but the confining shackles of sin have been taken away. Now we may enjoy the liberty that belongs to the child of God, and enjoy full fellowship with Him.

Some years ago when I was a student in seminary, living in the dormitory, one of my friends had a canary. When my friend studied, he would close the door of his room and open the cage door and let his canary fly around. The canary would go joyfully from place to place in the room and sing as though his heart would burst. He was enjoying a new liberty. On one occasion, after letting the canary out of his cage, my friend was called out of the room. One of his friends came into the room and felt that the room was pretty stuffy. So he went to the window and threw it open. The bird flew out into the dusk and a freedom which it had never known before. My friend was heartsick when he discovered that his bird was gone. He turned on all the lights in his room, put the cage on the windowsill, and propped open the door of the cage as wide as he could. He filled the cup in the cage with fresh seed and put bits of lettuce inside the cage in hope that the bird might be enticed back. But the bird did not return. When I asked if he had seen anything of his canary, he said, "No, I guess he is enjoying his newfound freedom too much to come back to the confines of his cage again."

Oh, child of God, what a tragedy it is that we who have been brought out from sin's domain into freedom should go back to the old bondage, to the old servitude, and voluntarily submit to slavery under the old master again! Thank God, we do not have to go back. We do not need to submit to sin's enticement. We can walk as new creatures of Christ Jesus in the light and the love and the liberty that has been given to us through Jesus Christ.

CHAPTER

9

WHAT IS MAN?

Romans 8:1-8

ONE OF THE MAJOR SECRETS of victory in any conflict is knowing your enemy. No commanding officer would send his troops into battle without first learning all he could about the adversary against whom he was fighting. No team engaged in an athletic contest would think of going into a game without trying to discover the tactics which the opposing team would use. No businessman would introduce a competitive product on the market without first trying to discover what his competitor was offering to the public. To be successful in any enterprise, we must be informed about our competitors or our adversaries. Many of God's children are totally defeated in their Christian life because they do not understand the conflict in which they are engaged nor the adversary against whom they fight. They have been betrayed by divisive tactics. They have focused all-out attention upon Satan, the evil one. They have been mindful of the wiles of the devil, and have failed to realize that the greatest enemy they face is themselves, the adversary within.

Three words or phrases are used in the New Testament to describe man. He is referred to as "the flesh"; he is referred to as "the old man"; he is referred to as "sin." We want to examine these words in order that we might understand ourselves and, understanding ourselves, see the nature of the conflict in which we are engaged. Such a study as this is not popular, for who can find any enjoyment in looking at the evil forces within him? We are not trying to present a popular message, but we are trying to present the truth of the Word of God so that you may understand the nature of the conflict. Only then can you fully appreciate the glorious provision which God has made for His children so that they can triumph over the enemy within.

THE TERM "FLESH"

The first and the most important of these words to which we direct your attention is the word *flesh*. In the New Testament, this word has a nontheological, or nonethical, usage and a theological usage.

In its first nontheological usage, the word *flesh* refers to the physical body in which the person dwells. Through this body a person expresses the mind, the emotions, and the will which constitute his personality. For instance, in I Corinthians 15:39 the apostle says, "All flesh is not the same flesh: but there is one kind of flesh of men, another flesh of beasts, another of fishes, and another of birds." There the apostle points out the fact that in creation God did not give every being the same kind of body. In this usage of the word, there is no ethical connotation at all. The word refers to a body made up of flesh and blood.

In its second nontheological usage, the word *flesh* is used to describe, or differentiate, classes of man. We find that it is used of both Jews and Gentiles as classes or groups. For instance, in Romans 1:3, Paul refers to God's "Son Jesus Christ our Lord, which was made of the seed of David according to the flesh." There "flesh" refers to a national designation. In His incarnation Jesus Christ was born of the seed of Abraham and was a Jew by race. In Ephesians Paul writes to Gentiles and says, "Remember, that ye being in time past Gentiles in the flesh, who are called uncircumcision by that which has called the circumcision in the flesh made by hands . . ." (Eph. 2:11). Paul's usage of the word *flesh* here has no ethical connotation. He is referring to "Gentiles in the flesh" as a division of the human race.

The third nontheological use of this word refers to mankind as a whole. In Romans 3:20, the apostle says, "Therefore by the deeds of the law there shall no flesh be justified in his sight: for by the law is the knowledge of sin." "Flesh," in that passage, means all mankind, the whole human race, created by God, possessed of bodies of flesh and blood. Now, when man is referred to as flesh, the term emphasizes his weakness, his corruptibility, his mortality—characteristics of a body which, because of sin, is passing away.

When we come to the theological usage of the word *flesh* we find that it is used to show us what we are in the sight of God as a result of Adam's sin. It is from the theological usage of the word that we gain a clear picture of what we are and an understanding of the nature of the enemy that dwells within.

First of all, the word *flesh,* in its ethical or theological sense, refers to one's own effort independent of God. It refers to that which a man does apart from divine aid, divine guidance, or divine empowerment. In Romans 4:1 the Apostle Paul says, "What shall we say then that Abraham our father, as pertaining to the flesh, hath found?" We might rephrase Paul's question this way: "What shall we say then that Abraham, our father, by his own power and strength, unaided by God, accomplished or achieved?" The answer, of course, is "Nothing." Again, in Philippians 3:3, the apostle uses the word *flesh* in this same sense when he says, "We are the circumcision, which worship God in the spirit, and rejoice in Christ Jesus, and have no confidence in the flesh." We have no confidence in the flesh. Why? Because the flesh represents man's effort apart from divine help or assistance. In Galatians 3:3 the apostle uses this word with the same force. "Are ye so foolish? having begun in the Spirit, are ye now made perfect by the flesh?" You will notice in that passage, the flesh is put over against the Holy Spirit, and the flesh there represents all that man does by himself, apart from divine aid. The flesh, then, is human nature, the sum total of all man's personality that, as a result of the fall, is corrupt—a mind darkened, an emotional capacity degraded, and a will that is deadened toward God. The words "according to the flesh" or "by the flesh" describe work, or merit, or righteousness produced by the natural man of his own mind, his own emotion, his own volition, apart from God's help. Of necessity, all that is of the flesh is under divine judgment.

The second theological usage of the word *flesh* emphasizes infirmity, weakness, and helplessness. In Romans 8:3 we read, "What the law could not do, in that it was weak through the flesh [or, it was weak because it depended on flesh, which is weak in itself], . . ." Again, in Romans 6:19 the apostle says, "I speak after the manner of men because of the infirmity [or, weakness or impotence] of your flesh." Paul there characterizes the flesh as the seat of weakness and inability. Now this refers to man, not as he came directly from the hand of God in creation but to man after the fall, for by the fall the strength that was given to man in creation was stripped away and man, because he was flesh, was characterized by weakness, by impotence, and by helplessness.

A third characterization of the flesh is seen in Romans 7:5, where the apostle says, "When we were in the flesh, the motions of sins which were by the law, did work in our members to bring forth fruit unto death." Now, when Paul says we were *in* the flesh, he does not mean "when we were alive," and that now we have passed beyond the land of the living. Rather, he is using the term *flesh* as a sphere, or a state, in which we had our existence. To be in the flesh is to be in sin. To be in the flesh is to be in an unsaved or unregenerate state. To be in the flesh is to be controlled by sin that uses this mortal body as the vehicle through which it translates its desires into action, and its affections into deeds. The apostle says then that not only does the flesh represent our natural effort apart from God, characterized by weakness and impotence, but the flesh is a state; it is a condition in which all unregenerate men live.

A fourth concept of *flesh* which we ought to observe is presented in Romans 7:18, where Paul says, "I know that in me (that is, in my flesh) dwelleth no good thing." The apostle is using "flesh" here for the sum total of the old capacity which a man has as a result of the fall. The flesh represents the old mind, the old heart, the old will. You will observe, in verse 18, that the apostle makes a distinction between the flesh and himself. He is not his flesh, but he is characterized by flesh. The Apostle Paul, because he has been saved, is a new man in Christ Jesus, and he is not to be equated with the flesh. Even an unsaved man is not equated with the flesh, for the flesh has no personality. But a man is fleshly because he is dominated and controlled by the flesh.

In Romans 8:3 we find another reference to the word *flesh*.

Here the apostle says that God sent His own Son in the "likeness of sinful flesh." Sin is not inherent in the flesh, that is, in the corporeal, or physical body which we possess. Because of a philosophy prevalent among the Greeks which held that all things material are corrupt and evil and only spirit is uncorrupted, the gnostics of Paul's day taught that Jesus Christ could not have had a material body, for that would have meant that Jesus Christ had a sinful body, because sin dwelt in the flesh itself. Paul in Romans 8:3 showed that Christ's physical body was not sinful flesh. He was sent in "the *likeness* of sinful flesh." Adam was created with a physical body, but Adam was not created a sinner. Adam lived in a physical body in the garden of Eden before the fall, but Adam did not have sin because he had a body. When Jesus Christ came into the world by the miracle of the virgin birth, He possessed a true, complete humanity. He possessed a man's body, but He did not have a sinful body.

What we are trying to show you is that your body of flesh is not sinful but is the vehicle through which sin operates to translate its desires into deeds. Having a physical body does not mean that a person must practice sin, for sin is not inherent in the flesh. But sin operates through this body as Paul makes clear in other passages. For instance, in Romans 13:14, Paul writes, ". . . make no provision for the flesh, to fulfill the lusts thereof." How does sin operate? It operates through the body. You find the same thing said again in Romans 6:12-19, "Let not sin, therefore, reign in your mortal body [that is, your flesh], that ye should obey it in the lusts thereof. Neither yield ye your members as instruments of unrighteousness unto sin: . . . For sin shall not have dominion over you: . . . as ye have yielded your members [that is, the physical parts of this human body] servants to uncleanness and to iniquity unto iniquity; even so now yield your members servants to righteousness unto holiness." The apostle, in the fifth chapter of Galatians, makes it very clear that the fruits of the sin nature manifest themselves through the physical body. This does not mean that there are no sins of the mind, for pride is a sin of the mind. Covetousness is a sin of the mind. Lust may be a sin of the mind. But the apostle says that when these sins of the mind demonstrate themselves, they do it through some member of this body.

That leads to the conclusion that this fleshly body is the vehicle through which sin operates, and apart from this body, apart from this flesh, sin cannot have an overt manifestation. We rejoice in the redemption that has been provided for us in Christ Jesus. Well do we sing, "Redeemed, how I love to proclaim it." How we praise God for the redemption that is in Christ! But redemption is not yet complete. I do not mean by that that we are not saved. But the apostle points out one portion of redemption that is still incomplete. In Romans 8:3 he says that "God . . . condemned sin in the flesh." Now, while sin has been condemned in the flesh, it does not mean the believer has been set free from the possibility of sin. The apostle says later, in verse 22, "We know that the whole creation groaneth and travaileth in pain together until now. And not only they, but ourselves also, which have the firstfruits of the Spirit, even we ourselves groan within ourselves, waiting for the adoption, to wit, the redemption of our body [or, the redemption of our flesh]." The apostle is anticipating resurrection. Not until we receive our glorified, resurrected body will redemption be complete. As long as we are in this mortal body, we are living in an unredeemed body; we are living in flesh which is the vehicle of sin.

The Apostle Paul makes a very perplexing statement in Romans 7:14, where he says, "We know that the law is spiritual, but I am carnal, sold under sin." The phrase "I am carnal" could be translated "I am fleshly." Now, what did the apostle mean? There are those who say that Paul had experienced salvation, as he testifies to that fact in the sixth chapter of Romans, but that he did not come into a full salvation experience until after the seventh chapter. They assert that in the seventh chapter he was living in weakness, ignorance, and immaturity. He was living in sin. He did not know the secret of victory over sin, and since he was practicing sin, he was carnal. I do not agree with those who take this view. Such a view suggests that a person cannot come to spirituality except by a long, difficult, and tedious process, that carnality is an essential part of our development and growth. The apostle is not speaking of his *experience* in Romans 7:14.

He is not telling us that he is practicing carnality, that he is doing this or that or the other thing that would be classified as carnal. Rather, he is telling us what he *is,* and he says ,"I am carnal." By that Paul means that he has experienced redemption from sin and is free from bondage to sin but that he still dwells in a body of flesh with all of the weakness, impotence, and helplessness to which the flesh is prone and that as long as he lives on this earth he will be a carnal being. He did not say, "As long as I live on the earth I will practice carnality." But he did say, "As long as I live in this body, I am carnal; I am a fleshly being with all of the potentiality and possibility to which the flesh is heir." We need to realize exactly the propensities of the flesh with which we are so intimately associated, because apart from resurrection, or translation, there will be no deliverance from this fleshly body. While the person has been redeemed, the flesh has not been redeemed, and we have to say, as Paul said, "We are carnal." We live with the flesh every moment of the day; it is impossible for us to put it off. It is something with which we must learn to live, and the provision which God has made for us in the victory that is ours in Christ takes into full account what the flesh is. Yet God's provision is sufficient to enable us to triumph over the flesh.

THE OLD MAN

The second word or phrase that the apostle uses to describe unregenerate man is "the old man." In Romans 6:6 Paul says, "Knowing this, that our old man is [has been] crucified with him, that the body of sin might be destroyed, that henceforth we should not serve sin." Our old man has been crucified! Again, the apostle uses the expression "the old man" in Ephesians 4:22, where Paul exhorts believers to "put off concerning the former conversation the old man, which is corrupt according to the deceitful lusts." Again, in Colossians 3:9, Paul says, "Lie not one to another, seeing that ye have put off the old man with his deeds." Now, the old man refers to the old sinful nature, the total personality, corrupted by the fall of Adam. "The old man" emphasizes the source of the corruption and takes us back to Adam, our first father, whose nature was corrupted by his disobedience and who passed on his nature to all his descendants.

"The old man" refers to the total unregenerate person, and the nature which he has received because of his connection with Adam, because he is a child of Adam. The term "the old man," like the term "flesh," refers to the old unrenewed self—the old mind, the old heart, the old will—which is corrupt, reprobate, blind, and lawless. The old man refers to what we were before God in salvation made each believing sinner a new man in Christ Jesus. "The old man" relates us to Adam, just as the phrase "the new man" relates us to Jesus Christ.

THE TERM "SIN"

The third word that is used to describe an unregenerate man is the word *sin*. Now, the word *sin,* on many occasions refers to the act which flows from the sin nature. We usually refer to these in the plural as sins. The word *sin* may also refer to the state in which all men are born because of Adam's sin. David says, "In sin did my mother conceive me." But the word *sin* also refers to the basic nature which men have as sinful human beings. The sixth chapter of Romans uses this word a number of times to refer to the quality of a man's nature, to the kind of person he is apart from the saving work of Jesus Christ. Romans 6:6: "Knowing this, that our old man is [has been] crucified with him, that the body of sin might be destroyed, that henceforth we should not serve sin." Now the apostle is not talking about a state, because you cannot serve sin as a state. He is not talking about individual acts, because you do not become a servant to individual acts. Rather, he is talking about the essential nature that is within us, and he uses the word *sin* to describe the quality, or kind, of nature which we possess. In verse 7 we read, "He that is dead is freed from sin [that is, free from necessary servitude to the sin nature]." In verse 10 we read, "In that he died, he died unto sin [that is, unto control by the sin nature] once." In verse 11 we read, "Reckon ye also yourselves to be dead indeed unto sin." Paul is not saying that we cannot commit a sin; rather he is saying, "Count it true that you died unto necessary or obligatory control by the sin nature." And so in this passage Paul emphasizes again and again the fact that the unbeliever is called by God "sin." In I John 1:8, the Apostle John says, "If we say that we have no sin, we deceive ourselves, and the truth is not in us." John is using the word *sin* as Paul uses it in the sixth chapter of Romans, to emphasize the fact that we have a nature within us that God calls sin, which we can refer to as "the sin nature."

When you put together the concepts contained in these three expressions—"flesh," "the old man," and "sin"—then you get a picture of the adversary against which we are called to war. We dwell in a corrupted body, a body characterized by weakness. We have flesh that is the instrument through which sin works. We derived it from Adam, our first father, so that it can be called "the old man." God calls the nature within us sin, because all that flows from that nature is sinful. That is why, in Galatians 5:19-21, where the apostle is writing concerning the sins that manifest themselves in a man, he calls these "the works of the flesh." First, you will notice that the works of the flesh are sensual—adultery, fornication, uncleanness, and lasciviousness. Second, the works of the flesh are perverted in regard to spiritual things, for men give themselves over to idolatry and witchcraft. Third, the works of the flesh are basically selfish, for the works of the flesh are hatred, variance, emulations, wrath, and strife. Fourth, the flesh is essentially intemperate, for men commit and give themselves over to revelings, and such like. You will notice that some of these works of the flesh are material, and others are immaterial. Some are deeply rooted in the mind, and others are translated into action; some works of the flesh are mental, and others are physical. This is indeed a dark picture. It is enough to bring about discouragement and despair if we concur in the divine estimate of the individual.

But the Word of God does more than portray accurately what we are in ourselves. It also brings to us the glorious message of liberation from the flesh, from the old man, and from sin, and it is that liberation to which we want to direct your attention in later chapters. This present study is neither comforting nor complimentary; yet it is essential, for unless we realize that we live every moment of every day with an adversary within that is seeking to manifest its basic nature through our flesh, we will not be prepared to turn to God to receive from Him the provision which He has made through the death of Jesus Christ and through the Holy Spirit for a life of victory and triumph over the flesh, the old man, and sin.

10

THE JUDGMENT AT THE CROSS

Colossians 2:9-17

How is it possible for a man to know freedom from sin, freedom from the dominion of a sin nature, freedom from the practice of sin, and deliverance from the power of Satan, the prince of the power of the air? The answer is, through the threefold judgment of the cross.

The cross of the Lord Jesus Christ is portrayed in Scripture not only as we often consider it, an emblem of the love of God, but more as the emblem of God's judgment upon sin. When God's love for the world is presented to us in the Scripture, that love is described in terms of the giving of a Son, the coming of a Saviour, the offer of salvation through the Lord Jesus Christ. But the cross stands as an emblem of the holiness of God, His righteousness, and justice. It was on the cross that the Lord Jesus Christ was judged that we might be set free from sin and delivered from the power of Satan.

We would like to emphasize three aspects of the judgment accomplished at the cross which became the basis on which we who accept Jesus Christ as Saviour are liberated from sin in our daily experience. If we, as the children of God are to live the life of Jesus Christ, by the power of the Holy Spirit, we must be delivered from Satan's domain, we must be delivered from the dominion of the sin nature, and we must be delivered from the consequences of our sin. And it was at the cross of Christ that God so dealt with Satan and the sin nature that believers can be liberated to walk in newness of life. There was a threefold judgment of the cross: the judgment on Satan, the judgment on sins, and the judgment on the sin nature.

JUDGMENT ON SATAN

When we read the twelfth chapter of John, we see that Christ is anticipating His death and His resurrection. He had told the disciples, in verse 24, that it would be necessary for Him to die in order that through His death He might produce new life. It was also necessary for Jesus Christ to die, according to verse 31, so that He, by His death on the cross, might pronounce judgment on the prince of this world. He said, "Now is the judgment of this world: now shall the prince of this world be cast out." The judgment of Satan, the prince of this world, is again referred to in John 16:11. There Christ, again anticipating the fruits of His death, says that the Spirit will convict the world of judgment because the prince of this world is judged.

When we were born the first time by a physical birth we were born into a world that is Satan's domain. How did it become Satan's domain? Sovereign authority over this world was entrusted by God to Adam at the time of creation. Adam, by willful disobedience against God, forfeited his right to rule; and Satan, the tempter, by usurpation became the god of this world. He is so referred to by the Apostle Paul in II Corinthians 4:4. In Ephesians 2:2, Satan is referred to as the prince of the power of the air. Satan, as a king, has innumerable hosts of angels arranged in hierarchies under his authority. Men, apart from Christ, are under the dominion of Satan. Even though Satan is a usurper, yet he rules his subjects as an absolute monarch.

The question arises then, "Does Satan have a right to rule?" Because Satan has ruled from the time of the fall of man to the present day, does it mean that he has attained permanent right to rule? If Satan has an absolute and an irreversible right to rule, then we have no right to expect to be delivered or liberated from bondage to him. If he has attained the right to reign, then we are wrong in rebelling against him and wrong in seeking to live a life pleasing to God instead of one that is pleasing to the present world ruler. The Old Testament anticipated a time when the Lord Jesus Christ, as God's King, would come to institute a kingdom on this earth. It prophesied a time when God's Messiah would put down every rebel and subject all authority to Him. It looked forward to a time when righteousness would cover the earth as the waters cover the sea. All these prophecies anticipated the judgment of Satan, the overthrow of his reign, and the liberation of his subjects. But men did not understand how this liberation would be accomplished until after Jesus Christ came into this world and went to the cross at Calvary. When the Lord Jesus Christ died, God passed judgment upon the usurper. And God declared through those who preached Christ that men might be liberated from the one who, for so long, had held men captive in his kingdom. Satan had not acquired a permanent right to men's obedience. He had not acquired an inalienable right to rule.

In Colossians 2:15, the Apostle Paul makes very clear that Jesus Christ, by His death, "spoiled principalities and powers." Now the word "spoiled" is a word which means to take a prey, to relieve someone of his possessions. Jesus Christ, by the judgment of the cross, removed from Satan that scepter which he professed to have as a permanent possession. Christ robbed the principalities and powers under Satanic authority of their professed rights. He made a show of them openly, triumphing over them. And when Jesus Christ went to death, He robbed principalities and powers of their authority, and by His resurrection He demonstrated that the judgment was a valid judgment because He triumphed over the powers of hell and death. All hell was concentrated upon the tomb of Jesus Christ to try to keep the One who slumbered in death within its grip. But death could not keep its prey, and Jesus Christ, by His resurrection, demonstrated the validity of the judgment of the cross as it fell upon Satan.

Even though Satan was judged at the cross, the execution of that judgment was postponed and will take place when Jesus Christ comes to this earth a second time to reign. Then Satan will be bound, and will remain bound for the thousand years of our Lord's reign. It is not until after Satan has been released at the end of the millennial reign for a brief season that the judgment at the cross is finally executed, and Satan is cast into the lake of fire forever and ever. Satan, although judged, is active. He is as active and vigilant in his reign today as he ever was. The difference, however, is that before judgment was passed upon

Satan no one had any assurance that he could be delivered from Satan's dominion. But since God passed judgment upon Satan at the cross, the one who trusts Jesus Christ as Saviour can be sure that Satan has no right to compel the child of God to obey. When Satan comes to tempt a child of God, he has the right and the authority to rebuke Satan as a tempter because judgment has been passed upon him and to remind him that he, as a judged and deposed monarch, has no right to continue issuing orders to you as though you still were in his kingdom and under his domain. The deliverance of the believer from sin in his daily life rests, first of all, upon the judgment on Satan, passed at the cross.

JUDGMENT ON SINS

In the second place, God at the cross passed judgment on the sins of the world. We have discovered from our study of the Scripture that man is not only in bondage to Satan by his natural birth but is also in bondage to sin. All of the fruits that flowed from his life were characterized and categorized by God as sinful. The works of the flesh were sinful in the sight of God. And when Jesus Christ went to the cross at Calvary, He went there in order that judgment might be passed by God upon the sins of the world. Sins as acts, sins as deeds, sins as transgressions, were brought under divine judgment. John the Baptist made this clear when he pointed to Jesus Christ and said, "Behold the Lamb of God, which taketh away the sin of the world" (John 1:29). And the Apostle John said that Jesus Christ "is the propitiation [that is, the covering over] for our sins [the sins of believers]: and not for ours only, but also for the sins of the whole world" (I John 2:2). In Hebrews 2:9, the writer said, "We see Jesus, who was made a little lower than the angels for the suffering of death, crowned with glory and honour; that he by the grace of God should taste death for every man." The value of the death of Christ is for those who personally accept Him as Saviour. But when Jesus Christ went to the cross so that sins might be judged in His body on the tree, the sins of the world were judged by God. When the Apostle Paul defined the gospel which he preached, he said, "I delivered unto you first of all that which I also received, how that Christ died for our sins according to the scriptures" (I Cor. 15:3). The first point of Paul's gospel was that Christ died for our sins. The sinner had incurred an indebtedness which he could not possibly pay. Eternity would be too short for a man to be able to discharge his indebtedness to God. When Jesus Christ went to the cross He bore our sins in His own body (I Peter 2:24), and while He hung on the cross, He said, "It is finished." The word translated "It is finished" is the word which when used in a business transaction meant "paid in full." Archeologists have uncovered a tax collector's office where they found a number of tax statements across the face of which had been written this same word. This word meant that the tax bill had been paid. And when our Lord said "It is finished," He was saying that our debt of sin had been paid for and could be cancelled because sin had been judged.

The apostle brings out this truth in Colossians 2:14, where he says that Jesus Christ, in His death, blotted out "the handwriting of ordinances that was against us, which was contrary to us, and took it out of the way, nailing it to his cross." No Roman citizen could be put in prison until an indictment containing a list of his crimes had been filed and the man had been tried to see whether that indictment was true. If a man was found guilty as indicted and was put in prison, it was the custom to nail that indictment over his prison cell so that any individual going through the prison could look at that indictment and know exactly why the prisoner was in prison. That indictment was a "handwriting of ordinances." Now, after the citizen had served his time and had paid the penalty for his crime, the chief jailer would take that indictment from over his cell and would write across the face of that indictment words to indicate that the debt had been cancelled through the man's imprisonment. And then that cancelled indictment would be given to the released prisoner. The released prisoner would return to his home and would post that indictment on his door. If any should question his right to be out of prison, he could point to the cancelled indictment and show that the debt had been cancelled and that he had a right to be free. Now, the apostle says, an indictment had been filed against us, an indictment that carried the record of our sin, transgression, iniquity, and unrighteousness. Because we could not cancel that debt, the Lord Jesus Christ took it to His cross so that if one were to pass by and ask the Lord Jesus Christ, "Why are you there?" He could refer to your indictment and mine and say, "That is why I am on this cross." And when Jesus Christ died, God wrote across your indictment and mine, "It is finished; it has been paid." Therefore all believing sinners have a right to post a cancelled indictment that has been signed in the blood of Jesus Christ declaring that they are free because Jesus Christ has paid the price.

The second great basis on which the believer is delivered from sin in his daily life in order that he may walk in the newness of life is that sins were judged at the tree.

JUDGMENT ON THE SIN NATURE

The third great area of the judgment of the cross is that a judgment was passed upon the sin nature. The sin nature was judged at the cross. In Romans 8:3, Paul states, "What the law could not do, in that it was weak through the flesh, God sending his own Son in the likeness of sinful flesh, and for sin, condemned [or judged] sin in the flesh." At the cross God judged sin (that is, the sin nature) in the flesh (that is, in the Lord Jesus Christ). This same truth is presented in Romans 6:6, where Paul says, "Knowing this, that our old man [you could substitute the words 'the sin nature' for 'old man' in this verse and do no violence to the text] is [has been] crucified with him, that the body of sin might be destroyed [disannulled]." The sin nature is not destroyed, as the English text suggests. But the sin nature has been rendered inoperative; it has been disannulled.

The question that faces one is this: Does the old sin nature with which I was born into this world have an inflexible, inalienable right to control my thoughts, words, and deeds? The sin nature has operated without opposition in untold multitudes of the sons of Adam. One might conclude that the authority of the sin nature could never be broken, that no one could rebel against its control. But when Jesus Christ died God actually passed judgment on our sin nature at the cross. Therefore God can say to all the redeemed that the right of the sin nature to

reign and to rule has been broken, and that those who believe
in Christ need no longer submit to its authority.

Certain facts should be observed in the light of this truth.
First, just as the judgment upon Satan does not mean Satan is
inactive and the judgment on sins does not mean that one can
no longer sin, so the judgment on the sin nature does not mean
that the sin nature can no longer operate. It is tragically true
that it operates and frequently controls us. Yet the necessity of
obeying the sin nature has been broken for the child of God because God has passed judgment upon that sin nature through the
death of Jesus Christ on the cross. The judgment on this sin nature did not change the essential character of the nature, did not
rehabilitate the sin nature, did not change it one iota. But the
judgment on sin has changed my relationship to the sin nature.
Before I became a child of God I was obligated to obey the sin
nature. Now, because I am a child of God, I know I need not
obey the sin nature because its power has been disannulled and
its right to rule has been broken. This sin nature, although
judged, is still active. There is no motivation of the will, no affection of the heart, no thought of the mind which the sin nature
does not seek to control. But even though the sin nature is active,
we have been released from obligation to obey it. For instance,
the President of the United States saw fit to remove Douglas
MacArthur, at the height of his career, from his command in
the Pacific. Douglas MacArthur did not lose his position as a
general, but his removal did mean that those who formerly had
obeyed him no longer had a responsibility to him. They then
were responsible to the general who had been named to succeed
him. MacArthur continued as a general, but as a general whose
authority was disannulled, whose right to command was cancelled. In like manner the sin nature once was our master and
overlord, but its authority was cancelled, and we who are children
of God have been delivered from bondage to it, even though it
continues active in our lives. We may choose to obey the old
commander, but it is not necessary to do so.

In the second place, we were delivered from the obligation to
obey the sin nature in order that we might be brought under
authority to Jesus Christ. We are not liberated from control

by the sin nature to embark upon a course of lawlessness and independence, in which we seek to please ourselves, but we were delivered from bondage to the sin nature in order that we might be brought into bondage to Jesus Christ. The Apostle Paul makes this clear in Romans 6:13, as he says, "Neither yield ye your members as instruments of unrighteousness unto sin; but yield [or, present] yourselves unto God, as those that are alive from the dead, and your members as instruments of righteousness unto God." We were delivered to be brought into bondage, bondage to the Lord Jesus Christ.

In the third place, we were delivered in order that we should not continue in sin. The purpose of this deliverance was not simply to deplete the ranks of those who followed Satan, nor to depopulate his kingdom. We were delivered from Satan and from sin and from the sin nature in order that we might practice righteousness. The apostle, in Romans 6:12, says, "Let not sin therefore reign [continue to reign] in your mortal body, that ye should obey it in the lusts thereof." We are to become servants unto righteousness.

The fourth observation is that this release itself does not give us the power to live a righteous, holy, God-pleasing life. The apostle points this out in Galatians 5:16 as he says, "Walk in the Spirit, and ye shall not fulfil the lust of the flesh." The fact of our release from Satan and from sin and from control by the sin nature does not give us the power to live the life of Christ. This life can be lived only by the Holy Spirit of God, who can produce in us the righteousness for which we were set free from dominion to Satan, to sin, and to the sin nature. One of the commonest errors among believers is the belief that, having been saved, we have the power to live a life of godliness and holiness by ourselves. It is only as we walk by means of the Spirit of God that the righteousness of Christ can be reproduced in us.

Finally, we discover in Romans 8:4 that this release from control by Satan and sins and the sin nature is what makes victory possible. The apostle said that sin was judged in the flesh "*that* [in order that] the righteousness of the law might be fulfilled in us, who walk not after the flesh, but after the Spirit." The release through the judgment of the cross makes victory possible. Our victory, our triumph, our reproduction of the life of Christ in our daily experience is inextricably tied in with the death of the Lord Jesus Christ for us. It is the cross of Christ that gives liberty—liberty from Satan's dominion, liberty from the condemnation of sin, liberty from control by the sin nature. The cross of Christ is God's means of victory, and all that the Spirit of God can do in and through the child of God has its basis in the judgment that was passed by God at the cross of Christ. You can never appropriate the power of the Spirit of God to live a life of holiness until, first of all, you have appropriated the freedom that is yours through the judgment—the judgment of Satan, and sin, and the sin nature—accomplished through the offering up of Jesus Christ for sin. In the light of this we understand what Paul meant in Galatians 6:14 when he said, "God forbid that I should glory, save in the cross of our Lord Jesus Christ, by whom the world is crucified unto me, and I unto the world." Paul had no basis for deliverance apart from the cross of Christ. We can well sing, "In the cross of Christ I glory, towering o'er the wrecks of time," because all the freedom which we enjoy is a freedom based upon the judgment of the cross.

PART

II

DESIGN FOR CONDUCT

CRUCIFIED WITH CHRIST

Galatians 2:15-21

THE CHRISTIAN LIFE is the life of Christ reproduced in the child of God, by the power of the Holy Spirit. Christian living is Christ living His life in and through the believer. The Christian life has its difficulties, its doctrine, and its deportment. In previous chapters we have seen the difficulties in the Christian life; the nature within us, the curse because of the fall, the blindness of our minds, the degradation of our emotions, the deadness of our will toward God. All put insuperable difficulties before the child of God in his purpose to live a Christian life. After having examined the scriptural teaching on the difficulties which we face, it is fitting that we should move into the area of the doctrines pertaining to the Christian life. It is at this point that many of God's children come far short of the provision which has been made for them in the Word of God. Just as there are doctrines that pertain to salvation by grace through faith, so there are doctrines that pertain to the living of the life of Christ by the child of God. Only after he has grasped the doctrines of the Christian life will he be ready to move into the area of practical deportment, or conduct, in the outworking of these doctrines in daily experience.

The child of God needs to recognize that certain responsibilities, obligations, and requirements are laid upon him by God. He needs to see himself under a divine fiat to fulfil the injunctions to "put off the old man" and to "put on the new" in daily life. But what is the basis by which we can fulfil these injunctions? What has God done in order that we might be liberated experientially from sin and dominion by the sin nature? Many different solutions have been propounded to answer such questions. For instance, there are those who have suggested that the best way to deal with this problem is to practice what might be called suppressionism—putting down the old man, denying the sin nature that is within us, and preventing the sin nature from manifesting itself through us by our own will power. Such a doctrine of the Christian life inevitably leads to legalism. A man sets up a series of laws and rules and determines to prevent the sin nature from manifesting itself. But suppressionism is not God's answer to the problem of sin in the believer's life. Man does not have power to control the old nature. He cannot control sin.

There are those who have propounded the doctrine of eradication. Those who accept this doctrine believe a man may have the sin nature eradicated or removed. They suggest that one may eventually come to the place where he no longer has a battle with the sin nature, for the sin nature has been eliminated. Sometimes we wish that this were true, and covet a second blessing that would eliminate the battle with sin. But this, of course, is the desire of the weakling who seeks to be removed from the battle completely, instead of equipping himself with the whole armor of God. Eradicationism is not taught in Scripture, and is no solution to the problems of the sin nature.

Some deal with the whole subject by giving it the silent treatment; that is, they treat the problem as though it did not exist. The idea seems to be that a child of God, apart from instruction in the Word of God, will somehow drift into a Christian life and will, by some mysterious process of osmosis, absorb the truths of the Word of God concerning the believer's new life. Many of God's children are struggling against insurmountable difficulties in living the life of Christ because of ignorance of the subject. Ignorance is certainly no solution to the problem of the sin nature.

There are those who teach self-crucifixion. They exhort the Christian to crucify himself as Christ crucified Himself, so that by putting himself to death, he will come to the end of the problem of the sin nature. A good many prominent teachers go astray at this point, for they give repeated exhortations to an individual to crucify himself. Self-crucifixion is a physical impossibility.

Jesus Christ could not crucify Himself. It had to be done to Him. The Word of God does not ask any believer to put himself to death.

THE PRINCIPLE OF IDENTIFICATION

God's solution is found in Romans 6:11: "Reckon ye also yourselves to be dead indeed unto sin, but alive unto God through Jesus Christ our Lord." God's solution is not suppressionism, nor eradicationism, nor silence that fails to instruct, nor self-crucifixion, but rather a reckoning, a believing, an acceptance of an accomplished fact. God's solution to the problem of sin in the believer's life is based on his identification with Christ.

Paul refers to identification with Christ when he says, "I am crucified with Christ: nevertheless I live; yet not I, but Christ liveth in me." The key phrase to which we direct your attention is the first portion of this verse, "I am [or literally, I have been] crucified with Christ." Identification with Christ in His crucifixion is a fact which Christians are to believe. When Jesus Christ died, we died together with Him. Identification with Christ involves not only crucifixion with Christ but burial with Christ, resurrection with Christ, ascension and glorification with Christ. We have been so identified with Him that God reckons us as having experienced cocrucifixion, coburial, coresurrection, coascension and coglorification.

How can this be? How can it be said that I, living nearly 2,000 years after Christ lived, have been crucified with Him? How can it be said that I have been resurrected with Christ? How can it be said of the believer that he has ascended and has been glorified with Christ when he is very much alive on this earth? The answer to these questions is found in the great truths involved in the doctrine of the baptizing work of the Holy Spirit. It is not our purpose to develop that doctrine in detail but rather to affirm what the apostle discloses in I Corinthians 12:13, the fact that "by one Spirit are we all baptized into one body, whether we be Jews or Gentiles, whether we be bond or free; and have been all made to drink into one Spirit." According to this passage, the baptizing work of the Spirit is that work whereby He joins those who have accepted Jesus Christ as personal Saviour to the body of which Jesus Christ is the living Head so that all that is true of the Head is also true of each member in His Body.

What does it mean to have been baptized? That question brings us to one of the most debated words in the Word of God, a word very much misunderstood because of the questions about the mode of baptism that inevitably arise when the doctrine of baptism is discussed. The Greek word *baptō,* from which we get the word *baptize,* means literally "to dip," "to plunge," or "to immerse." It is the word that was normally used by the fuller, or dyer, the man who prepared cloth. The fuller took raw, undressed cloth and put it into the dye vat. When that cloth was brought out of the dye vat, its entire appearance was changed. The fuller was said to have "baptized" the cloth.

This word, like many words, had both a literal and a metaphorical, or a symbolic, usage. When it was used literally, it had to do with dipping, plunging, putting something into something. But in its metaphorical usage it meant "to change identity," that is, to change appearance, to change the outward form in which this thing met the eye. This metaphorical usage of the word was its common usage in Greek. When the apostle uses the word concerning our relationship to Jesus Christ, he is using it in this widely accepted metaphorical way. Paul is not saying we have been dipped in a dye pot but, rather, we have changed our identity by forming a new union with Jesus Christ. May I use our English word *iron* to illustrate the literal and the metaphorical usage of a word? The word *iron* literally refers to a metal, and we commonly use the word in that way. But it also has its metaphorical usage. It may refer to courage, to hardness, or to strength of character. We refer to robustness of a man's physical body by saying he has an iron constitution. We say a man has a will of iron. In this usage the word means firmness, stubbornness, or obstinacy. We say a man rules with an iron fist, and in this usage *iron* refers to harshness, or severity of treatment. In our language, this word is used more frequently in its metaphorical sense than in its literal sense. This is also true of the word translated "baptize."

The thought of identifying one thing with another appears very early in the Word of God. For instance, in the sixteenth chapter of Leviticus we read about an act by which one identified himself with something else. This chapter gives us the ritual of the day of atonement. In the first portion of the ritual, the priest killed the goat which was the sin offering, and presented the blood. He then moved to the second portion of the ritual, that is, the separation of the scapegoat. We read in verse 20, "When he hath made an end of reconciling the holy place, and the tabernacle of the congregation, and the altar, he shall bring the live goat: and Aaron shall lay both his hands upon the head of the live goat, and confess over him all the iniquities of the children of Israel, and all their transgressions in all their sins, putting them upon the head of the goat, and shall send him away by the hand of a fit man into the wilderness: and the goat shall bear upon him all their iniquities unto a land not inhabited: and he shall let go the goat in the wilderness." Notice particularly that Aaron was to lay both his hands upon the head of the live goat. And while his hands were superimposed, he was to confess all the sins of the nation Israel. What did that imposition of hands signify? It signified that the one making the confession was identifying himself with the one upon whose head those sins were being confessed. The priest, representing the whole nation, confessed the sins of the nation. Then the priest, by laying on his hands, identified the nation Israel with this sin bearer. That was an act by which the nation was identified with the sacrifice.

We find a similar use of symbolism in the New Testament. In the thirteenth chapter of Acts we find the church at Antioch ready to send out Barnabas and Paul to the work of evangelizing the Gentiles. In Acts 13:2 we read, "As they ministered to the Lord, and fasted, the Holy Ghost said, Separate me Barnabas and Saul for the work whereunto I have called them. And when they had fasted and prayed, and laid their hands on them, they sent them away." Again we see the imposition of hands. Why? The believers at Antioch were identifying themselves with their emissaries, who were going forth to preach the gospel. This laying on of hands was an act of identification in which the church united themselves with their representatives. We find something similar in I Timothy 4:14, where Paul says to Timothy, "Neglect not the gift that is in thee, which was given thee by prophecy, by

the laying on of the hands of the presbytery." In II Timothy
1:6 Paul again refers to this laying on of hands: "I put thee in
remembrance that thou stir up the gift of God which is in thee
by putting on of my hands." The laying on of hands was an
act by which Paul and the church were identified with Timothy
as a minister of the gospel. In the Old Testament (in the relation
of the nation to the scapegoat) and in the New Testament (in
the relation of the church to the Lord's servants) the idea is the
same. The one identifies himself with the other so that a union
is constituted.

Another act of identification is described in the third chapter
of the Gospel of Matthew, where we are introduced to one who
bears the name John the Baptist, or John the Identifier. John
appeared in the wilderness to call out to himself a separated
people, to separate to the Messiah a believing remnant anticipating His coming. And John proclaimed, "Repent ye, for the
kingdom is at hand" (Matt. 3:2). Turn! Turn from your sin!
Turn to God and wait for the coming One! And then John said,
"I indeed baptize you with water unto [or, with a view to] repentance: but he that cometh after me is mightier than I, whose
shoes I am not worthy to bear: he shall baptize you with the
Holy Ghost, and with fire" (v. 11). John was practicing identification by baptizing. He identified a separated people (separated
from Pharisaism and from Judaism) with the Messiah. And
the sign of identification was water. When Christ came to be
baptized by John the Identifier, He received the sign of identification. John's baptism signified that these who once had belonged
to Judaism, who had been characterized by Pharisaism, had taken
on a new identity. They are identified by John as those who are
waiting for Messiah to come. The identifier put his identifying
mark on them, and those who received John's baptism were the
identified, or the baptized, ones.

We see the Apostle Peter using baptism as an identifying sign
in the second chapter of the book of Acts. Peter, after the death
and resurrection of Christ, stood up before the nation that had
been guilty of asking for the crucifixion of Jesus and proved to
these people that Jesus was both Lord and Messiah because God
had raised Him from the dead. They responded by asking,

"What shall we do?" And Peter replied, "Repent [that is, change your mind about this Jesus whom you deem to be a blasphemous, insane man], and be baptized [be identified] everyone of you in the name of Jesus Christ for [with a view to] the remission of sins" (v. 38). Peter told them that their nation was under judgment and they needed to save themselves from that "untoward generation." What would their baptism do? It would change their identity. It would separate them from the old nation, the old citizenship, their old religion. It would separate them unto the Lord Jesus Christ. Thus this baptism was an identifying sign.

IDENTIFICATION WITH CHRIST

When the Apostle Paul refers in I Corinthians 12:13 to the baptism of the Holy Spirit and teaches that all believers were baptized into one Spirit, he is saying that we have been identified with Jesus Christ and a union has been formed with Him. Now, this question arises: To what have we been joined? With what have we been identified? And here is a mystery so deep that we would be in complete ignorance concerning it did not the Word of God reveal it to us. The apostle teaches that when believers were baptized into one body by one Spirit, they were baptized into Christ's death, burial, resurrection, ascension, and glorification. Let us briefly note these great facts in Christ's redemptive work with which we, as believers, have been identified.

In Galatians 2:20 Paul says, "I am [I have been] crucified with Christ." What does that mean? When Jesus Christ died, I was so identified and united with Him that I died also. I was crucified with Christ. In Colossians 1:21-22 Paul says, "And you, that were sometime alienated and enemies in your mind by wicked works, yet now hath he reconciled in the body of his flesh through death, to present you holy and unblameable, and unreproveable in his sight." The apostle affirms again the fact that when Christ died, we died with Him. In Colossians 3:5 Paul says, "Mortify [put to death] therefore your members." Why? Because you "have put off the old man, with his deeds; and have put on the new man" (v. 9). The putting off is death, and the putting on is resurrection. Again, in Romans 6:3, Paul says, "Know ye not, that so many of us as were baptized into Jesus Christ were baptized into his death? Therefore we are buried with him by baptism into death: that like as Christ was raised up from the dead by the glory of the Father, even so we also should walk in newness of life." This is the first great fact: We were identified with Christ in His death, so that when Christ died, we died. Now this is not something we can prove, this is not something that, experientially, we can put to a test and demonstrate. This is a fact of divine revelation that we are called upon to believe. We were not consciously present. We have no sensory perception of our death with Christ, but it was nonetheless a real death. We were baptized by the Spirit into Christ Jesus, and by that act we were baptized into Christ Jesus, as we also were baptized into His death. Thus the first great work of Christ in which we were identified was His death.

Second, Paul says in Romans 6:4 that believers were also identified with Christ in His burial. "We are buried with him by baptism into death." In Colossians 2:12 Paul asserts the same truth. Burial removes the deceased one from the sphere in which he was born. We were born once into this world, over which Satan is prince. But by burial we are removed from this sphere. Just as burial is the consequence of death, and Christ's body was put into the grave because He had died, so we who have died with Christ have been buried with Christ. We were not conscious of our burial, we had no sense of the tomb closing over us; yet this burial is nonetheless real, a fact to be believed, a truth on which we can reckon.

The third great fact is the fact of resurrection. We were identified with Christ in His resurrection. In Romans 6:4-5 Paul says that "like as Christ was raised up from the dead by the glory of the Father, even so we also should walk in newness of life. For if we have been planted together in the likeness of his death [and the text states that we assuredly have], we shall be also in the likeness of his resurrection." In Ephesians 1:19 Paul prays that the believers to whom he wrote might know "what is the exceeding greatness of his power to us-ward who believe." What is the measure of His power? It is the power "which he [God] wrought in Christ when he raised him from the dead." In Ephesians 2:1 Paul affirms that we too have been raised by God's power. How can it be said that we have been raised? Because we were identified with Christ in His resurrection. This truth is asserted again in Ephesians 2:5: "Even when we were dead in sins [God] hath quickened us together with Christ (by grace ye are saved;) and hath raised us up together, and made us sit together in heavenly places in Christ Jesus." In Philippians 3:10 the apostle expresses the desire of his heart that he might "know him, and the power of his resurrection." In Colossians 3:1, the apostle exhorts the believers, "If ye then be risen with Christ [which is most certainly true of you], seek those things which are above, where Christ sitteth on the right hand of God." And the power that brought Christ to resurrection and was experienced by the apostle, can be experienced by any child of God, because believers have been resurrected with Christ.

In the fourth place, we discover from these same passages that not only have we experienced codeath, coburial, and coresurrection but we have experienced coascension and coglorification. Ephesians 2:6 tells us God "hath raised us up together, and made us sit together in heavenly places in Christ." In Romans 8:30 the apostle reminds those who have been predestinated and called by God that "whom he called, them he also justified; and whom he justified; them he also glorified." The apostle is not speaking of the future glory that awaits the child of God but of his present position before the Father as one who has been identified with Jesus Christ in His ascension and His glorification.

These are doctrinal facts which may be very familiar to you. Yet one may know the facts without realizing the purpose of this cocrucifixion, coburial, coresurrection, coascension, and coglorification. In Romans 6:9-10 the apostle says, "Knowing that Christ being raised from the dead dieth no more; death hath no more dominion over him. For in that he died, he died unto sin once: but in that he liveth, he liveth unto God." There the apostle is stating the reason for which we have been joined to Christ in His death, His burial, and His resurrection. We have been identified with Christ, baptized into Christ Jesus, in order that we might live unto God. We have been baptized into Christ Jesus so that we might be dead unto control by the sin nature. Just as a physical corpse no longer needs to respond to any com-

mand issued to it and just as that corpse need not obey any constituted authority that exercised control over the person when
he was living, so we who have died with Christ and have been
buried with Christ and have been resurrected with Christ need
not obey the old commander who once reigned supreme in our
lives. The power of sin has not been cancelled; the practice of
sin has not become an impossibility. But we are delivered,
through our death with Christ, from the obligation to obey the
commands of the sin nature. We have been liberated from servitude to sin. Ah, yes, it is possible to submit ourselves to the old
regime. We may obey a defeated dictator, but if we do, we do it
by choice and not by necessity. Before we were born into God's
family we had an ear that could hear only the commands issued
by the old sin nature. We were like a radio tuned to just one
wave length, the wave length that carried the commands of the
sin nature. But by the new birth we have been given a new capacity, or a new wave length, and now we must choose whether
we will take commands coming over the old wave length or the
new. We have been crucified with Christ so that Christ may live
His life through us.

Paul asserts this same fact in Romans 6:4, where he states that
we are buried with Christ so that "like as Christ was raised up
from the dead by the glory of the Father, even so we also should
walk in newness of life." The purpose of identifying us with
Christ in His resurrection was that we might be delivered from
sin's dominion so as to walk in newness of life. You see, beloved,
God was interested in far more than our salvation from sin's
penalty when He gave Jesus Christ to die for us. The death of
Jesus Christ, as we discovered in our previous study, was a divine judgment upon sin and upon the sin nature. Through the
death of Jesus Christ, God not only provided for our salvation but
for our walk in newness of life by identifying us with Christ in
His death, burial, and resurrection.

Beloved of God, get hold of this one great fact. God, in order
to terminate sin's control over you, put you to death with Christ.
In order to remove you from that old sphere in which you operated, God put you into a grave with Christ. And in order to
bring you into a new kind of life, God brought you in resurrec-

tion power, out of the grave with Christ, and raised you to glory with Christ. Cocrucifixion, coburial, coresurrection are yours in order that you might walk in newness of life; in order that Christ, who lives in you, might live His life out through you. This is not a doctrine to be proved logically but a fact of divine revelation to be believed. In Romans 6:11, Paul gives the only right response to this great fact: "Reckon [or, count it to be true] ye also yourselves to be dead indeed unto sin, but alive unto God through Jesus Christ our Lord." He is asking you who have been identified with Him to believe that you have been liberated from the obligation to serve sin. Your Christian life is based upon a fact to be believed. You died with Christ and you were resurrected with Christ in order that you might walk in newness of life. This fact, which is a doctrine, becomes real in your experience only when you count it to be true.

12

DEAD WITH CHRIST

Romans 7:1-14

IN THE CROSS provision has been made by an infinite God for all of the needs of sinners. All that any one could ever need has been fully provided for in the death of Jesus Christ. Christ died to pay the price for our sins. He died to discharge the indebtedness we owe to God. He died in order that He might liberate us from spiritual death and make us alive. He died that He might liberate us from control by the sin nature.

The doctrines of the Christian life must begin with the recognition that when we were born into this world the first time we were born into the kingdom of Satan. He was our god, and him we served. We were members of his family, and we looked to him as a father. By nature we were children of disobedience. We were born as bondslaves of sin. Sin was a ruthless, domineering master, and we obeyed its dictates. The glorious liberty that is in the gospel of Jesus Christ is set forth for us in the sixth and seventh chapters in Romans, where the Apostle Paul is showing believers the benefits of the death of Christ in respect to the Christian life. After the apostle tells believers that they were baptized into Jesus and that by being joined to Jesus Christ they were joined to His death, he proceeds to show that death with Christ sets believers free from dominion by the sin nature. The slavery to sin has been broken, and the obligation to obey sin has been cancelled.

EMANCIPATION

A hundred years ago slaves in America were set free by an emancipation proclamation, a judicial pronouncement by the chief executive in our land. God, who might have set the sinner free by a divine edict, by an emancipation proclamation, chose another means of liberation—death. And in order that we might be set free from bondage to sin, God put us to death with Jesus Christ. In Romans 6:6-7 the apostle says, "Our old man [that is, all that we were by nature through our first birth; all that we were because we were in Adam; all that we possess because we possess a sin nature] is [has been] crucified with him." And this identification of the believer with Jesus Christ in His death was in order "that the body of sin might be destroyed, that hence-forth we should not serve sin. For he that is dead [has died] is freed from sin."

When the apostle says that we died with Christ that the body of sin might be destroyed, he is not saying that the body of sin (that is, the sin nature) has been eradicated. He is not saying that we died with Christ in order that the sin nature might no longer be able to operate within us. Rather, he is saying that we died with Christ in order that the body of sin, or the sin nature, might be set aside as the master that controls us, the master we are obligated to obey. Paul is dealing with this question: Does the sin nature have the exclusive right to dominate and control us? And the apostle says that because we died with Christ, be-cause we were joined to Christ in His death, we are no longer obligated to serve the old master. The apostle states this truth positively in the seventh verse when he says, "He that is dead [has died] is freed from sin." This passage does not teach that the one who has died with Christ can no longer commit a sin, for the child of God can respond to temptation and succumb to mastery by sin. What the apostle is saying may be paraphrased this way, "He that has died with Christ is freed from the obligation to obey sin (a deposed general) when it issues orders to him." In both of these verses, you will observe the apostle is showing us that our death with Christ delivers us from compulsory obedience and submission to the sin nature which once dominated and con-trolled us. Just as by resurrection Jesus Christ was delivered from the power of death, so by our resurrection with Christ, death has no right to lay hands upon us, for we have been made alive in Christ Jesus. The apostle, in this sixth chapter, has been emphasizing the fact that we were brought into death with Christ, and brought into resurrection with Christ in order that the power of the sin nature over us might be broken. It was not eliminated. It was not eradicated. It was not rendered incapable of tempting us, but we are not compelled to submit to it as we were before we experienced death and resurrection with Jesus Christ.

The theme of the death of the believer with Jesus Christ and its practical effects in practical experimental living is again taken up in Romans 7. The apostle says, "Know ye not, brethren (for I speak to them that know the law,) how that the law hath dominion over a man as long as he liveth?" When the apostle introduces a thought with the words, "Know ye not?" he assumes the ignorance of those to whom he writes on that subject. Then he proceeds to dispel their ignorance. Thus present-day believers learn a great deal from the ignorance of the first century believers. In this case, the apostle recognized their slowness to perceive the twofold value of the death of Christ for the believer and the believer's death with Christ as that which liberates from sin's control. Therefore, the apostle went into detail to give an explanation before he applied this truth to their daily experience. And the doctrine that the apostle propounded is stated simply, "... the law hath dominion over a man as long as he liveth." By "the law" the apostle means any law principle, whether it be the Mosaic Law, the law of Rome, the law of marriage, or the physical laws by which our lives are governed day by day. This fact is evident and obvious, that a law can operate in reference to a man only as long as that man lives. When he dies physically, he is no longer under the laws that formerly applied to him. Those to whom the apostle was writing would recognize the fact that the law of Rome did not extend into the cemetery. When a man died physically, Rome's power over him was cancelled and broken. In like manner, the Law of Moses had authority over a man only as long as he lived. Moses could not descend into a grave to control a man after he had departed from this life. And the Apostle Paul, in verses 2 and 3, uses the familiar law of marriage to illustrate the same principle: law operates for those who are living, but death terminates the control of any law over any man.

Paul does not use Roman law or the Law of Moses for his illustration, but goes back to the original law of marriage ordained by God in the Garden of Eden, that one man and one woman would become one flesh for as long as they both live. The apostle uses this law of marriage as an illustration by saying, "The woman which hath an husband is bound by the law." What law? The law of marriage. So Paul says, "The woman which hath an husband is bound by the law [of marriage] to her husband." For how long? "So long as he liveth." That law operates as long as the two parties are alive. "But if the husband be dead, she is loosed from the law of her husband." What is the apostle teaching? That the law of marriage operates continuously until it is terminated by death; also that it is only death which breaks the control of the law of marriage over the wife. The apostle applies the fact in the fourth verse. "Wherefore [because of this fact that death breaks the control of any law over a man], my brethren, ye also are become dead to the law by the body of Christ; that ye should be married to another."

The apostle is using the law of marriage here as an illustration of the sin nature, which he calls the law of sin and death. The law of sin and death operates over a man until he dies. Now the apostle is not speaking of a man's physical death but of a man's death through union with the Lord Jesus Christ. When we were baptized into the body of Jesus Christ, so that we participated with Christ in His death, that old law (the sin nature which operated within us) was broken and its power was terminated. By our death with Christ, we have been set free from the obligation to serve the sin nature in the same way that a wife whose husband dies is set free from the law of marriage so that she may marry another.

It is not our good resolutions that break the control by the sin nature; it is not by joining a church that the power of the sin nature is broken; it is not reading the Bible that breaks the power of the sin nature; it is not fellowshiping with good people that breaks the power of the sin nature; it is not enactment of more laws and affixing penalties thereto that breaks the power of the sin nature. Only one thing can break sin's control over us. Death. When Jesus Christ died, you, as a believer in Jesus Christ, died with Him, and that death broke sin's control over you so that you might through resurrection with Christ walk in newness of life.

Romans 6:4 tells us that "like as Christ was raised up from the dead by the glory of the Father, even so we also should walk in newness of life." Resurrection has in view a new kind of life. The apostle asserts the same fact in the fourth verse of chapter 7, where he says, "Wherefore, my brethren, ye also are become dead to the law [that is, of the sin nature] by the body of Christ [by being joined to Him in death]; that ye should be married to another, even to him who was raised from the dead, that we should bring forth fruit unto God." The result of being joined to Christ in His death is liberation, and the product of being joined to Christ in resurrection is righteousness unto God.

A FACT TO BE BELIEVED

The burden of this study is that you should see how great is your deliverance, your emancipation. You who were born as slaves to sin have no power whatsoever to break the manacles by which you were chained. There is no power within you that can enable you to say even the weakest no to any order that the sin nature gives to you. But since you were joined to Jesus Christ in His death and His resurrection, God can announce that sin's dominion over you has been broken. By death you have been freed from the obligation to serve sin. This does not mean it is impossible for you to succumb to the enticements of sin. It does not mean that sins have become less attractive to that old nature of yours. But it does mean that the Spirit of God can operate through the new, divine nature, and bring you, who have been delivered from sin, into willing submission to Jesus Christ, so that He becomes the One who rules and controls you so as to produce His righteousness in you.

A very common misconception is that Christians are to put themselves to death. But death can be experienced by an individual only once. The secret of the Christian life is not repeated crucifixion—putting oneself to death again and again and again in order to be delivered from bondage to sin. Rather, God's secret is found in Romans 6:11, where you read that you are to reckon or count it to be a fact that you are dead indeed unto sin but alive unto God through Jesus Christ our Lord. When you were joined to Jesus Christ in His death, it was once for all. The apostle did not write in Galatians 2:20, "I crucify myself again and again and again and again, so that I might be free." But he says, "I have been crucified with Christ," and the effects of that crucifixion continue on and on and on. God is asking you to stand off and look at yourself as one who has died, and to deem yourself as one over whom sin's authority has been broken because when Christ died, you died; when Christ was resurrected, you were resurrected; and now you have been set free to walk in newness of life—resurrection life under control of the Spirit of God.

This is a fact from the Word of God. And like any fact, it is to be accepted and believed. The fact of Scripture is that the believer was set free from sin's power just as truly as a wife is set free from a husband when the husband dies. You were set free from the necessity to obey sin when you died with Christ. The fact is not changed by your acceptance or rejection of it, your belief or unbelief, your knowledge of the fact or your ignorance of it. God says you are crucified, and in God's sight you are a crucified one. God is not asking you to add to the value of the death of Christ by crucifying yourself again and again. God is asking you to accept His judgment on the sin nature and to reckon the fact to be true that you were joined to Christ in His death because God says it is true; also that death with Christ has broken sin's power over you so you have been liberated to walk in the newness of life. Such acceptance will change a man's whole attitude to the sin nature within him.

We believers, if we sin, do so not because we are obligated to do so but because we choose to do so. Christ set us free, but it is possible to be entangled again in the yoke of bondage. We may voluntarily submit to sin's enticements and walk in sinful paths. We do so not because the liberation was incomplete but because we do not reckon ourselves to have been crucified with Christ. We do not count ourselves as those over whom sin no longer has a rightful authority; we submit to a deposed commanding officer. When we choose sin, we become the servants of sin. It would be most helpful for any child of God, upon waking in the morning, to repeat Galatians 2:20 and say to himself, "I do not have to serve sin today because I have been set free." We need to remind ourselves constantly that God has liberated us, and then walk in righteousness and true holiness by the power of the Spirit of God.

I do not know of any doctrine that is more comforting or more helpful to the child of God than this scriptural doctrine of co-crucifixion with Christ. You see, God is not asking us to break the power of sin. God is not asking us by resolution and by determination to abstain from sin. God is telling us what He has accomplished. He is telling us that He has set us free, and this freedom is ours by faith. Just as we come into personal, intimate relationship with Jesus Christ by faith in Christ, so by faith we come into victory. We come into the experiential enjoyment of this freedom by faith in Christ, reckoning what God says is truth, reckoning that we have been crucified with Christ. Consequently, sin's power over us has been broken, and we can walk in newness of life.

13

RESURRECTED WITH CHRIST

Romans 6:11-23

THE ONE who, by faith, accepts Jesus Christ as a personal Saviour, is identified with Jesus Christ in all that He has accomplished. That one is joined to Jesus Christ in His death, in His burial, and in His resurrection. Believers have been joined with Christ in resurrection, so that they might walk in the newness of life. The apostle refers to this great theme when, in Ephesians 1:19-20, he prays for the saints, that they might know "what is the exceeding greatness of his power to us-ward who believe, according to the working of his mighty power, which he wrought in Christ, when he raised him from the dead." In Ephesians 2:5-6, Paul again affirms this truth when he says, "Even when we were dead in sins [God] hath quickened us together with Christ, . . . and hath raised us up together, and made us sit together in heavenly places in Christ Jesus."

THE FACT OF CORESURRECTION

The apostle recognizes the fact of his resurrection with Christ when he reveals the great desire of his heart in Philippians 3:10: "That I may know him, and the power of his resurrection, and the fellowship of his sufferings, being made conformable unto his death; if by any means I might attain unto the resurrection of the dead." The desire of the apostle's heart is not that some day he might be brought to physical resurrection but rather that the resurrection life of Jesus Christ, in which he has become a partner by identification with Christ, might manifest itself through him day by day in a new kind of life.

Identification with Christ in death, burial, and resurrection is referred to by Paul when he writes to the Colossians. He says, "If ye then be risen with Christ [the original text infers, you most certainly have been], seek those things which are above, where Christ sitteth on the right hand of God" (3:17). All the commands and injunctions of the apostle in the third chapter of Colossians are based upon the assumption that believers have been identified with Jesus Christ not only in death and burial but in resurrection as well.

Perhaps the most important New Testament passage bearing upon our resurrection with Christ is found in the sixth chapter of Romans. In the third verse Paul states the fact that we who were identified as living members of the body of Christ by being baptized into Jesus Christ by the Holy Spirit were baptized into His death. We have experienced a cocrucifixion with Christ. "We are buried with him by baptism into death: that like as Christ was raised up from the dead by the glory of the Father, even so we also should walk in newness of life. For if we have been planted together in the likeness of his death, we shall also be in the likeness of his resurrection" (vv. 4-5). Once again we need to note the fact that the apostle is not primarily emphasizing the truth concerning the physical resurrection of the body, important as that teaching is in the Word of God. Paul's thought in Romans 6:5 is rather the newness of life that will be manifested in the child of God because he has experienced a cocrucifixion and a coresurrection with Jesus Christ. Because he died with Christ, he has been liberated from obligation to obey the old man (v. 6). He that has died (v. 7) has been freed from control by the sin nature. The apostle's next concern is that those who have died with Christ should live unto God.

The apostle develops this thought by using the experience of Christ as an illustration. He says, ". . . Christ being raised from the dead dieth no more, death hath no more dominion over him. For in that he died, he died unto sin once: but in that he liveth, he liveth unto God" (vv. 9-10). Death could not claim the Lord Jesus Christ, as it claims all humanity because they are sinners. Jesus Christ alone among men was separate from sinners, holy, harmless, and undefiled. He died not because death had a right to lay hold of Him but because by an act of His will He sub-

mitted to death and dismissed His soul from His body. Our Lord
Jesus Christ submitted to death in order that He might redeem
us who were spiritually dead, and in order that we might be made
alive in Him. On the third day He emerged triumphant over
physical death by His resurrection from the grave. After He had
been resurrected, death had no more dominion over Him and
could not again reach out its cold hand, grip Him, and hold Him
in its power. Death did lay hold upon Him for the three days
that He was in the grave, but when Jesus Christ came forth from
the grave, He was delivered from death's power. After the resurrection Christ was not subject to anything that death could do to
Him.

THE RESPONSE OF FAITH

Because Christians have been identified with Christ in His resurrection, they are expected to walk in newness of life—to live a
new kind of life, and this is the kind of life that need not submit
to sin's control. But in order to live this kind of life the believer
must exercise faith. For this reason the apostle, after presenting
the great fact of the believers' identification with Christ, calls
upon believers to reckon themselves "to be dead indeed unto sin,
but alive unto God through Jesus Christ our Lord" (v. 11).
The word translated "reckon" in Romans 6:11 is a word which
literally means "to count a thing to be true." So Paul says, "In the
light of the fact that I have presented to you, I call upon you to
count it to be true that you yourselves have died unto sin's dominion, that you have been made alive unto God because you
have experienced a coresurrection with Jesus Christ our Lord."
The fact: you died and rose again. The faith: your response to
the fact that God declares to be true.

THE POWER OF THE HOLY SPIRIT

In the eighth chapter of Romans, you will discover the force
by which this fact operates in a believer's life. In Romans 8:3,
Paul writes, "What the law could not do, in that it was weak
through the flesh, God sending his own Son in the likeness of
sinful flesh, and for sin, condemned [or, judged] sin in the flesh:
that the righteousness of the law might be fulfilled in us, who

walk not after the flesh, but after the Spirit." The force by which
the resurrection life of Jesus Christ is manifested in the life of
the child of God is the Holy Spirit. The fact: you died and were
resurrected with Christ! The faith: you count this fact to be
true! The force: you permit the Holy Spirit to live His life
through you. The resurrection life of Jesus Christ is lived by the
Spirit's power in your life—moment by moment and step by step.

In Galatians 5:16 Paul gives the injunction, "Walk in the
Spirit, and ye shall not fulfil the lust of the flesh." This could
be translated more literally, "You be constantly walking by means
of the Spirit, and you will not fulfil the lusts of the flesh." We
need to remind ourselves again and again that the child of God
of himself cannot walk in newness of life. He has been redeemed;
he has been given a new nature; he has a new mind so that he can
know the truth of God; a new heart so that he can love God; and
a new will which gives him the capacity to obey God. But of
himself he has no power to put into operation that life that has
been implanted by the miracle of regeneration. However, as he
continually walks by the power of the Spirit of God, the resurrection life that is his in Christ will be manifested. His attitude
should be that of the Apostle Paul: "I can do all things . . ."
(Phil. 4:13). You will notice Paul does not say, "I can do all
things because I have been born into God's family." No, he says,
"I can do all things through Christ which strengtheneth me." The
Holy Spirit indwelling the child of God reproduces the life of
Jesus Christ in that believer, and Christ in the believer manifests
His life through that believer. The idea that we have the wisdom, the strength, and the power, to live the life of Christ day by
day because we have been born into God's family has brought
about the downfall of many of God's children. We must reckon
on the fact that we have been crucified and resurrected with
Christ, and then we must permit the Holy Spirit to live the resurrection life of Christ through us.

How can the Holy Spirit live His life through me? What is
the key to understanding what is meant by permitting the Holy
Spirit to live the resurrection life of Christ in me? Again we return to Romans 6 to get an answer. In the thirteenth verse Paul
says, "Yield yourselves unto God." Again, in the sixteenth verse,

"Know ye not, that to whom ye yield yourselves servants to obey, his servants are ye to whom ye obey; whether of sin unto death, or of obedience unto righteousness?" Again, in the nineteenth verse he says, "As ye have yielded your members servants to uncleanness and to iniquity unto iniquity; even so now yield your members servants to righteousness unto holiness." The apostle emphasizes again and again the principle of *yielding*. By using this word the apostle shows how the Holy Spirit can live the life of Christ through the child of God. While walking by the Spirit has to do with divine enablement and empowerment, yielding to the Spirit has to do with the Spirit's direction or control over us. Apart from this act of yielding to the Spirit's control, the believer will experience no manifestation of the resurrection life of Christ.

THE SACRIFICE OF SELF

Paul reveals the secret of permitting the Spirit to do His work in us of conforming us to the Lord Jesus Christ when he says, "Yield yourselves unto God."

This word *yield* or *present* can be illustrated from several passages in the New Testament. I would like to refer you, briefly, to three passages. First, this word *yield* or *present* is used in II Corinthians 11:2 of the presentation of a bride to the bridegroom at the marriage ceremony. Paul says, "I am jealous over you with godly jealousy: for I have espoused you to one husband, that I may present you as a chaste virgin to Christ." The word translated "present" is the identical word translated "yield" in Romans 6. In fulfillment of a marriage contract, the father of a bride would take the hand of his daughter and would put that hand into the hand of the father of the groom, who in turn would put her hand into the hand of the bridegroom. By that act the bride was presented to the bridegroom, and she became his possession. The apostle, using that same word in Romans 6, is emphasizing that just as there can be no lawful marriage apart from the consent of the wills of the two parties involved, so, apart from the consent of the will of the child of God to present himself to the Spirit's control, there will be no manifestation of the resurrected life of Christ in that child of God.

Second, this word is used in Colossians 1:22, where Paul writes that Christ purposes "in the body of his flesh through death, to present you holy and unblameable and unreproveable in his sight." The Lord Jesus Christ will offer believers as a gift to the Father. We have become the Father's possession. We have been put at the Father's disposal. We have been brought into intimacy with the Father, and the Father's home will become our dwelling place. And the apostle uses this word *present* to show that we have been put at the disposal of the Father by this act of the Son. In like manner we are to present ourselves to the Father so that the Spirit may manifest the life of Christ in and through us. We are to place ourselves at God's disposal. This is the meaning of "yield yourselves . . . and your members" in Romans 6.

Third, we direct your attention to Romans 12:1, where Paul says, "I beseech you therefore, brethren, by the mercies of God, that ye present your bodies a living sacrifice, holy, acceptable unto God, which is your reasonable service." The word translated "present" in Romans 12:1 is the same word translated "yield" in Romans 6. And Paul's climactic exhortation is "Present your bodies a living sacrifice." In the Old Testament it is recorded that every sacrifice was to be bound with a cord to the altar. This principle was stated in Psalm 118:27, where we read, "God is the LORD which hath showed us light: bind the sacrifice with cords, even unto the horns at the altar." An animal offered as a sacrifice was not a voluntary, or a willing, sacrifice. The animal brought to that scene of death could smell death in the spilled blood, and out of fear of death would turn and run back to the herd from which it had been taken to be offered as a sacrifice to God. No animal was a voluntary sacrifice. It was not until the Lord Jesus Christ came, as "the Lamb of God, that taketh away the sin of the world," that the world knew anything about a voluntary, or a willing, sacrifice. Twice in the tenth chapter of Hebrews, once in verse 7 and again in verse 9, Christ said, "I come to do thy will, O God." And Jesus Christ was a willing sacrifice. His blood had value before God above all the blood on Jewish altars because His blood was a voluntary sacrifice. In Romans 12:1 God is asking His children for willing, or voluntary, sacrifices. God is not asking for a sacrifice of blood, for the blood of Christ shed for the sin of the world was sufficient to cover every need. But

God is asking for a willing sacrifice, the sacrifice of oneself. So the apostle exhorts the brethren, in view of all the mercies of God, that they present their bodies a living sacrifice. It will be acceptable to God because it is a willing sacrifice to Him. This, Paul says, is your logical service to God in view of what God has done for you through Jesus Christ.

While the Old Testament tells us nothing of a voluntary sacrifice, the Old Testament does tell us about a living sacrifice. The beasts that were sacrificed to God upon Israel's altars were dead sacrifices. But on the altar on Mount Moriah, where Abraham offered his son, Isaac, we see a living sacrifice. In perfect obedience, Abraham went on a long journey to the appointed place of sacrifice. He made his way up Moriah's hill. There he built an altar. There he consecrated to God his son. And when, in obedience to the command of God, Abraham was about to offer Isaac as a dying sacrifice, the hand of God stayed the hand of Abraham, and Isaac stepped down off that altar to live as one who had been sacrificed to God. Isaac was sacrificed not when the knife touched his heart but when he was put upon that altar by his father in obedience to God's command. And when Isaac stepped down off that altar, he was one who had been sacrificed to God but who lived. God is asking His child to make himself a living sacrifice. The child of God is to be one who is presented, one who is yielded to God. Apart from such a presentation, there will be no continuous manifestation of the resurrection life of Christ in the believer.

The presentation of Romans 12:1 is viewed as a once-and-for-all presentation because of the tense of the verb in the Greek. So we might render the verse this way: "I beseech you, brethren, in view of the mercies of God, that you *once and for all* present your bodies, a living sacrifice, holy, acceptable unto God, which is your reasonable service." God is calling upon you who know Him to come face to face with your responsibility to Him, and to register this once-and-for-all decision: "Father, right now, I am presenting myself as a sacrifice to you." When one presents himself to God, he at that moment takes on the designation, or the character, of one who has been sacrificed. From that point on, he need not sacrifice himself again and again. He need only reaffirm, continually, the fact of his once-for-all presentation as a sacrifice to God.

It may well be that you are stumbling and falling in your Christian life because you never have given yourself, or presented yourself, to God by an act of your will. God the Holy Spirit cannot continuously empower you to righteousness and true holiness, cannot manifest the resurrection life of Christ in you, until you have first of all yielded, presented, submitted yourself unto God. But when you, recognizing your responsibility and loving the God who has laid that responsibility upon you, by an act of will present yourself, then you become one who has been sacrificed and yet lives. The Christian life begins when one accepts Jesus Christ as personal Saviour. One begins living the Christian life when he presents himself as a sacrifice to God so that he may continually be walking by the Spirit. Have you ever done this?

14

FILLED WITH THE SPIRIT

Ephesians 5:18

WHILE I WAS SERVING a pastorate in the northwestern corner of Pennsylvania my brother came to visit me in the early spring of the year. While he was there, twelve inches of new snow fell upon the deep snow which was already on the ground. The time came for him to go to a neighboring town to take a train back to Philadelphia. Because of the road conditions we allowed extra time so that we might get to the station in plenty of time. We were proceeding cautiously when with no warning at all the car skidded, turned around, and landed in a deep bank on the opposite side of the road, headed in the wrong direction. We were prepared for such emergencies, for we never traveled without a shovel and a bucket of sand or ashes in the trunk of the car. We began to remove the snow, but found it was deeper than we had anticipated. As we were working rather hurriedly, a car came along. The driver saw the predicament we were in and very courteously stopped, rolled down the window, and called out, "Do you need any help?"

Do you know what I said? "No, thank you. We'll make it ourselves." I shall never forget the look my brother gave me. Even though I shouted after the car as it drove away that we did need help, it was too late. I was too independent for my own good! And there was nothing to do but to dig through some six feet of snow to try to clear the wheels. How often a similar situation is true in our lives. When help is offered, we would rather do without it than admit that we need to depend on somebody else.

The Apostle Paul was facing just such a situation as that with the believers to whom he was writing when, in Ephesians 5:18, he said, "Be not drunk with wine, wherein is excess; but be filled with the Spirit." In the previous chapters of this epistle the apostle laid requirements upon God's children that no one un-aided by the Holy Spirit can fulfil. No man, by his own efforts, can bring his whole life into conformity to Jesus Christ. No man by himself can be a living epistle to proclaim Jesus Christ, to be read and known by all men. And yet when God offers help in the fulfillment of those requirements which have been laid upon us, we, with self-confidence, look to Him who offers divine assistance and say, "No, thank You; we can make it ourselves." In the commandment given to us in Ephesians 5:18, the apostle is of-fering us assistance from God in fulfilling His requirements.

We want to direct your attention, first, to the meaning of being filled with the Spirit. Then we will consider the means by which one is filled with the Spirit. Finally, we will see the results of being filled with the Spirit.

DEFINITION

To discover the meaning of being filled with the Spirit, let us look first at some references in the Word of God to something being filled.

Several words in the original text are translated by this one English word *filled*. The common concept which is basic to all of these words is the thought of filling up a vessel by putting something into it. An empty glass into which water is poured could correctly be said to be filled with water. Now, of course, it would be a mistake to say that that glass is empty. For unless it is in a vacuum, the glass is not empty at all; it is filled with air. And the water that is poured into that glass drives out what previously had been filling it and fills it with something new. And when the apostle speaks of a person being filled with the Spirit, he is speaking of the Spirit supplanting that which was once within, then taking over so that that person is filled with the Spirit of God.

Several references will illustrate this. We read in Luke 5:26, following Christ's miracle of healing the paralytic, that "they were all amazed, and they glorified God, and were filled with fear, saying, we have seen strange things today." They were filled with fear. The people were accustomed to seeing paralytics. What they had never seen before was a paralytic instantaneously cured of his paralysis. And as they saw that manifestation of divine power, they were filled with fear. Their complacency, their indifference, and their doubt were removed and they were filled, or possessed by fear. And as a result they said, "We have seen strange things this day."

Again, we read in Luke 6:11, following the account of the miracle of the healing of a man with a withered hand that "they were filled with madness; and communed with one another what they might do to Jesus." They were filled with madness! Christ had presented Himself publicly as the Messiah, the Saviour, the King. There religious leaders were perfectly complacent in their own religion; they were working for their salvation by observing the traditions of men, and were content to trust their works. When Christ manifested the power of God in the midst of them, their self-righteousness no longer sufficed and their self-satisfaction gave way to madness, so that instead of being controlled by indifference, complacency, and self-satisfaction, they were filled with anger. They gnashed on Him with their teeth, to do away with Him if it were possible to do so.

The word *filled* is also used in Acts 2:4, where we read that the men in the upper room were all filled with the Holy Ghost. They were *filled* with the Holy Ghost! The same thought found in the previous references is found here. Filling these men with something new supplanted what previously filled them. They had possessed natural power before, but then that natural power had been supplanted, or superseded, by a new divine power, and they were filled with the Holy Spirit. If those men in Luke 5 had continued to be filled with their indifference to the need of the man, they would not have been filled with fear. If those of Luke 6 had continued to be filled with self-complacency because of their own righteousness, they would not have been filled with madness. And if the disciples in the upper room had continued to be filled with their own abilities, their own strength, wisdom, and power, they would not have been filled with the Holy Spirit.

Being filled with one thing prevents being filled with another. This thought is common in these three passages: filling has the idea of filling up something by removing what was there. What is filled is possessed or controlled by the new thing that fills.

A second word which is translated "filled" in the New Testament has this same basic concept of filling up, or taking possession of, but it seems to add the thought that that which fills an object or a person motivates or moves a person to a certain course of action. The emphasis is not just on the act of filling up but on the result of being filled. In Acts 6:5 it is recorded, "The saying pleased the whole multitude: and they chose Stephen, a man full of faith. . . . " Stephen was filled up with faith, and his faith manifested itself in good works before the congregation of believers so that they knew he was possessed with, or controlled by, faith. We read in Acts 5:3 that when Ananias brought in the purchase price of his field and laid it at the disciples' feet, Peter said, "Ananias, why hath Satan filled thine heart to lie to the Holy Ghost?" Ananias was filled with Satan. The filling by Satan produced a lie, deception, and fraud. Because he was filled, he was moved to a certain kind of action. Again, in John 16:6, after Christ told the disciples of His approaching death, He said, "Because I have said these things unto you, sorrow hath filled your heart." They were filled with sorrow. This sorrow completely dominated them, so much so that they considered themselves orphans. Hence Christ's promise in John 14:18, "I will not leave you comfortless" or "I will not leave you orphans." Again, we read in Acts 4:31 that "when they had prayed, the place was shaken where they were assembled together; and they were all filled with the Holy Ghost." As a result of the filling with the Holy Ghost, they spoke the Word of God with boldness. Now when we put these two ideas from the original text together to form our concept of *filling*, we see that there is that which comes into a man's life which expels what was there and fills and controls that life so that the individual, so filled, is possessed and controlled by that which fills him. Whether that which fills be madness, fear, sorrow, Satan, faith, or the Holy Spirit, the old control is terminated and a new emotion or person dominates.

The apostle, in this fifth chapter of Ephesians, is bringing to us the truth that God the Holy Spirit, who came to dwell in the body of the child of God the moment he accepted. Jesus Christ as a personal Saviour, came into that life in order that He might possess it, in order that He might own it, in order that He might control it. The individual who is filled with the Holy Spirit is not the one who is indwelt by the Spirit but the one who is controlled, or led, by the Spirit of God. To be filled with anything is to be possessed or controlled by that thing so as to be moved. The man who is filled with the Holy Spirit is under the control of the Spirit of God so that his life is ordered by the Holy Spirit.

On three occasions in the Word of God drunkenness and the filling of the Holy Spirit are contrasted. Let us consider these as background for understanding Paul's teaching in Ephesians 5.

First, let us look in Luke 1:15. In this chapter we have an angel announcing the birth of John the Baptizer. John was to come as the forerunner of the Messiah in fulfillment of the prophecy of Malachi. Concerning the person of John, and the power in his ministry, the angel said, "He shall be great in the sight of the Lord, and shall drink neither wine nor strong drink; and he shall be filled with the Holy Ghost, even from his mother's womb" (Luke 1:15). John was not to be controlled by wine or strong drink. But, on the other hand, he was to be controlled by the Holy Spirit of God, and this from the moment of his conception. We learn then from this angelic announcement that there are two different powers or forces which may control a man. A man may be controlled by alcohol, or a man may be controlled by the Holy Spirit of God. Both will do the same thing. They will produce a new kind of behavior, a different kind of behavior from that which is normal. And John's power was not the power of alcohol. It was the power of the Holy Spirit.

Next, in the second chapter of Acts we read about the Holy Spirit's coming into this world to take up His residence in the church. At this time the believers were filled with the Holy Ghost (v. 4). There was something in the ministry of the apostles, something in their message that was not natural, and it called for an explanation. Now if a man comes with a supernatural message and with a supernatural power, that man is to be believed and his message is to be received. If a man comes professing to be a messenger from God and is empowered by someone, or something other than God, that man is to be rejected and his message scorned. Peter stood up on the day of Pentecost to deliver a message to the nation Israel. This was the same nation which had rejected Jesus Christ, the nation which had said, "We will not have this man to rule over us." And Peter's address is summarized in verse 36, "Let all the house of Israel know assuredly, that God hath made that same Jesus, whom ye have crucified, both Lord and Christ [Messiah]." Now if Peter preached a divine message by the power of the Holy Spirit, his message was to be believed and the men who heard were responsible to act on it. However, the religious leaders questioned Peter's authority, for they had come to the conclusion that Peter was drunk. They recognized that they were seeing and hearing a man controlled by a power outside of himself. We read in verses 12-13, "They were all amazed, and were in doubt, saying one to another, What meaneth this? Others mocking said, These men are full of new wine." "These men are drunk!" Now the extent of their slur is brought out in the original text, because these leaders did not use the normal word for wine, the intoxicating beverage, they used the word for the newly pressed juice of the grape. They were ridiculing these men by inferring that they were such babies that when they took a little sip of grape juice they became drunk. Who wants to listen to prattling babies who have gotten drunk on grape juice? Peter refuted their words by pointing out that it was but the third hour of the day (verse 15). Since this was a holy day, no Jew would have used any alcoholic beverage from sundown the evening before until sundown that night. Hence, it was impossible, since they were law-abiding Jews, to explain their actions as the effect of wine. So he says, "This is not drunkenness, this is not control by alcoholic spirits, as you suppose, but this is that which was prophesied by Joel, for Joel prophesied that the Holy Spirit of God would take up His residence in men and would control men and use them for God's glory." Thus we find that Peter contrasted control by alcoholic beverages with control by the Holy Spirit of God.

In Ephesians 5:18 we find this same contrast where Paul gives a prohibition, "Be not drunk with wine" before he gives the command, "Be filled with the Spirit." Now why should the disgusting spectacle of drunkenness be mentioned in the same breath with the glorious experience of being controlled and moved by the Holy Spirit of God? Because both of these will do the same thing. Either will completely transform a man. Whether he is under the control of alcohol or under the control of the Spirit of God, his conduct, or behavior, will be different from what it was before he was so controlled. When alcohol takes control, the man's walk is different. The proverbial test of whether a man is intoxicated is whether he can walk the chalk line. Why? Because if a man is controlled by alcohol, he cannot walk that chalk line. When alcohol controls, a timid individual who normally is afraid of his own shadow is ready to fight anyone; one who couldn't be coaxed into singing a song will sing at the top of his lungs; one who may be as shy and retiring as a mouse is temporarily transformed into a voluble, outgoing person. How? Because he is controlled by alcohol, and such control transforms the man by removing his inhibitions.

What the apostle is trying to show us by way of contrast is that when one is under the control of the Spirit of God, his life is so altered that, whereas he otherwise could not conform to the demands of divine righteousness by his own strength, yet when controlled by the Spirit of God, the Spirit does produce a new kind of life. The Spirit of God can conform him to Jesus Christ in his walk. The Spirit of God can cause that man to be a witness for Jesus Christ, and timid lips become lips that speak forth with authority. The individual is transformed by the Spirit of God who fills, or who controls, him. And God's ideal for His child is to have His child so under the control of, or so possessed by, the Spirit of God that the life of Christ is manifested by the Spirit's filling.

It is unnecessary to try to prove that the child of God is living in a degenerate world. He is tempted to accept standards that do not conform to the standards of the Word of God; he is surrounded by practices that are contrary to the teaching of Scripture; he is despised because the Lord Jesus Christ is despised, and persecuted because Jesus Christ was rejected of men. Yet the difficulty of the situation in which we find ourselves does not remove the obligations to holiness and righteousness and godliness imposed upon us by a holy and righteous God.

The economic future of the world is uncertain. No one can predict what will happen. The political situation is such that men are grasping for some solution. Religiously, the world is in a turmoil. Those who name the name of Christ seem to be diminishing in number. Unbelief and apostasy seem to be increasing on every hand. How is the child of God to stand up under the religious, political, economic, and social pressures that are put upon him? God has provided His child with One upon whom he can rely so as to be sustained through every trial and pressure.

In the upper room our Lord told His disciples that it was necessary for Him to go away. In view of this, He promised, "I will pray the Father, and he shall give you another Comforter, . . ." The word translated "Comforter" is a word which means "a helper, one who has been called alongside to help." May I illustrate the meaning by saying that the Holy Spirit has come to be a crutch. While a crutch is a sign of the user's weakness or helplessness, yet the crutch is also his strength. The child of God is like a disabled person who has no power to stand alone, or to walk as he ought, and needs a crutch. God has given Someone upon whom the child of God can lean, or depend.

But that illustration doesn't satisfy, because a crutch is an *external* support. God the Holy Spirit has come to dwell within to be an *internal* support. The Apostle Paul refers to this in II Corinthians 3:5, "Not that we are sufficient of ourselves to think any thing as of ourselves; but our sufficiency is of God." In this same epistle God said to Paul, "My grace is sufficient for thee: for my strength is made perfect in weakness" (12:9). What was to be Paul's sufficiency? On what was Paul to lean? The grace of God! He was to be sustained and empowered by the Holy Spirit. I am certain that many of you have gone to Philippians 4:13 in a time of testing, discouragement, trial, defeat, or need, and you have echoed those words, "I can do all things through Christ which strengtheneth me." God has promised divine assistance. His grace, His power, His strength, are made available to the child of God. When the child of God is walking by means of the Spirit of God, he has One upon whom he can lean, who can sustain in every experience of life.

Even though God has given us Christians One who can sustain and uphold us, many of us do not avail ourselves of the Helper He has provided. We expect non-Christians to run to something for support, because they do not have the Holy Spirit to indwell, to fill, to possess, to empower, and to help them. And men of the world have many props and crutches which they lean upon, on which they are dependent. But what a tragedy when the child of God abandons the Helper and trusts that upon which the world leans to see him through some trying experience.

One of the supports on which some people of the world lean is alcohol. The alcoholic is not an alcoholic in the terms of the amount he drinks but because of the fact that he has to depend on alcohol to see him through experiences that are too much for him. He has become totally dependent upon it. Many times you have watched someone under stress, who nervously has tried to get hold of a cigarette. Why? Because to him the cigarette was a crutch. Why do Christians depend on the help that the cigarette gives instead of the help that is available from the Spirit of God? Now, a cup of coffee may become a crutch. If the cup of coffee is absolutely essential to you to enable you to face some situation, then you are using coffee as a crutch. Food or sweets may become crutches. Overfed Christians are a silent testimony to the fact that they depend upon something other than the Spirit for comfort. Many under some strain or pressure run to some diversion—the newspaper, a magazine, a novel, or television. Because they do not know how to avail themselves of the power of God that is available, they have to depend upon these, or similar, crutches.

The question to ask is "Why do I use these things? Am I expecting them to do for me what the Holy Spirit of God should be doing? Am I asking them to do what only God the Holy Spirit can do?" If that is true in your experience it would be good to build a rubbish pile right now. When things that we have used as substitutes for the blessed experience of being filled with the Spirit of God are put away, we can cast ourselves in dependence upon Him. We must remember that when we trust the world's supports, we will get whatever temporary support there is in such things, but we will not at the same time enjoy the help of the divine Comforter. Be not drunk with wine. Do not depend upon any of the world's supports, but be filled with the Spirit.

CHAPTER

15

YIELDING TO THE SPIRIT

Romans 6:11-23

WHILE I WAS A STUDENT at seminary our president, Dr. Lewis Sperry Chafer, came into class one morning with a twinkle in his eye. He had just returned from an extended trip. He said that at the close of one of his meetings an individual came to him and said, "Oh, Dr. Chafer, I have just received the baptism of the Holy Spirit. Tell me, have you ever had the second blessing?"

Dr. Chafer said, "Yes, I have. In fact I have had the third."

The questioner looked at him rather surprised and said, "I have heard of a second blessing, but I have never heard of a third. What is that?"

Dr. Chafer said, "Well, come to think of it, I guess I have had the three-thousandth blessing instead of just the third." The questioner was nonplussed and gave Dr. Chafer a look that showed she thought he was beside himself. Then Dr. Chafer used the occasion to explain to this questioner the difference between the baptizing of the Holy Spirit and filling of the Holy Spirit.

In Ephesians 5:18 the apostle gave the command, "Be filled with the Spirit." How can one be filled with the Holy Spirit? How can one obey this injunction, "Be filled with the Spirit"?

BAPTISM AND FILLING

First, let me remind you that there is a difference between being baptized with the Spirit and being filled with the Spirit. The Apostle Paul writes in I Corinthians 12:13, "By one Spirit are we all [A.S.V., were we all] baptized into one body, whether we be Jews or Gentiles, bond or free; and have all been made to drink into one Spirit." The baptizing work of the Spirit of God is the work by which a believer in Christ is joined as a living member to the body of which Jesus Christ is the head. That is quite different from Paul's injunction in Ephesians 5:18, where he commands, "Be filled with the Spirit." It is not our purpose to investigate the baptizing work of the Spirit of God. We would like to point out several contrasts to enable you to see that the apostle is speaking of two different things when he speaks of these two works of the Spirit. According to I Corinthians 12:13, the baptizing work of the Spirit takes place once and for all. It takes place the moment one accepts Jesus Christ as personal Saviour. On the other hand, the filling of the Spirit is continuous, and can be an often repeated experience for the child of God.

Second, the baptizing work has taken place in the past for you who know Jesus Christ as personal Saviour. It took place in your experience the moment you accepted Jesus Christ as your Saviour. For you it is a past act and event. But the filling of the Spirit spoken of in Ephesians 5:18 has to do with the present and with your daily walk and experience.

Every single child of God has experienced the baptizing work of the Spirit. Paul said, "We have all been baptized into the body of Christ" (I Cor. 12:13). There is no such thing as an unbaptized believer, for all who accept Jesus Christ as personal Saviour are without exception joined to the body of which Jesus Christ is the head. But the filling of the Spirit is true only of some. If all believers had been filled, it would be unnecessary for Paul to command those to whom he wrote to be filled. Again, we find that the baptizing work of the Spirit affects our union with Christ. But the filling of the Spirit releases the power of God through the individual's life and has to do with our practice, not our union with Christ.

Next, we find that no individual is ever commanded to be baptized with the Spirit. But on the other hand, believers are commanded to be filled with the Spirit. That shows us that the baptism has to do with our position in relationship to Jesus Christ, while the filling has to do with our experience in the things of the Spirit of God. Now, with these contrasts in mind, we can see why Dr. Chafer felt it necessary to show the inquirer that it would be impossible for any believer to have a second baptism. On the authority of the Word of God we can declare that if you have accepted Jesus Chirst as personal Saviour you are already blessed "with all spiritual blessings . . . in Christ" (Eph. 1:3) except the new, glorified body. That awaits our translation, or our resurrection. But no other gifts have been withheld by God. Since you perhaps have not entered into the blessings provided, we purpose in this study to bring you who have been blessed with all spiritual blessings into the experience of those blessings so that you will know the joy of being continuously filled or controlled by the Spirit of God.

PRELIMINARY CONSIDERATIONS

In considering Paul's injunction, "Be filled with the Spirit," several important facts should be observed.

First of all, the grammatical construction is important. The words "Be filled with the Spirit" are an imperative, a command issued to God's children, not a plea. We are not to debate whether we should be filled. This is not something that we can take or leave. God has given this command because it is His purpose that every child of His should be controlled by the Spirit of God.

Then we notice that the apostle used the present tense. This verb used in the phrase "Be filled with the Spirit" expresses a continuous action going on and on. It is difficult to translate this into smooth English, but what the apostle says is: "You believers be constantly being filled with the Spirit." This is rough English, but good theology. This is not a once-for-all action, as was the baptism by the Spirit, which does not need to be repeated. After we have been joined to the body of Jesus Christ by the Holy Spirit, that relationship can never be terminated, and we do not need to be baptized a second time. But the believer should be continuously kept filled with the Spirit of God. And this should be a daily experience, an hourly experience, a moment-by-moment experience in which the Holy Spirit is controlling us so that we are consciously under His authority, under His dominion and control.

Then, too, the Greek verb translated "be filled" is in the passive voice, which means that somebody else is to do the filling. We are not commanded to fill ourselves but rather to permit the

Holy Spirit of God, who indwells us as His temple, to possess and control us so that, by the Spirit of God, we are being continuously kept filled with the Spirit. We do not need to get more of the Holy Spirit; instead we need to let the Holy Spirit have all of us. We are not exhorted to get more of the Holy Spirit than we received when we were born into God's family, but we are commanded to permit God the Holy Spirit to possess and use us. The Apostle Paul's command is that we should be controlled not by wine but by the Holy Spirit of God so that He who is resident in us may be president over us, that He who has come to dwell in us may be permitted to dictate to us.

AN ACT OF FAITH

How can we who have been born into God's family and have been baptized into the body of Christ experience the filling of the Spirit? How can we be brought under control of the Spirit of God so that the Spirit is dictator in our lives? We can find an answer to these questions in a word spoken by our Lord on the occasion of His coming to the city of Jerusalem for the Feast of Tabernacles: "In the last day, that great day of the feast, Jesus stood and cried, saying, If any man thirst, let him come unto me, and drink. He that believeth on me, as the scripture hath said, out of his innermost being shall flow rivers of living water. (But this spake he of the Spirit, which they that believed on him should receive: for the Holy Ghost was not yet given; because that Jesus was not yet glorified)" (John 7:38-39).

In this invitation we have an indication of how a child of God may be filled with the Spirit. It begins with a desire. There must be a thirst. Christ said, "If any man thirst." Apart from thirst a man will not drink, and no man will ever be controlled by the Holy Spirit until he desires to be controlled, to have every area of life brought under the Spirit's authority. It is a tragedy that so many Christians are satisfied with so little. They are content with their present experience, content with the knowledge they have, content with past victories. They have no desire to be conformed to Jesus Christ, to manifest the righteousness of God day by day. In their complacency they never lift a voice to cry to God for anything beyond that which they already have. I am mindful of the spiritual thirst of Moses, David, and the Apostle Paul. Moses, after he had been on the mount with God, prayed, "Shew me now thy way, that I may know thee" (Exodus 33:13). David cried out, "As the hart panteth after the water brooks, so panteth my soul after thee, O God." Paul revealed his thirst in Philippians 3:10 when he expressed this desire: "That I may know him." And our Lord said, "Blessed are they which do hunger and thirst after righteousness: for they shall be filled" (Matt. 5:6). As long as you are satisfied with the blessings you have enjoyed, as long as you are satisfied with the kind of life you are living now, you will not thirst to be brought under the Spirit's control so that the Spirit may empower you to new life and to new manifestation of the holiness of Jesus Christ and the righteousness of God in your daily experience. We need to become so dissatisfied over our present state of spiritual attainment that we will come to Him and say, "Lord, I can't do it. I cannot attain to that which is your goal and purpose for me as your child. But I want to turn my life over to the Holy Spirit and let Him empower me so that the righteousness of Christ might be manifested through me." You must have a desire for what God wants to give you.

When a person responds to our Lord's invitation in John 7:37, "If any man thirst, let him come unto me," he admits his own defeat by coming. And we let our stubborn pride and our self-esteem hinder the Spirit from controlling us because we are independent by nature. Jesus Christ said you will never be brought under control by the Spirit of God until you come to the end of yourself, until you give up your struggling, your trying, your hoping, and your promising, and admit defeat and come to Him. Why is it that men are so reluctant to come to Jesus Christ for salvation when He offers them the forgiveness of sins, when He offers them the gift of eternal life, when He offers them a position as the sons of God in the family of God? Because they are too proud. A man may say, "It is an insult to my morality, an insult to my intellect, an insult to my religion." And men will not come to receive the gift because of stubbornness. Why is it that we who have accepted His gift of eternal life do not come to avail ourselves of the provision which God has made in the Holy Spirit that we might live to the glory of God? Because of pride and stubbornness. We don't want to admit to ourselves or to God or to anyone else that we can't live the Christian life. So we keep on struggling. With grim determination we say, "I can, I can, I can. I didn't, but I'll try, I'll try, I'll try." And we will not confess our inability and come unto Him, and drink.

Not only must a man come but he must drink. "Let him come unto me, and drink." This is the act of appropriating that which God has provided. The Apostle Paul said, in Ephesians 5:18, "Be not drunk with wine wherein is excess, but be filled with the Spirit." A bottle of intoxicating beverage may be put in front of a man but that man will never get drunk by staring at the bottle or handling it. He will not become intoxicated until he imbibes enough of it so that it can take over the control of all his faculties and senses. No man will ever be controlled by the Spirit of God apart from the conscious act of submitting himself to the Spirit's domination and control. "If any man thirst, let him come unto me, and drink." In John 7:38-39, our Lord explains what He means by drinking: drinking was His symbol of believing, His symbol of acknowledging a fact. Belief, or faith, appropriates all that God has provided.

GOD'S METHOD OF CONTROL

In Romans the sixth chapter, the apostle has a good deal to say concerning the method by which one is filled or controlled by the Holy Spirit. In the eleventh verse he asks us to believe a fact, to reckon something to be true: our relationship to Jesus Christ in His death and resurrection. The same principle holds in regard to control, or filling, by the Holy Spirit. We need to acknowledge certain facts. When we were born into God's family we received everlasting life, the forgiveness of sins. The moment that we accepted Christ as Saviour, we were joined to the body of which Jesus Christ is the head. The very moment that we accepted Christ as personal Saviour, God the Holy Spirit took up residence in our body and made it His temple. These are facts to be believed. On the basis of these facts, a response is demanded of the child of God. It comes to us in the word *yield*. "Let not sin therefore reign in your mortal body, that ye should obey it in the lusts thereof. Neither *yield* ye your members as instruments of unrighteousness unto sin: but *yield* yourselves unto God, . . ." And the word translated "yield" in this passage of Scripture is the same word translated "present" in Romans 12:1, where Paul says, "I beseech you by the mercies of God, that ye *present* your bodies a living sacrifice, . . ." And the word *yield*, or the word *present,* is the word which means "to turn yourself over to another; to submit yourself to another." The apostle says, in verse 13, that we are to present ourselves, or submit ourselves, unto God. Again, he says, in verse 16, "Do you not know that to whom you present yourselves servants to obey, his servant ye are. . .?" You may present yourselves unto sin, or you may present yourselves unto righteousness. When you submit yourself to righteousness you become the servant of righteousness. The call to such service is found in verse 19, "I speak after the manner of men . . . as ye have yielded your members servants to uncleanness and to iniquity; even so now yield your members servants to righteousness unto holiness."

A pastor has no more joyous experience than to preside at a marriage ceremony. In the course of the ceremony the pastor will turn to the husband-to-be and say, "Wilt thou have this woman to be thy wife?"

And his response is, "I will."

He turns to the bride and says, "Wilt thou have this man to be thy husband?"

And she says, "I will." When the man and the woman make such promises, they become husband and wife; they are married. The pastor cannot marry. The pastor can only preside at the wedding and declare that this man and this woman are now married, according to the law of God and of the state. Essential to the marriage is the consent of will of each of the two parties to be married.

Now the apostle uses that same concept to show us how we may be controlled by the Spirit of God. Until the child of God consciously submits to the authority of the indwelling Spirit and presents himself to the Spirit's control, he cannot be controlled by the Spirit. The experience of being controlled by the Spirit will not be yours until you yield yourself, present yourself, submit yourself to the Spirit's control. "Be filled with the Spirit."

CHAPTER

16

LIBERTY IN THE CHRISTIAN'S LIFE

Romans 14:1-13a

THE BIBLE is a timeless book. We soon discover, as we read its pages, that the sins which faced Noah, Abraham, David, Peter, and Paul are the sins we face today. The commands and the prohibitions given to these saints of old in the Word of God are as applicable today as they ever were. Times change, but men do not change. Societies change and customs change, but the principles by which God governs a man's life never change. The Word of God, because it deals with principles governing our conduct, is as timeless today as when it was delivered to men of old.

The Apostle Paul, writing to the Romans, has presented to them the glorious truths of their freedom from sin's condemnation and their liberty to walk in newness of life in Christ Jesus. He has presented to them the great fact of imputed righteousness and the outworking of that righteousness in the righteousnesses which will be produced by the Spirit of God. In Romans 14 and 15 he lays down certain principles to guide God's children in questionable things. There are today—as well as then—certain practices which, if indulged in, will jeopardize Christian growth and Christian testimony. Had the Apostle Paul been specific about certain practices of his own day, we might have assumed these portions of the Word do not apply to us today because those problems no longer exist. But in the area of doubtful things the apostle has given certain timeless principles by which the child of God may determine the fitness of any habit, practice, or course of conduct—principles by which he may determine what is right and what is wrong.

The first principle to which we direct your attention, found in Romans 14:1-13a, is the principle of *freedom in Christ Jesus.*

THE MOSAIC LAW

When God called Abraham out of Ur of the Chaldees, God separated a man unto Himself. It was God's purpose to make of Abraham a great nation, and He set Abraham and his seed apart by the promise which He made with Abraham, as recorded in Genesis 12:1-9, so that Abraham's seed should be a peculiar people. At the time God brought the nation out of Egyptian bondage and instituted Mosaic Law, God said, "Ye have seen what I did unto the Egyptians, and how I bare you on eagles' wings, and brought you unto myself. Now therefore, if ye will obey my voice indeed, and keep my covenant, then ye shall be a peculiar treasure unto me above all people: for all the earth is mine: and ye shall be unto me a kingdom of priests, and an holy nation" (Exodus 19:4-6). God, who had set apart Abraham unto Himself, and who had set apart Abraham's seed unto Himself as a peculiar treasure, intended that the children of Israel should be unto Him a kingdom of priests and a holy, that is, a set-apart, nation. Now, in order that the children of Israel should have this peculiar characteristic of a kingdom of priests and a holy nation, God gave instructions to Moses, saying, "These are the words which thou shalt speak unto the children of Israel. And Moses came and called for the elders of the people, and laid before their faces all these words which the LORD had commanded him" (Exodus 19: 6-7). And that law which the Lord gave to Moses, which Moses in turn gave to the children of Israel so that they should be a kingdom of priests and a holy nation, was designed to govern their entire life.

In order that the children of Israel should be a witness to the glory and holiness of God before the nations of the earth, God gave laws that governed every aspect of their lives. The calendar of events for each year was very carefully set before the people. There were holy days and Sabbath days. The command to keep the Sabbath day was a religious law given for the purpose of setting Israel apart as God's peculiar people. No other nation was a sabbath-keeping nation. In addition to the religious laws,

God gave dietary laws to Israel. God did not call certain animals unclean because they were unfit for human consumption, nor did He call other animals clean because they were more nourishing. But God set a division between clean and unclean so that, as Israel used that which was clean and refrained from using that which was unclean, they should be a distinctive nation. God's laws regimented the kitchen of the Jewish home, dictating what foods could be put together and what foods could not be put together; what could be eaten and what could not be eaten. There were laws concerning dress. God told the nation Israel, through the Law of Moses, what they could wear and what they could not wear. He told of the composition of the cloth that went into their dress, what could be combined and what could not be combined. God laid down certain marriage laws. These were designed by God to preserve Israel as a peculiar people and a holy nation. Thus we see that every part of the life of the Jew was circumscribed by laws—laws designed to produce a holy nation, a nation set apart unto God.

As the centuries passed, the Mosaic Law became a burdensome thing to the Jews. The Pharisees were so conscious of a man's responsibility in the light of God's revealed law that they had tried to codify and systematize all of the laws within the law of Moses for the Jews. By the time of Christ's ministry, they had arrived at 365 negative commandments, and 250 positive commandments. They said this was the sum total of the law, and taught that it was every Jew's obligation to keep these commandments which they said summarized the law of Moses.

FREEDOM FROM THE LAW

We discover, as we read the account of our Lord's life, that He anticipated the passing of the law. The law of Moses was for the Jewish nation, and when that nation rejected Jesus Christ as Messiah and Saviour, they were no longer a peculiar people set apart unto God. Hence the laws which were designed to accomplish that in their experience no longer served a useful purpose. The rending of the veil of the temple at the time of the crucifixion of Christ (Matt. 27:51) was God's sign that that which was instituted to set the nation apart unto God was being done

away. It is this to which the writer to the Hebrews refers in
Hebrews 8:13: "In that he saith, A new covenant, he hath made
the first old. Now that which decayeth and waxeth old is ready
to vanish away." The apostle has in mind the Mosaic Law when
he refers to that which decayeth and waxeth old, and is predicting
the destruction of Jerusalem and the temple in the year A.D. 70.
Thus we see that the nation Israel, which for countless generations had been under a law which governed every aspect of their
life, through rejection of Christ lost their position as a separated
nation, a holy nation. And the law which governed them and set
them apart was annulled.

This fact was revealed to the Apostle Peter on the occasion recorded in Acts 10, where we read: "Peter went up on the housetop
to pray about the sixth hour: and he became very hungry, and
would have eaten: but while they made ready, he fell into a
trance, and saw heaven opened, and a certain vessel descending
unto him, as it had been a great sheet knit at the four corners,
and let down to the earth: wherein were all manner of fourfooted
beasts of the earth, and wild beasts of the earth, and creeping
things, and fowls of the air. And there came a voice to him, Rise,
Peter: kill and eat." As Peter looked into the sheet let down
from heaven, he discovered that it was filled with animals which
the Law of Moses forbade the Jews to eat. And Peter recoiled
in horror from breaking the law of Moses. When God said,
"Kill, and eat." Peter replied, "Not so, Lord; for I have never
eaten anything that is common or unclean." Then came a great
revelation to the Apostle Peter. "The voice spake unto him again
the second time. What God hath cleansed, that call thou not
common. This was done thrice: and the vessel was received up
again into heaven." God revealed to Peter that the distinction
between clean and unclean, the distinction between common and
sacred, had been obliterated because God had done away with
the law which made those distinctions for the nation Israel as a
nation set apart to Himself. This setting aside of the prohibition
against eating unclean creatures shows that the uncleanness was
not in the animal itself but was rather in the divine arrangement
by which God said, "You may eat this, and you may not eat this."

After God took away the law, the distinction between clean and unclean no longer obtained.

It was very difficult, as you can well imagine, for Peter to accept this divine revelation. Peter shared with those of Cornelius' household and later with the apostles and brethren the message that had been delivered by God to him. But we discover, when we turn to the Epistle to the Galatians, that while Peter had a theoretical knowledge of the fact that God had broken down the middle wall of partition and had made all things clean experientially, or practically, it was difficult for him to act on the basis of what he had come to know doctrinally. In Galatians 2:11, Paul, speaking of his contact with Peter in the city of Antioch, wrote, "When Peter was come to Antioch, I withstood him to the face, because he was to be blamed." Now why did the Apostle Paul oppose the Apostle Peter in this face-to-face encounter? We find out why in verse 12: "For before that certain came from James, he [that is, Peter] did eat with the Gentiles." Peter had been practicing what God had revealed to him on the housetop in Joppa (Acts 10), that the distinction between Jew and Gentile, the distinction between clean and unclean no longer obtained and that Peter was free to eat with Gentiles, and even to eat Gentiles' food. But when Jews from Jerusalem came up from Antioch, Peter "withdrew [that is, from the Gentiles] and separated himself [from the Gentiles and from Gentile food], fearing them which were of the circumcision." He was afraid of what the Jews would think of him because he, the apostle to the Jews, was eating with Gentiles. When Peter withdrew, he denied the liberty which God gave (Acts 10) and built again a barrier or wall between himself and Gentile brethren. He put himself back under the Mosaic Law, observing the distinctions that had been cancelled by the death of Christ. Not only did this have an effect upon Peter, but "the other Jews dissembled likewise with him" (v. 13). That is, the other Jews who were with Peter followed him in his defection from the truth that all things were clean, and they, like Peter, built a wall between themselves and the Gentiles "insomuch that Barnabas also was carried away with their dissimulation [with their insincerity]." And Paul said, ". . . when I saw that they walked not uprightly according to the truth of the gospel, I said unto Peter before them all, If thou, being a Jew, livest after the manner of Gentiles, and not as do the Jews, why compellest thou the Gentiles to live as do the Jews?" There the Apostle Paul strongly rebuked Peter because Peter had denied the liberty from the Law of Moses that is included in the gospel message.

As we come to the Epistle to the Romans we find this same problem confronting that assembly of believers. While the Roman church was principally a Gentile church, there were numbers of Jews in the assembly. The Jews had one background, and the Gentiles had an entirely different background. The Gentiles were apt to look at the Jews and ask, "Why do they observe those customs?" And the Jews looked at the Gentiles and said, "How can they eat those awful things?" So the Apostle Paul had to write to this assembly of believers to lay down certain principles in this area of doubtful things in order that the brethren in the assembly might not be divided over these matters. The first principle that the apostle laid down is the principle of freedom from the restrictions in the Mosaic Law because the law had been done away as the operating principle by which God separated a people unto Himself. God today, no less than in Abraham's or in Moses' time, is concerned about a peculiar, set-apart people for His name. It is God's purpose that you and I should be a part of a peculiar people, a holy nation, a kingdom of priests. But God's method of obtaining that holy nation is not to institute a new set of laws, a new set of dos and don'ts as a substitute for the Law of Moses. He conforms us to Christ by the Holy Spirit in order that, through the transforming work of the Holy Spirit, we should be a royal priesthood, a holy nation, a kingdom of priests, to His honor and glory.

FREEDOM IN CHRIST

These principles found in Romans 14, laid down by Paul to guide Christians in that day, serve a valid purpose today. Paul began, in Romans 14:1, by saying, "Him that is weak in the faith receive ye, but not to doubtful disputations. For one believeth that he may eat all things; another, who is weak, eateth herbs." The apostle recognized that there was a danger that some brethren would set up a list of requirements in the area of doubtful things, and make those requirements tests of fellowship. The apostle said, "Receive any brother, even though he is weak in the faith, but do not receive him for the purpose of becoming entangled in a debate about doubtful things." The apostle recognized that in any assembly of believers there would be two classes of people—those who were weak in the faith and those who were strong. The weak brother was the brother who did not have faith to believe that God had made all things clean and acceptable. The strong brother was the brother who accepted God's revelation and believed that all things were allowable for him because God had set aside the law that made things clean or unclean. The weak brother could not accept the fact of revelation, and the strong brother welcomed the revelation and acted on it. When the Apostle Peter received the revelation recorded in Acts 10, and went and told the brethren of that revelation, and then sat down to eat with Gentiles, he was manifesting himself a strong brother. But later, when certain Jews came from James, he became a weak brother because he could not accept the fact that his fellowship with Gentiles had God's blessing. We must be very careful about our definition of who is a strong brother and who is the weak. It is related to the question of faith in the revelation which God has made.

The apostle pointed out three things when he gave this first principle, the principle of freedom in Christ. First of all, the brother (weak or strong) is to refrain from judging his brother The weak brother must refrain from judging the strong brother who has accepted God's revelation that all things are clean and he may eat. The strong brother must refrain from judging the weak brother who cannot exercise faith to believe that he may eat anything. You see, the danger of judging and despising a brother confronted both, and either the strong brother or the weak brother might fall into this snare. Therefore, the apostle said, "Let not him that eateth [because he has faith to believe that all things are clean] despise him that eateth not" (v. 3) . The word *despise* means "to look down the nose at."

One brother would say, "I believe the revelation which God made to Peter. I believe I can eat anything. What is the matter with that spiritual infant that he can't see it?" And he would look down his nose at the Jewish brother who did not have faith to believe that he could eat ham with his eggs.

On the other hand, Paul said, "Let not him which eateth not, judge him that eateth."

While the strong brother was munching a ham sandwich, the weak brother would look at him and say, "How in the world can he eat meat from a pig?"

So the apostle said, "You both have to be careful. The man of faith must not look down his nose at the one who does not have faith. And the one who doesn't have faith to eat certain foods has no right to judge the one who has faith to eat them."

Why were both courses of action forbidden? Because God has received both the strong brother and the weak brother. You see, it was a matter of no consequence to God whether they ate or didn't eat. Eating could not bring a man to God, and refraining from eating could no longer set a man apart to God. God had accepted both the weak and the strong because of their faith in Jesus Christ; therefore whether one ate or did not eat was a matter of no consequence.

The second thing that the apostle pointed out about this principle of freedom in Christ is found in verses 4 to 9. Both the weak and the strong must recognize that Jesus Christ is Lord. The title "Lord" implies the right to command. The right response to a lord is obedience. What the apostle pointed out in this passage is that God has not appointed the strong brother as a lord to the weak brother, so that the weak brother will obey the strong; nor has he appointed the weak brother as a lord so that the strong brother has to serve him. God has not abrogated, or set aside, His rights. So the apostle says, "Who art thou that judgest another man's servant? To his own master he standeth or falleth" (v. 4). Paul was saying, "It is none of my business what your master permits you to do. If your master permits you to do something that my master does not permit me to do, it does not give me the right to condemn you because you do what your master lets you do. Just as soon as you step into the realm of a judge to condemn another man's servant for what his master lets him do, you are taking over the prerogatives of his lord. No one has

the right to do that." Then Paul gave an illustration. He said,
"One man esteemeth one day above another: another man esteemeth every day alike" (v. 5). He was referring to the observance of the Sabbath day under Jewish law. The Gentiles had
never observed a sabbath; the Jews were required to observe innumerable sabbaths. Many Jews, after they were saved, could not
break the habit of observing the Sabbath day, and they continued
to observe the Sabbath as a day set apart unto the Lord. Other
Jews, when the Sabbath came, felt free to do many things they had
not dared to do before they were saved. The apostle said, "He
that regardeth the day, regardeth it unto the Lord: . . ." (v. 6).
That explains why the Apostle Paul frequently attended Jewish
services on the Sabbath day and why many Christian Jews, in the
early days of church history, still observed Jewish ritual and ceremony. They were observing it to the Lord. Then the apostle
continued by saying, "He that regardeth not the day, to the Lord
he doth not regard it." Both men had the Lord before them in
their conduct. And then Paul referred again to the matter of
eating: "He that eateth, eateth to the Lord, for he giveth God
thanks; and he that eateth not, to the Lord he eateth not, and
giveth God thanks." So the apostle has shown us that it is the
Lord who determines for each of His servants what He wants
that servant to do. Paul concluded this portion of his thought by
saying, "To this end Christ died, and rose, and revived, that he
might be Lord both of the dead and living" (v. 9).

The third aspect of this principle of freedom in Christ is found
in verses 10 to 12, where the apostle says that the right to judge
is the Lord's. "Why dost thou judge thy brother? or why dost
thou set at nought thy brother? for we shall all stand before the
judgment seat of Christ. For it is written, As I live, saith the
Lord, every knee shall bow to me, and every tongue shall confess
to God. So then every one of us shall give account of himself
to God." No believer shall be examined or asked to give account
of himself to another believer. Each individual is answerable to
the Lord, his Master, and has the responsibility of conducting his
life so as to please the Lord who has called him to Himself. When
a believer lives so as to please somebody else, that person becomes
his judge, and Christ is deposed from His rightful place as sov-

ereign Lord of his life. The conclusion is drawn in the first part of verse 13, "Let us not therefore judge one another any more."

In this passage the apostle is not speaking about sin. No child of God has any right to think that it is a matter of no consequence if he commits sin. Sin never has God's approval and that which is expressly forbidden in Scripture and is classified as sin is as much sin in the life of the child of God as in the life of the sinner. Here the apostle is not dealing with sin but is talking about those practices that in themselves are not sinful; those things that, whether we do them or don't do them, are a matter of in- difference to God.

Paul recognized certain dangers which faced the church. These dangers also face the church today. The first danger is that any assembly of believers may become so divided over these incon- sequential questions as to produce disunity among those who have been brought into the family of God. The second danger is that Jesus Christ may be set aside from His place as head and that others may usurp that place and seek to control the lives of the members of the body according to their own conscience. The third danger is that an individual or an assembly may set up a list which substitutes for the Law of Moses as a law governing the Christian life. When one puts himself under a law, whether it is the Law of Moses or a self-imposed law, and when he obeys that law, thinking that through the observance of that law he will please God, then he has become a legalist. One is not a legalist because he conforms to the standards of God's holiness. One be- comes a legalist when he uses a law as a means of producing right- eousness in his daily experience. And the apostle was concerned lest believers should set up for themselves laws, thinking that by conformity to a law they would be pleasing to God. God has re- moved the Mosaic law as that which set a people apart for Him- self. He is concerned that His people be a holy, set-apart people and this is accomplished as the righteousness of Christ is repro- duced in the life of the child of God by the power of the Holy Spirit. The Christian life is not a lawless life. The Christian life is a disciplined life, a life controlled by the Spirit of God and not regimented by law, either the Law of Moses or a self-imposed law.

CHAPTER

17

GIVING NO OFFENSE

Romans 14:13b-23

THERE HAD NEVER BEEN a declaration of independence, or a proclamation of liberty, that equaled the proclamation made by the Apostle Paul as a messenger of God's grace. His proclamation was made to those who were in bondage to the law and to those Gentiles who had been in bondage to the licentious practices surrounding heathenism. To the Jews, he proclaimed liberty from the law, which for countless generations had controlled every aspect of the life of the Jew, and he announced that things formerly forbidden by the Law of Moses were now lawful. To the Gentiles, who had practiced lawlessness and knew nothing of the restraints of law, the apostle likewise came with a message of liberty—that God had cleansed all things and had made all things acceptable to Himself. This was the message that the apostle penned to the Christians at Rome as, in the fourteenth chapter of the Epistle to the Romans, he introduced the problem of doubtful things. When we mention doubtful things, you will recognize immediately that the apostle was not dealing with things that are sinful in themselves, for anything that has the intrinsic character of sin is forbidden the child of God. But doubtful things may be put to sinful uses. The apostle did not deal with things that are inherently worldly, but with things that could be used for worldly ends. He did not deal with things that are carnal in themselves but with things that could be corrupted to a carnal use. Every generation of believers has had to make decisions about doubtful things. The Apostle Paul made no effort to draw up a list of things which were acceptable, and a list of those which were unacceptable. But he did lay down certain principles that are timeless, which, if properly applied to the conduct of the child of God, will settle for him questions about doubtful things.

In our last study we considered the basic principle of freedom in Christ. The Law of Moses has been done away, for by the death of Christ the rule of the law over an individual was broken. The apostle put a new standard before believers. No longer was the standard for the Jew conformity to law but rather conformity to Christ. To the lawless Gentiles the apostle presents the same basic principle. The goal of their lives was not to be conformity to a set of standards to overcome their Gentilism but rather conformity to a Person. As a consequence of this freedom in Christ, one brother must refrain from judging another brother. Each individual is responsible to the Lord, and the Lord will direct each one of His children in what He permits that child to do. It is exclusively the Lord's right to judge, and He, in a day of reckoning with His servants, will judge their conduct. Therefore, no believer has any right to sit in judgment upon that which another believer's Lord permits him to do.

THE WEAKER BROTHER

Now let us consider the second principle that the apostle presents in Romans 14, from the latter part of verse 13 through verse 21. The principle is, *give no offense.* Believers must *give no offense* in their behavior. The first principle might be erroneously interpreted. For instance, someone might adopt this attitude: Since God has declared all things clean, and all things that formerly were forbidden are now acceptable to God, it makes no difference what I do. Thus we see that the doctrine of liberty in Christ may be misinterpreted to give license to the child of God. The second principle was delivered to us to forestall our turning our liberty in Christ into license and lawlessness. The first principle is the basic principle which the child of God is asked to believe. When we by faith accept the truth that God has broken down the distinction between that which formerly was unclean but now is clean, when we accept the liberty which we have in Christ, we have honored God by our faith. There are those who erroneously teach that in order to keep from being legalists we must actually practice things formerly forbidden, also that if we voluntarily restrict our liberty we are putting ourselves back under law and becoming legalists. But the Apostle Paul, in Romans 14:13-20, showed that there is a principle that supersedes and takes precedence over the first principle of liberty—the principle of refraining from giving a brother offense or causing a brother to stumble.

In developing this second great principle, Paul first said believers should "judge this rather, that no man put a stumbling-block or an occasion to fall in his brother's way" (v. 13). "It is good neither to eat flesh, nor to drink wine, nor any thing whereby thy brother stumbleth, or is offended, or is made weak" (v. 21). You will notice the apostle used three expressions in verse 21 to describe what might happen to a weak brother as a result of our actions. A brother might be caused to stumble, be offended, or be made weak. In the mind of the apostle there was a distinction in these three. A brother stumbles when he patterns his life after the liberty of another believer and does not have faith to accept the fact that God gives him liberty to do that which the brother is doing. When a brother does this, he falls into sin. Because "whatsoever is not of faith is sin" (v. 23), that which he does becomes sin for him. The apostle said that it is good for Christians to abstain from exercising their liberty so as to cause a brother who patterns his life after our conduct to fall into that which is sin for him because he cannot accept God's declaration that all things are clean or acceptable.

Next, it is good for a Christian to abstain from doing anything that causes the brother to be offended. We offend a brother when we permit the brother to see us exercise liberty which we have which he in turn does not have, so that our testimony is jeopardized before that brother. The difference between stumbling and offending may be stated this way. If, when we exercise liberty, a brother does what we do, but without the faith we have that this is acceptable conduct, then he stumbles into sin. However, if the brother sees us do that thing and refrains from doing it because he does not feel free to do it but is caused to question or set aside our Christian testimony because of what we have done, then we have offended the brother. You see, we did not lead him into sin in this instance, because he did not do what we did. But, since we have caused him to question our Christian life, our Christian experience, or our liberty, we have given offense to this brother.

In the third place, the apostle says that it is good for a Christian to abstain from doing anything by which a brother is made weak. This brother is viewed as being in spiritual childhood; he is spiritually immature. He has not learned the truths of freedom in Christ, but he is studying the Word of God. He is reaching out to lay hold of the revelation which God has made. But if he sees a brother do that which he does not have liberty to do and is offended by it, he may be driven back into infancy or into immaturity. Let me illustrate it this way. Suppose one of those new Jewish believers saw an older Jewish believer sitting down to eat some meat that was specifically forbidden by the law of Moses. The older brother had learned what was revealed to Peter in the vision of Acts 10 and could sit down to a roast pork dinner and enjoy it tremendously. The weaker brother had also heard about the revelation given to Peter and began to question whether that meant he could even eat pork. He was repelled at the thought. When he went to the house of the stronger brother and saw the brother eating pork he was again repelled and asked, "If I accept the liberty that was revealed to Peter, am I *required* to eat pork? If that's what it means, I don't want anything to do with God's declaration that all things are clean, because even to think of putting a bite of that pork into my mouth nauseates me." And He would have been driven from the truth of liberty in Christ and would have wanted to put himself under the law so as to protect himself against the liberty that the stronger brother had. That brother was made weaker because he was offended by the stronger brother.

RESPONSIBILITY OF THE STRONGER BROTHER

The apostle, in covering these three areas, has put a tremendous responsibility upon the believer to whom the Spirit of God has brought the truth of liberty in the gospel.

First, we must so guard our conduct that a weaker brother does not follow our pattern of life so as to fall into sin. Second, we must so conduct our manner of life that that weaker brother is not given cause to discount our Christian testimony. Third, we must so conduct ourselves that the weaker brother is not turned from the truth of the gospel by that which our liberty permits. These requirements are very stringent, they are inflexible. In the mind of the Apostle Paul there is no reason which the strong brother can use to justify causing a weaker brother to stumble, to be offended, or to be weakened in his Christian growth.

Second, we must realize that things in themselves do not defile (v. 14). The apostle says, "I know, and am persuaded by the Lord Jesus, that there is nothing unclean of itself: but to him that esteemeth anything to be unclean, to him it is unclean." The key thought is in the phrase "there is nothing unclean of itself." This takes us back to our previous study. God made a distinction between clean and unclean animals, not because there was anything harmful or unhealthy in the unclean animal but because He wanted the people governed by those laws to be a people set apart unto God. God prescribed the dress of those who lived under the law, not because a combination of fibers rendered one unclean in his person but because God wanted to put a distinction between those who were set apart to the Lord and those who weren't. If a child of God cannot accept this fact of revelation "that there is nothing unclean of itself," and continues to believe that certain things or certain practices are unclean, then to him they are. The defilement is not in the thing itself, but in the attitude of the child of God toward it. The distinction between the strong brother and the weak brother is in this very area. The strong brother, by faith, can accept God's declaration that all things are clean and acceptable. The weak brother cannot bring himself to believe this declaration of God and to accept, for instance, that lamb was no better in God's sight than pork. It was his attitude toward the thing that made it unclean for him. What the apostle was trying to show is that the child of God who has become strong in the faith cannot argue that since God has made all things clean he can go ahead and eat anything he wants. No. The strong brother must take into consideration the attitude of the weak brother. The strong brother has no right to say,

"My poor weak brother can't believe that he can eat pork, but I know that pork is clean, therefore I'll go ahead and eat it." The strong brother must say, "I know my weak brother can't accept the fact that he can eat pork. To him it is unclean. Therefore, I will not eat the pork lest I lead my brother to stumble by doing as I do, or offend my brother by nullifying my testimony, or cause him to turn from the whole truth of liberty because of his weakened state."

Third, the apostle pointed out, in verses 15 to 20, that the strong believer who recognizes that all things are clean is responsible to *relinquish the use of his liberty* for the good of the weak brother. This is difficult, for there is a stubbornness in every one of us that leads us to say, "I know my rights, and nobody is going to take them from me." Such an attitude is a manifestation of the old nature, which exerts itself stubbornly in this matter of Christian liberty and freedom, and says ,"I know that God permits me to do these things. I don't care what my weaker brother says. It's his fault if he can't grow up." The apostle says that the stronger brother is to relinquish his own rights in order to avoid stumbling, offending, or weakening his brother. "If thy brother [that is, the weaker brother who does not have faith to believe that all meats are clean] is grieved with thy meat [because you eat it], now walkest thou not charitably." If you eat in front of him meat that he cannot eat and he is conscious that you are eating such meat, you sin against love. Your liberty may lead that brother into sin. If you do not relinquish your rights, then you sin, because you sin against love in wounding the conscience of the weaker brother. "Destroy not him with thy meat, for whom Christ died." This destruction does not refer to the loss of the soul but to the prevention of growth in the Christian life. It's the same as making him weak (v. 21). "Let not . . . your good be evil spoken of" (v. 16). The "good" of verse 16 is the liberty which the strong brother has. Why not permit your liberty to be reproached? Because the kingdom of God is not meat and drink. Meat is not the essence of the life that God has given us. God has not saved us so that we can eat and drink. That is not the essence of salvation. The essence of salvation is righteousness and peace and joy in the Holy Ghost. There were some of these

Jews who could not see anything beyond a ham sandwich in their salvation. They viewed salvation as giving them the right to eat the things that were forbidden, the right to wear what they couldn't wear before, the right to marry whom they could not marry before. To such people, the apostle said, "Is that all your salvation means to you? Haven't you grasped the fact that the gospel of Christ is concerned with righteousness and peace and joy in the Holy Ghost?" "He that in these things serveth Christ is acceptable to God, and approved of men" (v. 18).

GOALS IN VIEW

In verse 19 the apostle applied this principle and gave the believer two goals in the light of the truth presented: "Let us therefore follow after the things which make for peace, and things wherewith one may edify another."

The first goal is to "follow after the things which make for peace." The union of Jews and Gentiles into one body and into one fellowship of believers created tremendous practical problems for those who were so recently saved out of Gentile heathenism and out of Judaism. The Gentile would look at the Jew, who still retained some of those old attitudes toward certain meats, and would turn up his nose at the Jew and say, "Why don't you go ahead and eat it? Even Peter said it is clean."

And the Jews would sit across the table and look at those converted Gentiles and say, "How can they do it? How can they eat that stuff?" There was division and friction in the assembly because the Gentile was insisting on his right to eat certain things the Jew hesitated to eat. Paul said that in the area of doubtful things the goal of the believer ought to be to follow after the things which make for peace. The Gentile in that assembly, if he followed this injunction, would say, "If my dear Jewish brother cannot yet accept the fact that certain meats are clean, then when I eat with him, I won't eat anything but lamb. That won't cause him to stumble, or to be offended, or to be made weak at all." And on the other hand, the Jew would say, "It is hard for me to give up this custom but if it is going to promote the unity of believers, I won't insist that we continue a kosher diet when we are together." Now he might say, "At home we will have nothing but kosher food, but when we are together as believers, we will eat what is set before us, asking no questions, for conscience' sake." This would be following that which makes for peace.

The second goal was to follow the things wherewith one might edify another. The Jew was to eat, and the Gentile was to refrain from eating, with a view to building up the faith of the other. If an assembly of believers of such heterogeneous backgrounds came together, determined to conduct themselves so as to promote the peace of the brotherhood and to edify the brothers, how different that fellowship dinner would be! Surrendering of their rights, for the good of the brethren, would produce peace and unity, and would build them up in the faith.

The apostle dealt with a situation prevalent in his own day, but this same principle is pertinent for us today. Doubtful things do not fall in the category of sin. They are doubtful because Scripture does not specifically forbid them. Had it done so, they would have been removed from the category of doubtful things completely. We, by faith, accept the fact that God no longer continues a distinction between clean and unclean, between acceptable and unacceptable. By faith we lay hold of our liberty in Christ, and we stand in that liberty and will not permit anyone to bring us into bondage to any law that forbids what God permits. But we do not have to *practice* that liberty in order to *possess* that liberty. A second, and higher, principle supersedes the practice of liberty. We consider our brother's good, and we so order our lives that we do not lead that brother into sin and hence cause him to stumble as he patterns his life after ours by practicing that which he does not have liberty to do. We make it a goal to refrain from jeopardizing our Christian testimony by doing that which God may permit us to do but that which another believer does not feel free to do. We refrain from conduct that will prevent a weak brother from going on to maturity. For instance, our conduct may make him feel that maturity requires that he do what we do and he just cannot accept God's revelation that such conduct is permissible. To surrender one's own right to practice liberty is not to put oneself under law but to pattern one's life after the Lord Jesus Christ, who surrendered His rights in order that we might have salvation.

CHAPTER

18

A GOOD CONSCIENCE BEFORE GOD

Romans 14:22—15:3

THERE ARE MANY AREAS in the life of a child of God in which he is called upon to make a decision concerning doubtful things. The Apostle Paul, in writing to the Christians at Rome, gave certain age-long principles by which we who are children of God may determine what is right and what is wrong for us in the area of doubtful things. The first principle that the apostle laid down, in the fourteenth chapter of Romans, is the principle that God, who had made a distinction in the Mosaic Law between what was to be considered clean and unclean, what was acceptable and unacceptable, has now abrogated that distinction. Therefore, all things are lawful. In the second place, the apostle lays down the principle that no child of God is to use his liberty to be a means of causing a brother to stumble into sin.

In Romans 14:22—15:3, the apostle applies these principles and gives some practical exhortations concerning the outworking of the principles that he has previously predicated. In his thinking there are two classes of believers—the weak and the strong. The strong brother has sufficient faith to accept God's declaration that the things that were previously forbidden are now declared clean and may be used by a child of God as unto the Lord. The weak brother, on the other hand, perhaps because of his background or because of insufficient training in the Word of God, is weak because he cannot accept the revelation which God has made that all things are to be received with thanksgiving and used as unto the Lord. Paul recognized that no congregation would be made up entirely of weak brethren or strong brethren. Were the assembly of believers either all weak or all strong, there would be no problem, and no conflict between the two groups. But because in every fellowship there will be some who may be characterized as weak brethren and others who may be characterized as strong brethren, it was necessary to lay down certain injunctions lest the weakness of one or the strength of the other should be a cause of division and destroy the unity of the assembly. It was to that end the apostle wrote that the weaker brother was not to judge the strong brother for eating. Nor was the strong brother to condemn the weak brother for not eating. This injunction to the two was intended to preserve the unity of the body of believers in that given locale.

THE DANGER OF LIBERTY

In the particular verses that occupy our attention, the apostle gives further injunctions which lay down a third principle in the matter of doubtful things. The third principle may be summarized by saying it is of utmost importance that both the weak brother and the strong brother *have a good conscience before God* in their manner of life in respect to doubtful things. To be more specific, notice in verse 22 that the apostle first of all addresses a question and then gives a charge to the stronger brother. He says, "Hast thou faith? Have it to thyself before God." Now the faith here is not faith to accept Jesus Christ as personal Saviour. It is not even faith to walk by faith before men. The faith in the apostle's mind in verse 22 is that particular aspect of faith which has been set before us throughout this chapter, the faith to accept God's revelation that the restrictions have been removed from the things previously forbidden by the law and these things may now be used unto the Lord. The apostle addresses this brother and says, "Do you have faith to accept the revelation made through Peter [Acts 10] that God has cleansed all things and made them acceptable?" And to the man whose response is "Yes, I have faith to accept that fact," the apostle addresses this injunction, "Have that faith to thyself before God."

There is today, as there evidently was in the apostle's day, an erroneous conception that any limitation placed upon one's liberty, either by another brother or by the individual himself, is to put that one under the law and to impose a legal system upon the believer. Growing out of that attitude is the idea that if a believer knows he has liberty to do these things he must of necessity do them. The reasoning is that if he knows he can do them but does not do them then he is a legalist, he is in bondage to the law, and consequently does not enjoy the liberty which is his in Christ. Now, the apostle wants to correct that misapprehension and to affirm that one's liberty is primarily a matter of one's attitude in private, and not his conduct before an assembly of believers. The apostle says, "Have this faith to yourself before God, because just as soon as you acknowledge to God that you believe His Word that the things previously forbidden are now acceptable to you, you have been delivered from bondage to the law. You are free as soon as you recognize the liberty that is yours." Paul says, "It is not necessary for you to flaunt your liberty before others in order to be delivered from legalism, or bondage to the law."

The apostle recognizes that the great danger in the assembly of believers is not that weak brethren will refrain from eating. The great danger that confronted the assembly which would divide it was that the strong brother would insist upon exercising his liberty to show to all men that he had been delivered from the law. So Paul says, "I want to warn you stronger brothers, lest you either offend the weaker brother (that is, lose your testimony before him because he does not have the same faith that you have) or cause your weaker brother to stumble as he patterns his life after your freedom and falls into sin because he does not have the same faith that you have." May I repeat it, the danger to the unity of the assembly is in the stronger brother insisting on exercising his rights.

After the apostle addressed this word of caution to both the strong brother and the weak brother, he says, in verse 22, "Happy is he that condemneth not himself in that thing which he alloweth." Or, "Blessed is that man who does not stand self-condemned by that thing which he lets himself practice." Now this would be applicable to the strong brother in that the strong brother could consider himself happy, could congratulate himself, if he ordered his life so that the weaker brother did not become offended by his conduct or stumble into sin. You see, if I, as a stronger brother, exercised my liberty and then noted that you, as a weaker brother, followed me and defiled your conscience because you followed me, then my conscience would be grieved because I had not walked circumspectly before you in love. If I cause offense to you, or cause grief to you, it brings condemnation to my heart. The apostle says the strong brother is blessed if he surrenders his liberty and does not stand self-condemned in doing something which will be to the detriment of another brother.

But this word is applicable, on the other hand, to the weaker brother, for the apostle says to the weaker brother, "You will be blessed if you do not stand condemned because you patterned your life after the stronger brother when you did not have the stronger brother's faith." This is the way this would work. If I am the weak brother and you are the strong brother, and I see you eating something that I do not have faith to believe, in spite of the declaration of the Word of God that I can eat, but I eat it because you eat it, then I would stand self-condemned and I would be miserable in heart because I had tried to live my life by your faith and I had found it utterly impossible to do so. I, as a weak brother, will be happy if I do not pattern my liberty after your liberty, without your faith. If I do, I will condemn myself for eating that which I have no faith to eat. The principle, then, is that each man ought to conduct himself so as to have a good conscience before God in these matters.

In verse 23, Paul explains why it is that a weaker brother who patterns his life after a stronger brother, without the stronger brother's faith, actually falls into sin. He says, "He that doubteth is damned if he eats" The word *damned* here does not mean "condemned to eternal punishment." This verse does not say that this brother has lost his salvation but rather that he stands self-condemned, or reproved by his own conscience. The doubter of verse 23 is not a man who does not have faith but is the weak brother who cannot bring himself to believe God's declaration that the law has been terminated and that all things formerly declared unclean have now been declared clean by God. If this man eats that about which he has doubts he will stand self-condemned, reproved by his own conscience because he cannot eat in faith. Then Paul adds these important words: "whatsoever is not of faith is sin." Notice carefully that this expression "whatsoever is not of faith is sin" is delivered to the weak brethren. They have been born into the family of God and are enjoying fellowship with God. But Paul says to them, "If you pattern your conduct by the conduct of another believer, without that believer's faith, you will fall into sin. That which was allowable for the strong brother is not allowable for you as a weak brother—not because it is wrong, not because the meat that you eat is any less clean than the meat that the strong brother eats, but it becomes sin for you because you eat doubting God's declaration that it is clean." Each man must satisfy himself concerning what God the Holy Spirit will allow him to do in the area of doubting things. He must examine his life in respect to his faith in God's declaration that all things are acceptable and clean.

THE SACRIFICE OF LIBERTY

This matter of a good conscience will eliminate certain actions from our practice because of the possible effect on a weak brother, who may say, "Because you did it, I am going to do it." In so doing, he will sin, because "whatsoever is not of faith is sin."

The Apostle Paul has very little to say to the weaker brother, for the danger to the life of the assembly was not so much through the failure of the weaker brother to eat, but rather through the insistence of the stronger brother on eating. The apostle tells the stronger brethren how they should act toward the weaker brethren. "We then that are strong ought to bear the infirmities of the weak, and not to please ourselves." "To please ourselves" means to use the liberty which we have, and to ignore the weaker brother or to despise him for his weakness. This would be a natural reaction. However, the apostle says that the strong ought not to please themselves, but they ought to bear the infirmity of the weak. "To bear" means literally "to bear aloft" the infirmities of the weak. This means more than merely putting up with the infirmities of the weak. It means assuming, so as to impose upon oneself, the infirmities of the weak. No strong believer has any right to exercise any liberty which a fellow believer does not have the faith to accept for himself. Even though you are the strongest brother among the strong in the assembly, you are to impose upon yourself the same restrictions that the weak conscience of the weakest brother imposes upon him, lest you lead your weaker brother to be offended or to fall into sin. This is difficult. It is hard to keep from judging the weaker brother. It is difficult to follow the principle that we are voluntarily to put limitations upon our liberty according to the conscience of the weakest brother. It means we will have to sacrifice, for the good of the weaker brother, something that we know we have perfect liberty to do. This is the crux of this whole problem of doubtful things. We believe we have the right to do certain things. We know, from the Word of God, that God has no objection to our doing them. But we voluntarily surrender our rights on the basis of the principle that we who are strong ought to impose upon ourselves, as our burden, the limitations of the weak brother. We are not to please ourselves.

In the second verse, the apostle tells why we ought to impose such limitations upon our liberty. He says, "Let every one of us please his neighbor [in surrendering our rights] for his good to edification." The strong brother should give up that which he knows God permits him to do because he is concerned with his weaker brother's spiritual welfare. The ultimate goal in seeking the good of the brother is the brother's edification, or his being built up in faith, being strengthened in faith. This was the concern of the apostle, when he asked the strong brother to surrender the use of his liberty until such a time as the weak brother could be taught the truth that all things are clean and acceptable, and until the weak brother could accept the strong brother's faith as his own faith. The surrender of one's liberty was viewed as temporary. The strong brother was to surrender his liberty until such a time as the weak brother had been taught and had grown in faith. Then the weak brother could join the strong brother in the use of this liberty. When the strong brother gives up his liberty, he is to begin a work of teaching, edifying, and instructing in the Word of God with a view to building the weak brother in knowledge and faith.

SELF SCRUTINY

The principle which the apostle has put before us is of intensely practical value in the life of the assembly. We believe that this principle is meant to bring our lives under the closest scrutiny—not scrutiny by another brother but by ourselves. The strong brother is to consider the effect of his conduct upon a weaker brother in the assembly. The strong brother is to ask himself questions like these: Will this jeopardize my testimony? Will this lead an immature believer into sin if he sees me do it and then does it himself? Observing this principle will cause the weak brother to examine his conscience in the light of the Word of God to see whether those limitations which he places upon himself are limitations placed by God or his own limitations due to a lack of spiritual growth and a lack of faith. If the weaker brother sees that the Word of God permits certain conduct, but his conscience won't let him do it, then he needs to put himself under the teaching of the Word so that he may grow in faith, for "faith cometh by hearing, and hearing by the word of God."

Too many Christians have come to feel that the greatest virtue is in proving that they have liberty. According to the Word of God, that is not the greatest virtue. The greatest virtue is to enjoy your liberty as given by God and yet not use that liberty, in order to avoid offending a weaker brother. You give up your liberty for his good, with a view to building him up, to bring him out of babyhood into maturity in Christ Jesus. The apostle wrote, "None of us liveth to himself, and no man dieth to himself." Your every word and action has an effect on someone. Perchance you have dropped a pebble into a placid body of water, causing eddies to spread out in an ever widening circle. You could have refrained from dropping the pebble and thus could have prevented the eddies, but once you released that stone, there was no stopping the eddies. Before you exercise your liberty, pause and consider the effect of your action. Impose upon yourself the weakness of the weakest brother with a view to his good and his edification. The Lord Jesus Christ is the classic example of one who considered not Himself, who did not insist upon His own rights, who surrendered the liberties that were intrinsically His for the good of those He came to save. And may the mind of Christ so control you in the area of doubtful things that you will consider your brother with a view to his edification.

DO ALL THINGS TO THE GLORY OF GOD

Romans 15:1-7

THE APOSTLE PAUL was concerned over the possibility of division in an assembly of believers over matters of Christian conduct in the category of doubtful things. In order to avoid such division in the assembly and preserve unity, the apostle laid down certain principles to guide God's children in decisions concerning doubtful things.

The first principle, stated in Romans 14, is that there is freedom, or liberty, for the believer in Christ. The rule of the law has been terminated. The law is no longer the operating principle by which God distinguishes between clean and unclean. The second principle is that no believer, even though he is free from the law, has any right to do anything that would cause the weak brother to be offended by his conduct or cause a brother to sin if that weak brother patterns his conduct by the life of the stronger brother. The third principle applies to both the weak brother and the strong brother. Each must be satisfied in his own conscience concerning the course of action which he follows. The strong brother must be satisfied that he has the right to exercise his liberty, and the weak brother must not try to pattern his life according to the strong brother if he does not have the strong brother's faith. Every man must be satisfied in his own conscience. This imposes certain obligations upon the strong brother, and Paul says, in chapter 15, "We then that are strong [that is, the strong brothers] ought to bear the infirmities of the weak, and not to please ourselves." The strong brother is obligated to impose upon himself the conscience of the weak brother and to adapt his life to the weakness of the weak brother.

The apostle now states the fourth and final principle that takes precedence over all the other principles—the principle that all that we do is to be done to the glory of God. This principle is summarized in Romans 15:6: "That ye may with one mind and one mouth glorify God, even the Father of our Lord Jesus Christ." This principle applies to both the weak brother and the strong brother. If the strong brother exercises his liberty and eats meat, he is to eat to the glory of God. If the weak brother, for conscience' sake, refuses to eat meat, his refusal is to be to the glory of God. If the two brothers, differing as they do in the interpretation of what is lawful or unlawful, do all things to the glory of God, they will not be judging one another, nor will they offend and be offended.

PLEASING ANOTHER

In verse 2, the apostle says that everyone is to please his neighbor for his good, with a view to his edification. The apostle has asked the strong believers to surrender voluntarily the *exercise* of their liberty. He does not ask them to give up their liberty. He does not ask them to repudiate their liberty. When the strong brother imposes upon himself the limitations of the weaker brother's conscience, this does not mean that the strong brother becomes a weak brother. It does not mean he denies his faith that God made all things clean. But he will lay aside the exercise of his liberty to please his brother, for the brother's benefit. He will do this until the weaker brother can be built up in faith to believe that all things are now clean.

Basically, the problem is one of selfishness. The problem would arise in the assembly when a strong brother, selfishly, wants to exercise his liberty, and when a weak brother, selfishly, refuses the strong brother the right to exercise his God-given liberty. Both are selfish. One is insisting that the other conform to his thinking. The apostle says, "If you are to glorify God together, then you must be concerned not with yourselves, not with that which pleases you, but that which will be for your brother's good." It would not be for the weak brother's good to have the strong brother take the hand of the weak brother and lead him in the path of the strong brother's freedom, for if the strong brother drags the weak brother along, he is led into sin because he does not have faith that this conduct is lawful for him. And if the strong brother insists that the weak brother conduct his life according to his standards, it will be to the weak brother's detriment, not to his good. So Paul says, "Set aside your own selfish desire, your insistence on your own way, your manifestation of your liberty, and be concerned with your neighbor's good with a view to building him up, or edifying him in the faith. Impose upon yourself all his limitations and restrictions until you can teach him in the faith, and bring him to the place where he can exercise the same liberty which you enjoy. With a view to glorifying God, let each one try to please his neighbor instead of pleasing himself."

PROMOTING UNITY

The principle of doing all to the glory of God is concerned not only with seeking to please one's brother instead of himself but also with promoting the unity of the assembly. "The God of patience and consolation grant you to be like-minded one toward another according to Christ Jesus: that ye may with one mind and one mouth glorify God" (Rom. 15:4-5). Now what does the apostle mean when he prays that God may grant the believers to be like-minded one toward another? The apostle is not inferring that after a period of time all believers will come to the same settled convictions concerning these doubtful things so that there will no longer be any division. The goal in the assembly is not to impose one set of standards upon every believer. But the goal is for them to be like-minded one toward another according to Christ Jesus. What Paul is emphasizing goes back to the first principle stated in Romans 14. To be like-minded means that the stronger brother will not condemn nor look down upon, nor consider himself superior to his weaker brother. To be like-minded means the weaker brother will not condemn or discount the testimony of the stronger brother because of what God permits that stronger brother to do. To be like-minded does not mean to come ultimately to the same conclusions but rather to acknowledge that the Master may allow one servant to do one thing and another servant to do another thing, and to agree that that which God allows you to do is none of my business, and what the Master allows me to do is not your responsibility. In the closing chapter of John's Gospel, Christ was asked, "Lord, what will you have that man do?" And Christ's reply, in effect, was, "That is none of your business. You be concerned with My will for you. You have enough to do to discharge My will for you without worrying about My will for him." In matters within the Christian assembly this same principle applies. With a view to the glory of God there should be unity of minds but not conformity of decision about these doubtful things.

The apostle, in the fourteenth and fifteenth chapters of Romans, dealt with the problems that resulted from integration. This present generation is not the first generation to battle with these problems. Without doubt, the problems of integration in the first century church were far greater than the problems of integration that face this nation today. The problem the apostle faced was the problem of integrating Jew and Gentile. He instructed both that in their Christian living they must be careful lest through their liberty they destroy one for whom Christ died. The apostle stated certain principles to guide them in their conduct. In presenting these principles, the apostle was deeply concerned with the unity of the assembly of believers, but he had a higher goal than unity of the assembly. His goal was that all things should be done to bring praise, honor, and glory to the name of the Lord Jesus Christ. In certain situations unity is achieved at the expense of sound doctrine; in others unity is achieved at the expense of sound practice. But the New Testament concept of unity is never unity by denying the faith; it is never unity at the expense of countenancing sin in the life of the assembly; it is always a unity that is based upon the Word of God; a unity that is based upon the Person of Jesus Christ, a unity that arises out of a meeting of minds because believers in the assembly have the mind of Christ. And when the apostle presented the principles that should guide a believer's conduct, he summarized our responsibility by telling us to do all things to the glory of God. We, as believers, can do no better than to take this as our guide, that whatever we do, we do all to the glory of God.

Any course of conduct can be tested by this principle. Can I do this thing for the glory of God? If I practice this thing, will God be honored? If this thing is a part of my life, will I attract others to Jesus Christ, or will I repel them from Jesus Christ? We must realize that frequently the world has far higher standards for the Christian and expects far more of a Christian than Christians themselves do. Many things that we could countenance in the name of liberty, the worldling would never countenance for a Christian and would consider to be out of harmony with his Christian testimony. In this matter of living the Christian life, we have a responsibility not only to the saints but to the world which watches us most critically and is far more ready to point an accusing finger at us than are the saints in the assembly. Therefore the apostle says, "If you would give no offense and if you would cause no man to stumble, either in the assembly, or outside it, then set this as your goal: Whatsoever you do, in word or deed, do all to the glory of God."

20

HOW FAR CAN A CHRISTIAN GO?

I Corinthians 8:1-13

THE CHURCH IN ROME was threatened with division because of the conflict that arose between Jews and Gentiles due to their different social, cultural, and religious backgrounds. The conflict made it necessary for the Apostle Paul to lay down certain principles to guide both groups of believers in Christian conduct. These principles were given to guide them in the area of doubtful things so that one believer should not be judging another believer, so that there should be no division in the assembly, so that a weaker brother should not be offended or caused to stumble, so that there should be no loss of testimony, and so that God would be glorified through the life of those believers.

When we turn to Paul's letter to the Corinthians, we find the apostle was facing a different situation. A conflict had arisen in the Corinthian church. The conflict was not between Jews and Gentiles, for the people in the Church had, almost without exception, been brought to the Lord out of the same social, cultural, and religious background. Gentiles who had been converted from pagan heathenism made up the assembly, and they were facing a problem concerning doubtful things which caused the apostle to state the same principles that we have studied in the Epistle to the Romans. And in the eighth and ninth chapters of I Corinthians we see how the principles which Paul applied to the problems between Jew and Gentile in Rome were equally applicable to the problems that arose among the Gentiles in Corinth.

Corinth was a center of heathen paganism and the site of great temples erected to Greek deities. Many of the deities worshiped in Corinth were worshiped by offering meats to the gods. The flesh of the animal would be taken to the temple, presented to a priest, and would be placed by the priest upon the altar. The meat remained in the temple for only a short time and was soon taken to the market place and offered for sale. Meat that had been in the idol's temple was later offered for sale in the market at reduced prices. The housewife who came to the market would notice a difference in the prices of what appeared to be identical cuts. She would ask why one piece of meat should be so much more expensive than the other. The butcher would tell her that the expensive piece had come directly from the slaughterhouse, but the cheaper cut had come from the idol temple. Suppose two believers, Mrs. A and Mrs. B, went together to the market. Mrs. A would reason, "Funds are short at our house. I don't see any reason why I should not buy that bargain piece of meat, because I know that an idol is nothing. An idol could not feast on that piece of meat even though it was on the altar. The idol has not changed the meat nor destroyed the nutritive value of it. I will buy that bargain piece of meat and serve it to my family." Mrs. B, confronted with the same situation, would reason, "I used to be a worshiper of that god. Many times I brought flesh into that temple and gave it to the priest, who offered it to that god. I will not, under any circumstances, touch meat that has been in an idol temple because it reminds me of my past life and my past idolatry. I'll have nothing to do with it." And so she would buy the more expensive cut lest she defile her conscience by eating the meat that had been offered to idols. So far there had been no conflict between the two women, for each had a good basis for doing what she did. Mrs. A was exercising the liberty given her. Mrs. B was zealous to have a good conscience before God and sought to avoid giving offense to anyone. The conflict would arise when Mrs. A and Mrs. B began to judge each other. Mrs. A would accuse Mrs. B of needless extravagance in paying the higher price. She would question her narrow conscience and question her spiritual maturity because her conscience was so easily defiled. On the other hand, Mrs. B would accuse Mrs. A of trafficking with idols and neglecting to maintain separation from that which they had been saved from. The conflict between the two would erupt into an open conflict in the assembly of believers, sides would be taken, and one group would accuse the other of a lack of spirituality and maturity, and the other group would accuse the first of a lack of separation. You would have the meat-eaters, and the nonmeat-eaters, those who insisted upon buying hamburger that hadn't been in a temple rather than sirloin that had been in the temple. Thus the assembly would be divided.

Paul applies to this situation in Corinth the same principles that were applicable to the Jews and Gentiles in Rome. It is so encouraging to see that the one set of principles is applicable to any society, to any culture, in any day. We don't need a different set of principles today, for these are universally applicable.

PRINCIPLES OF CONDUCT

In I Corinthians 8:1-6, the apostle stated the principle of liberty in Christ. He began by saying, "Now as touching things offered to idols, we know that we all have knowledge." Knowledge, as he explained in this passage, is the knowledge that an idol is nothing. A believer, by buying idol meat, is not approving the idolatrous system carried on in the temple. The apostle says, in verse 4, "As concerning therefore the eating of those things that are offered in sacrifice unto idols, we know that an idol is nothing in the world, and that there is none other God but one . . . to us there is but one God, the Father, of whom are all things, and we in him; and one Lord Jesus Christ, by whom are all things, and we by him" (vv. 4, 6). The knowledge which these believers had gave them liberty to use the idol meat. The apostle knew that putting that meat in the idol temple could not contaminate it so that it could not be used by a believer. To use it or not to use it is a matter of conscience. Because they knew that an idol is nothing, and knew that there was but one God, it made no difference whether that meat stayed overnight on an idol altar, or whether it stayed overnight in the butcher's shop. Thus Paul affirmed the principle of freedom in Christ.

In verses 1 and 2 the apostle said that knowledge can be a dangerous thing: "Knowledge puffeth up, but charity edifieth. If any man thinketh that he knoweth any thing, he knoweth nothing yet as he ought to know." A person's knowledge of his freedom is not to be the determinative factor in his Christian conduct. My knowing I *can* do something does not mean that I *should* do something. Because God has declared all things clean, we will not permit anyone to take away our freedom, to impose law upon us, or put us under a legal system that says we cannot. But we are not obligated to exercise our freedom. There is a second principle which takes precedence over the first principle, as indicated by verses 7 and 9: "There is not in every man that knowledge: for some with conscience of the idol unto this hour eat it as a thing offered unto an idol; and their conscience being weak is defiled. . . . Take heed lest by any means this liberty of yours become a stumblingblock to them that are weak." This second principle, which Paul also affirmed in Romans 14, was the principle that no believer should use his liberty to cause a weaker brother to stumble or to be offended. The fact that we have liberty and *could* do something, does not mean, in view of another believer's weaker conscience, that we *should* do that thing. Though some had knowledge, yet Paul recognized (v. 7) that not every man had the same knowledge. Paul equated knowledge with the faith to believe that a thing is acceptable. Therefore, Paul gave this warning: "Take heed lest by any means this liberty of yours become a stumblingblock to them that are weak" (v. 9) .

The danger involved in causing a weaker brother to stumble is clearly outlined in verses 10 to 11. "If any man see thee which hath knowledge sit at meat in the idol's temple [that is, he sees you using the idol's meat, and as a result concludes that you are joining yourself to the idol], shall not the conscience of him that is weak be emboldened to eat those things which are offered to idols; and through thy knowledge shall the weak brother perish for whom Christ died?" The weak brother concluded that if the strong brother could eat the meat from the temple so could he. He instructed his wife to bring the cheaper cuts home. But when he ate such meat his conscience was defiled because he was patterning his conduct by another's liberty. The result is described in verse 11. The word *perish* does not mean the weak brother lost his salvation. In Romans, chapter 15, Paul said we were to consider the weaker brother with a view to his good, and with a view to his edification, or being built up in the faith. The thought is the same here. A brother who patterns his conduct in doubtful things by the stronger brother's manner of life, does something he doesn't have faith to believe God will permit him to do, defiles his conscience, and so there can be no development, no progress, no growth, no edification in the doctrine of grace.

Paul adds another thought in verse 12 which cannot be emphasized too much. "When ye sin so against the brethren [that is, by insisting on using your liberty, and exercising your rights, regardless of what it does to the weaker brethren]. . . ye sin against Christ." May I quote it again? "Ye sin against Christ." The believer who says, "I *can*, therefore I *will*," and will not assume the conscience of the weaker brother but insists on doing that which he believes is right for him regardless of how it affects his testimony or the brethren is guilty of sinning against Christ. So, then, the second principle is the principle that no believer has the right to exercise his God-given liberty if it means he is going to cause his brother to stumble, because if he causes his brother to stumble, he is not only sinning against the brother but is committing sin against Christ.

The third principle is given to us in verse 13 and is then illustrated in chapter 9. The principle is that of surrendering one's right, or surrendering one's liberty, for the good and the edification of the brother. "Wherefore, if meat makes my brother to offend, I will eat no flesh while the world standeth, lest I make my brother to offend." The apostle is going beyond what would be expected or demanded in this situation. If the believer would be offended because Paul ate idol meat, the simple remedy would be for Paul to eat the other kind. But Paul said, "If my brother saw me eat idol meat and it caused him to offend, I would give up all meat, because I might eat the non-idol meat and the brother might think that I was eating idol meat. Therefore I would go beyond what would be expected of me, because my desire is to avoid causing the weak brother to perish and, consequently, causing me to sin against Christ." This is going "the second mile" in order to please the brethren, surrendering one's own right for the good of the brethren.

Next, the apostle cited some illustrations of rights which he surrendered for the good of the brethren. In chapter 9 he affirmed the fact that he was an apostle. Because he was an apostle he had certain rights and liberties, as indicated by his question in verse 4. "Have we not power to eat and to drink?" The answer would be "Yes, God has declared all things clean; you can eat and drink what you want to." In verse 5 he asked another question. "Have we not power to lead about a sister, a wife, as well as the other apostles, and as the brethren of the Lord, and Cephas [Isn't it permissible for me to be married]?" And the answer would be "Yes, you have the right to be married." And Paul asked a further question, "Have we not power to forbear working [Should not the churches support us because we are apostles]?" The answer would be "Yes, you have that right." What was Paul's response? "Though I be free from all men, yet have I made myself servant unto all, that I might gain the more" (v. 19). Paul became a servant by assuming the limitations which the weakest brother had concerning these matters of conscience. Paul did not say, "I demand that the weaker brother recognize that I am an apostle and have certain liberties." No, he put himself into the servant class and submitted to their conscience. He said, "Unto the Jews I became as a Jew, that I might gain the Jews; to them that are under the law, as under the law, that I might gain them that are under the law; to them that are without the law, . . . that I might gain them that are without law. To the weak became I as weak, that I might gain the weak: I am made all things to all men, that I might by all means save some. And this I do for the gospel's sake" (I Cor. 9:20-23a). Thus the apostle gives his own personal testimony about how these principles affected his life. In effect, the apostle said, "I gave up meat and lived on vegetables in order that I might not give offense. I did without the companionship of a wife. I labored making tents when it was the obligation of the brethren to contribute to my needs. I imposed upon myself the conscience of the weak brother and gave up those things in which I personally would have found delight. I even observed days and months and years of the old Jewish calendar that I might win those that are under the law." Why did he do all of these things? "For the gospel's sake" (v. 23).

How would Paul have summarized his teaching concerning the problem of which meats the Christian housewife in Corinth should have bought? Something like this: "First of all, it doesn't matter to God. In the second place, you must be satisfied in your own conscience about which meat God wants you to buy. If God gives you liberty to buy meat that is cheaper because it has been offered to idols, eat it and enjoy it. If God won't let you, then get the more expensive meat. Each believer in this matter must have a knowledge concerning what God wants him to do. In the third place, you be careful lest you cause another brother to stumble by the use of your liberty, for if you do, you sin against Christ. It is far better to give up the use of your liberty than it is to cause a brother to offend."

DANGERS TO AVOID

These principles are applicable to situations today. Most of us are not bothered as to whether we should eat ham, or not eat ham, as were the Christians in Rome. Most of us are not bothered about the problem of which meat to buy, as were the Christians in Corinth. These are not the problems which we face. But there are other problems upon which believers are divided today. Now what are we to do about these things? Are Paul's principles applicable? In different parts of the country Christian groups have different standards concerning what is right and what is wrong. If you were to try to draw up a list of the so-called doubtful things, it would vary tremendously according to locale. Certain doubtful things have, for some time, been debated. What should the believer do about movies and television? What should the believer do about dancing? What about tobacco? What about cards? What about wine? What about cosmetics and makeup? How high or how low should a hemline be? These doubtful things fit into many different categories. Some fit into the social realm, like makeup, attire, dancing, and mixed bathing. Others fall into the area of amusements, like cards and movies. And others are classified as pleasures and habits. How are we to decide these things? The first thing we must decide is whether these are doubtful things. We have to face the issue. Are they forbidden by the Word of God? Is there something inherent in them that would violate the principles of the Word of God? If so, then they are removed from the area of doubtful things. May I illustrate? Where I grew up, smoking was always included at the head of the list of doubtful things. All of the recent medical evidence of the relation between smoking and cancer and the effects of smoking on the body, has removed smoking from the area of doubtful things. How can one call doubtful that which medical science says destroys the body? We are forbidden by the Word of God to destroy the body which is His temple.

Many Christians say, "You cannot be a Christian and do this, and this, and this." A legalistic code is imposed on believers that stifles individual liberty and nullifies the individual's conscience in these matters. One could be a Christian and go to the movies. One could be born again and use wine. One could be born again and dance. One could be born again and play cards. One could be born again and use cosmetics. To say that one cannot be a believer and do these things is to make salvation depend upon works instead of upon the grace of God. To say one cannot be a Christian and do these things is to impose a legalistic system upon a person that is not taught in the Word of God. Institutions and assemblies of believers may find it necessary in order to maintain their testimony, to impose standards. It may be right for a Christian organization to impose restrictions for the sake of its testimony. But to say one cannot be a Christian if he does these things is to deny the doctrines of grace and the freedom of the individual conscience. This is the first danger to be avoided, the danger of legalism.

The second danger is that of lost testimony or of causing a brother to sin. If God gives me the liberty to do something, I have perfect liberty to do it. I could do it, but that does not mean I should do it. If a believer does what I do without liberty from God to do it, then I have caused that individual to sin. It would be better to forego that which could be enjoyable to me, or relaxing, rather than to prevent a fellow Christian from growing in grace and in the knowledge of our Lord and Saviour. I do not become more spiritual by foregoing my liberty, but I show concern for my testimony and for my brother lest he be offended or be led into sin by my conduct. It is a fallacy to think that giving up these things is an evidence of spirituality. Many Christians believe that if they went to the movies, a dance, or a card party; if they took a sip of wine or wore makeup, they would not have any more spirituality than a bedpost. Dr. Homer Hammontree used to say that there is a city that has two million inhabitants, not one of whom drinks, smokes, dances, or plays cards. But not one of them has a bit of spiritual life. He referred to the Greenwood Hills Cemetery in New York City. Refraining from doing certain things is not synonymous with spirituality. To be spiritual is to be controlled by the Holy Spirit of God. Spirituality is an attitude toward the Holy Spirit and toward the Word of God, and not toward things. Spirituality will certainly produce a different kind of life and will remove offensive things from the life of the child of God, but we cannot equate spirituality with the observance of certain prohibitions.

The question finally resolves itself to this, "Should I do it simply because I could do it?" The question is not "How much can I do?" The question is "How much *should* I do in view of the danger of offending my brother and, consequently, causing me to sin against Christ?" How much are we willing to give up for the gospel's sake? That was Paul's great consideration. Paul's consideration was not "How much can I do and get away with and still be recognized as an apostle?" Paul's concern was "How much can I give up for the gospel's sake?" That ought to be the attitude of the child of God. How far can a Christian go? First of all, in the light of the teaching of the Word of God, a Christian can go only as far as the limits set by his weaker brother. It isn't a question of exercising his God-given liberty. It is a question of assuming the weakness of the weaker brother—with a view to his edification.

In the second place, the believer can only exercise his liberty to the extent that his testimony is not jeopardized. One of the greatest dangers believers face today is the danger of losing their testimony before the world by being so much like the world that they have nothing to offer it. We will never attract men to Jesus Christ by being like the world. If all we have to offer is what the world already has, they won't want it or feel a need for it. The only way we can attract men to Jesus Christ is by having something that the world doesn't have, thus creating an appetite in them for what God has to give through Jesus Christ. And that appetite comes not by being like the world but by being different from it. Peter didn't hesitate to call us a peculiar or a set-apart people. Some Christians don't want to be considered peculiar. To others, being peculiar is a badge of honor. Jesus Christ stood out from His whole generation as singular and unique. And God is asking us to stand apart, to surrender some of the liberties that God has given us, in order that we might attract people to Jesus Christ. The question is not "Can a believer do this?" The question is "Can I give this up for the gospel's sake to maintain my testimony before other believers, and before the world?" Will you dare to be different by refusing to conform to the world for the gospel's sake?

21

THE GOAL OF THE CHRISTIAN

John 17:1-10

WHAT IS THE GOAL in the Christian life? When the Apostle Paul dealt with doubtful things he concluded by stating that all things are to be done to the honor and glory of God. If we eat, let us eat not to demonstrate our liberty but to glorify God. If we refrain from eating, let us do that not for our own glory in surrendering our liberty but for the glory of God. One of the many bumper stickers that catch my attention is one that says, "Do not follow me. I am lost." And because many Christians have no clear goal in view, it is impossible for them to accomplish anything in the Christian life. Because we are so nebulous in our thinking about what constitutes Christian living, we have to confess we are lost and know not where we are going. If we are to glorify God, we must understand how God is glorified.

TO THE GLORY OF GOD

In the seventeenth chapter of John's Gospel we are given an intimation as to what it is to glorify God. We recognize that God is a God of infinite glory, and it is impossible to add anything to the infinite glory already inherent in God. In what sense, then, can an individual glorify God? Jesus Christ, in His conversation with the Father just before His death, said, "I have glorified thee on the earth: I have finished the work which thou gavest me to do." Jesus Christ glorified the Father because, in perfect obedience to the will of the Father, He had completed the work which the Father had given Him to do. Now what was the work to which Christ referred? We find the answer in verses 6 and 8, where Christ said, "I have manifested thy name unto the men which thou gavest me out of the world: . . . I have given unto them the word which thou gavest me." The Lord Jesus Christ was sent into the world to reveal the Father to men. He glorified the Father when He revealed the Father to men. Having revealed the Father to men, He could say to the Father, "I have glorified thee on the earth: I have finished the work which thou gavest me to do." John 1:18 records that "the only begotten Son, which is in the bosom of the Father, he hath declared [or revealed] him." Jesus Christ came into the world in order that the world, which was ignorant of God, might have a revelation of God. And when Jesus Christ revealed God to men, Jesus Christ glorified the Father. When men received the revelation which Christ gave, and responded to that revelation by honoring, worshiping, obeying, and adoring the One who was revealed, they glorified God. And those who received the revelation were called upon to manifest the glory of God to the world as Jesus Christ had glorified the Father during the years of His earthly sojourn. So, when the Apostle Paul says, "Ye are bought with a price: therefore glorify God," he is saying, "You who have received the Father are responsible to manifest the Father to those who are in ignorance and in darkness."

How is God working in His child to glorify Himself? First of all, the child of God glorifies God through the very fact that he has received Jesus Christ as personal Saviour. His salvation glorifies God. Three times in the first chapter of Ephesians, the apostle emphasizes the fact that our salvation brings glory to God. In Ephesians 1:6 we see that all that the Father has done has been planned to be to the praise of the glory of His grace. In verse 12 we discover that all that the Son had done was done with this in view: that we should be to the praise of His glory. In verse 14 it is stated that all that the Holy Spirit accomplishes in and through the child of God is unto the praise of His glory. The apostle there emphasizes the fact that the salvation by grace which has been offered to us by the Father through the Son and accomplished by the Holy Spirit brings glory to God. We find this same truth emphasized in Romans 9:23 where Paul states God's purpose to "make known the riches of his glory on the vessels of mercy, which he hath afore prepared unto glory." The apostle is emphasizing there the fact that God has chosen men unto salvation, so that they should be vessels, or instruments, through which God would make known the riches of His glory. God is glorified because He saves sinners. God did not select the good, the kind, the nice, the upright, the righteous, and save them because of what they were. But God saves sinners, those who deserve nothing. And His reaching down in grace, mercy, and love to redeem sinners brings glory to Himself.

God's being glorified through saving sinners is emphasized again in I Timothy 1:16, where Paul writes, "Howbeit for this cause I obtained mercy, that in me first Jesus Christ might shew forth all longsuffering for a pattern to them which should here-after believe on Him to life everlasting." The salvation given to Saul of Tarsus manifested the patience of God with a stubborn rebel, seeking him, finding him, and bringing him to Himself. We see, then, that the kind of salvation which has been provided for us is a salvation that glorifies God.

In the second place, one glorifies God the Father through a daily life that is lived in conformity to the Person of Jesus Christ. The fact that we have been graced with salvation puts upon us the obligation to walk worthy of God, so that through that trans-formed walk God will be revealed and glorified. Paul emphasized this when he wrote, in I Thessalonians 2:12, "That ye would walk worthy of God, who hath called you unto his kingdom and glory." Again, in I Corinthians 10:31, he wrote, "Whether there-fore ye eat, or drink, or whatsoever ye do, do all to the glory of God." The apostle was concerned with the daily life of these believers, and his great desire for them was that those who had been brought to Christ through a salvation which glorified God, should so conduct themselves in their manner of daily life that their lives should bring glory to God.

In the third place, we find that God will be glorified through the unending ages of eternity as He brings many sons into glory. The apostle emphasizes this fact in Colossians 3:4, where he says, "When Christ, who is our life, shall appear, then shall ye also ap-pear with him in glory." The phrase "in glory" does not describe *where* we shall be, but *how* we shall be. It may be paraphrased this way, "When Christ shall appear, then shall ye also appear with him, glorious ones." Paul is focusing his attention upon the end of our salvation, that is conformity to Christ in glory, which means that we shall be found to His praise and honor and glory through the ages of eternity. This same truth is presented in Hebrews 2:9-10, where we read, "We see Jesus, who was made a little lower than the angels for the suffering of death, crowned with glory and honour, that he by the grace of God should taste death for every man. For it became him, for whom are all things, and by whom are all things, in bringing many sons unto glory, to make the captain of their salvation perfect through sufferings." Jesus Christ offered Himself as a sacrifice and died to bring many sons unto glory. Jesus Christ was resurrected to be the firstfruits of a great harvest of glorified ones who shall be transformed into His likeness, so that through the ages of eternity we should bring glory to the Father.

When we gather these passages together, we find that the believer glorifies God through the salvation that he has received by grace, through the new life that he lives, and through being one in whom the promise is fulfilled that is given us in the Word of God that when Jesus Christ "shall appear, we shall be like him; for we shall see him as he is." The preeminent goal of the believer is the goal of bringing glory to the Father.

IN THE LIKENESS OF CHRIST

The question will logically arise, "How can a redeemed sinner glorify God?" In Galatians 2:20 the apostle writes, "I am crucified with Christ: nevertheless I live; yet not I, but Christ liveth in me: and the life which I now live in the flesh I live by the faith of the Son of God, who loved me, and gave himself for me." Christ liveth in me! The child of God, of himself, cannot glorify God. But as Jesus Christ lives His life through us as children of God, Jesus Christ can do through us what He did when He walked here among men. He can glorify the Father by revealing the Father. We will be the instruments, or the channels, through which Jesus Christ glorifies God. It was Jesus Christ's purpose to glorify the Father as He walked among men, and it is just as much the purpose of Jesus Christ to glorify God today. But instead of doing it through His own Person, He does it by living through those who have been redeemed by the grace of God unto the glory of God. And if we are to glorify God, we must reproduce the likeness of Christ.

This brings us to our relationship to the second Person of the Godhead. We glorify the Father by manifesting the likeness of Jesus Christ. The One who dwells within lives His life through us to glorify God. Perhaps the first passage that would come to mind in this connection is I Peter 2:21, where the Apostle Peter says, "For even hereunto [or, to this end] were ye called: because Christ also suffered for us, leaving us an example, that ye should follow his steps." And then Peter shows us the submission that characterized the Lord Jesus Christ. Peter refers to Christ's submission to the Father to emphasize the truth that as the child of God submits to the Lord Jesus Christ in his daily experience, Christ will manifest His life through that child to the glory of the Father. This theme occurs repeatedly through Paul's writings. For instance, we read in II Corinthians 3:18, "We all, with open face beholding as in a glass the glory of the Lord, are changed into the same image from glory to glory, even as by the Spirit of the Lord." Why is the Lord Jesus Christ revealed to us? In order that we might be changed, or transfigured, into the image of Jesus Christ. We cannot, with these natural eyes, look upon His glorified face. Yet the glorified, risen, ascended Christ is revealed to us through the Word of God, which is like a mirror, reflecting His glory, and God intends, as we look at the One revealed therein, that we be conformed to that image, so that Jesus Christ might glorify the Father through us. Again, in II Corinthians 4:11, Paul says, "We which live are alway delivered unto death for Jesus' sake, that the life also of Jesus might be made manifest in our mortal flesh." Think of it! Jesus Christ so transforms the Christian that His life is manifest through his body, to the end that God might be glorified. The life of Jesus is made manifest in our mortal flesh. "For all things are for your sakes, that the abundant grace might through the thanksgiving of many redound to the glory of God" (v. 15). Paul shows in verses 11 and 15 that it is God's purpose that the life of Jesus be made manifest in our mortal flesh to the end that glory might redound to God. In I John 2:6, John says, "He that saith he abideth in him ought himself also so to walk, even as he walked." When God purposes to glorify Himself through us, He does so by manifesting the life of Jesus Christ through these bodies. As Christ lives His life through us, God is revealed to men who see Jesus Christ in us and thus God is glorified.

That brings another question to mind. Since it is God's goal for my life that I should glorify God, and since God can only be glorified as the life of Christ is reproduced in this mortal body, how can I manifest Christ as I live day by day? And that question leads us to our relationship to the third Person of the Godhead, the Holy Spirit. I, of myself, cannot manifest the life of Christ, for I am not Jesus Christ. I do not have His perfection. I do not have His holiness. I do not have His wisdom and knowledge of the Father. I live in an unredeemed body with a sinful nature, and I live in the midst of an unredeemed world. How can I glorify God by manifesting forth the life of Christ? The child of God can reproduce the life of the Lord Jesus Christ only by the power of the Holy Spirit of God. Again and again the apostle emphasizes this theme as he writes about the Christian life. He says in Romans 8:5, "They that are after the flesh do mind the things of the flesh; but they that are after the Spirit the things of the Spirit. For to be carnally minded is death; but to be spiritually minded is life and peace. Because the carnal mind is enmity against God: for it is not subject to the law of God, neither indeed can be. So then they that are in the flesh cannot please God. But ye are not in the flesh, but in the Spirit, if so be that the Spirit of God dwell in you. Now if any man have not the Spirit of Christ, he is none of his. And if Christ be in you, the body is dead because of sin; but the Spirit is life because of righteousness. But if the Spirit of him that raised up Jesus from the dead dwell in you [and he certainly does], he that raised up Christ from the dead shall also quicken your mortal bodies by his Spirit that dwelleth in you. Therefore, brethren, we are debtors, not to the flesh, to live after the flesh. For if ye live after the flesh, ye shall die; but if ye through the Spirit do mortify the deeds of the body, ye shall live." There the apostle is emphasizing that if we manifest that which is our nature, we manifest the flesh, we manifest that which is dead, we manifest that which can bring no glory to God. But if the Spirit of God takes charge of this mortal body, the Spirit of God will reproduce the life of Jesus Christ, and use this mortal body as His instrument to reveal Christ so that God might be glorified.

This fact was emphasized again by the apostle in Ephesians 1:19. It was his desire that the believers he addressed should know "what is the exceeding greatness of his power to us-ward who believe, according to the working of his mighty power, which he wrought in Christ, when he raised him from the dead." Now if you compare this passage with Romans 8:11, you will discover that the Holy Spirit who raised Jesus Christ from the dead, is the power that works in us to quicken our mortal bodies to do God's will. That is why in Ephesians 5:18 Paul says, "Be not drunk with wine [that is, under the control of wine] . . . but be filled with [that is, under the control of] the Spirit." As one is controlled by the Holy Spirit, the Spirit will reproduce the life of Christ so that God might be glorified. Galatians 5:16 is crucial here: "This I say then, Walk in the Spirit [or literally, walk by means of the Spirit], and ye shall not fulfil the lust of the flesh." Only as we walk in conscious dependence upon the supporting power of the Holy Spirit can the life of Christ be manifested in these mortal bodies.

The apostle reveals his own spiritual secret in Philippians 3:10, where he says that it was the great desire of his heart to know Christ and to know the power of His resurrection. A paraphrase of what the apostle says would read, "I want to know Him. Then I want to know experientially the power that brought Jesus Christ to resurrection." Paul's great goal is to know Him so that he may be like Him, and then to be so related to the Holy Spirit that the power that brought Jesus Christ from the dead may be the power that operates in his life, so that the One that he loves is the One whose life is manifested through his mortal body. Then men will not see Paul; they will see Jesus Christ and, seeing Jesus Christ, they will come to know the Father so that God the Father will be glorified as He is manifested through his body. Then the apostle, in Colossians 1:11, prays that the believers might be "strengthened with all might, according to his glorious power [that is, the Holy Spirit's power], unto all patience and longsuffering with joyfulness." What the apostle is emphasizing here is that when God's power, that is, the Holy Spirit's power, operates in the child of God, He will be glorified because the Holy Spirit produces the patience, longsuffering, and joyfulness of Jesus Christ in us.

Men are characterized by many goals. They want security; they want happiness; they want material prosperity; they want power and influence; they want a reputation. All of these things satisfy the flesh. They do not fulfil the purpose of God, because God's purpose for your life is to reproduce the life of Jesus Christ in you, so that men may look at you and see the Lord Jesus Christ revealing the Father, thus bringing honor and glory to God. There can be no higher goal. There can be no higher ambition. There can be no higher purpose than that which the Word of God puts before us as the chief end of the child of God, to glorify God. The greatest goal in the believer's life is not his own enjoyment of his salvation. His highest goal is not learning the truths of Scripture, nor even teaching and preaching the Word. His greatest goal is to live Jesus Christ so that men may know the Father. God is glorified through the transformation in the life of His child that enables Him to use that child to reveal Himself to men, so that as men respond to that which has been revealed of Christ, they might honor and glorify the Father. Jesus Christ could say, "I have finished the work that thou gavest me to do." May God the Holy Spirit so possess and control us, and so reproduce Jesus Christ within us, that we can say, at the close of each day, "I have finished the work you gave me to do today. The Spirit has reproduced the life of Christ in this mortal body, to the glory of God."

PART

III

DESIGN FOR CONFLICT

22

THE CHRISTIAN AND THE WORLD

Romans 12:1-21

THE CHILD OF GOD faces a number of difficulties on his journey from earth to heaven. The first great difficulty is sin itself. He is beset on every hand by temptations which entice him away from the path of conformity to the Lord Jesus Christ. The Word of God makes it very clear that sin can have no rightful place in the life of the child of God. The child of God has no right to entertain any thought, deed, or word that is contrary to the holiness of the Lord Jesus Christ. Such things are forbidden in the Word.

The second great difficulty comes in the great area of doubtful things, things that in themselves are not sinful but which may be put to sinful uses, or sinful ends. The Word of God lays down principles to guide God's child in the decisions concerning his conduct but does not deal with specifics. God's child is constantly faced with decisions whether it is right for him to do this, that or the other thing. In such matters believers are to be guided by the principles of the Word.

A third difficulty is in the area of worldliness. It is this problem to which we direct your attention now. When this world was created by God, it was created to be the instrument through which God would manifest His glory to all created intelligences. With the rebellion of Adam against the authority of God, this world, which had been designed and created to serve God's end, was appropriated by Satan to serve his purpose, to promote his ends, and to further his rebellion against God. Our problem, then, is the problem of how a child of God can use that which has been appropriated by Satan to be used against God. How can we use the things that are in the world without promoting the program and the purposes of the evil one?

THE WORLD SYSTEM

We need to remind ourselves that when we were born, we were born into the world. When we speak of being born into the world, we are not thinking of the world as a geographical place but rather as a state or a condition. The Word of God repeatedly refers to the world as a state or condition of existence. The world has its prince, Satan, whom Christ referred to as the "prince of this world." Paul referred to Satan as "the prince of the power of the air." This world is ruled by a government operating under the control of Satan, its head. Paul also called Satan "the god of this world." This world has its own false religious system which demands worship, loyalty, and submission to Satan as its god. This world is the instrument which was appropriated by Satan and is used to promote his goals, his aims, his ends, and his ambitions. If Satan is to accomplish his purpose of overthrowing the kingdom of God and of elevating himself as a god and a prince in this world, he must have some means through which he operates. This organized system with Satan as its prince and its god is the means which he uses to accomplish these ends. When we were born into this world as worldlings, we were born under Satan's authority. He is the god who controlled, guided, and directed our lives. His purposes became our purposes. His standards became our standards, his ethics were our ethics, his morality or righteousness was our standard of morality or righteousness, for we were in the world. The Apostle John, in I John 5:19, gives us very graphically, God's picture as he says that the whole world is cradled in the lap of the evil one. Our English translation says, "The whole world lieth in wickedness." But John pictures a nurse who is holding a child to her bosom, and John says this whole world system (*kosmos*) is cradled in the lap of the evil one.

The world as a system is marked or characterized by ignorance. In I Corinthians 1:21 Paul says, "The world by wisdom knew not God." The world system into which we were born did not know the true God but knew only the god of this world, who transforms himself into an angel of light so as to deceive men. In II Peter 2:20, Peter speaks of the defilement of the world. This system, under the control of Satan and serving his purposes, is marked by defilement. Further, in II Peter 1:4, Peter refers to "the corruption that is in this world through lust." The world, as a system is characterized by corruption, and those who are in the world partake of the defilement and the corruption of the world system. In I Corinthians 11:32, Paul tells us that the world as a system is set apart to judgment. Our Lord Himself in John 12:31 announced that the prince of this world was to be judged at the cross. The system of which Satan is the prince and the god was to come under a divine judgment. God created man for Himself, and God purposed that His creatures should enjoy fellowship with Him. But with the rebellion of Adam, God's purpose could not be realized or accomplished in either the world or the citizens of the world. Therefore, the world and its citizens came under divine judgment.

THE BELIEVER'S RELATIONSHIP TO THE WORLD

One of the glorious truths of the gospel is that the death of Christ has changed the believer's relationship to the world. The death of Christ has so many ramifications that it is impossible for us to comprehend in a small scope of time, or with our limited minds, all that God accomplished through the death of Christ. Not only did Christ's death provide redemption from sin, propitiate God, and reconcile the world, but the death of Christ makes possible a change in a man's relationship to the world, if he believes and is brought into a relationship to Jesus Christ. Believers can say with the Apostle Paul, "Our conversation [or, our citizenship] is in heaven" (Phil. 3:20). Paul is emphasizing one of the benefits of the death of Christ. We who were born into this world as citizens of this world have had our citizenship transferred. Even though physically and geographically we are on the earth, we are no longer of the world, for we have been given a new citizenship in a new state which is ruled by a new Prince, even the Lord Jesus Christ. This state is not characterized by ignorance but rather by a knowledge of God. This state is not characterized by defilement and corruption, for we have been made clean and righteous through the death of Christ. Those in this state have been delivered from divine judgment because, as Christ is in relationship to judgment, so are we, even though geographically we are still on the earth, or in the world.

We want to call your attention to some of the things that take place in a man's relationship to the world at the time that he accepts Christ as his personal Saviour. First, our Lord spoke of this changed relationship when He said in a prayer to His Father, "I have manifested thy name unto the men that thou gavest me out of the world: thine they were, and thou gavest them me; and they have kept thy word . . . they are not of the world, even as I am not of the world" (John 17:6, 11). To His disciples Christ said, "If ye were of the world, the world would love his own; but because ye are not of the world, but I have chosen you out of the world, therefore the world hateth you" (John 15:19). In these passages, which are but a few of many to which we could direct your attention, we see that by faith in the Lord Jesus Christ believers have been taken, positionally, out of the world. They have been brought into the kingdom of God's Son. Their citizenship has been transferred, and those who once were worldlings are now citizens of Heaven. The Apostle Paul's favorite phrase for this in the Book of Ephesians is that we who once were in the world are now "in the heavenlies." One result of our receiving Jesus Christ as a personal Saviour is that we were taken out of the world.

Another result of the death of Christ that affects the believer's relationship to the world is indicated in Galatians 6:14, where the Apostle Paul says, "God forbid that I should glory, save in the cross of our Lord Jesus Christ, by whom the world is crucified unto me, and I unto the world." One who has gone through crucifixion can no longer respond to stimuli as he did before death laid hold of him. Because the Apostle Paul was crucified with Christ, the world could no longer dangle its baubles before his eyes to attract him. He was separated from the world by a judicial act because of his cocrucifixion with Christ. He had been taken out of the world and had been separated from it as much as a man who had gone through crucifixion and had been buried was separated from the world. By his reference to crucifixion, Paul shows very graphically that the world has no right to attract the child of God, and the child of God has no right to respond to the attractions of the world, because he is one who has died with Christ and has been buried with Christ. Just as one who is in the tomb cannot respond to a voice from the world of the living, so the child of God has no right to respond to the voice of the world.

Our Lord makes it very clear in John 17 that believers who have been taken out of the world and who have been judicially separated from the world are sent by the Lord into the world to be witnesses to men who are in the world system. In verse 11 Christ said, "I am no more in the world, but these are in the world, and I come to thee. Holy Father, keep through thine own name those whom thou hast given me, that they may be one, as we are." And then He said, in verse 18, "As thou hast sent me into the world, even so have I also sent them into the world." Now why was Christ sent from Heaven into this earth? John 1:18 tells us that He was sent into the world to reveal the Father. Jesus Christ was sent in order that He might bring a knowledge of God to those who, because they were worldlings, were ignorant of God. And we who have been called out of the world and separated from the world have been left here in the midst of worldlings in order that we might reveal the Father to them. The Apostle Paul said that we are ambassadors for Christ. An ambassador is a personal representative of an absent sovereign. And as ambassadors we have been sent into the world to do that for which Christ came into the world: to reveal the Father to men. This thought was presented by the Apostle Paul in Philippians 2:14 when he said, "Do all things without murmurings and disputings: that ye may be blameless and harmless, the sons of God, without rebuke, in the midst of a crooked and perverse nation, among whom ye shine as lights in the world; holding forth the word of life." We are to shine as lights before worldlings so that the worldlings, who are in darkness, may be drawn to the Light that they see shining in and through us. If we are so conformed to the world that the worldling can see no difference between our conduct and his, then he will see no light. The only way that we

can hold forth the word of life is for our life to be so separated
from the world that the worldling sees a marked contrast. That is
why the believer is "to keep himself unspotted from the world"
(James 1:27).

Paul says, in Romans 12:2, "Be not conformed to this world."
And the word *conformed* means, literally, "to be stamped out in
the mold of." A piece of metal that is put into a press will bear
the image of the mold, and every piece that comes out of the mold
will be identical. If the child of God bears upon himself, upon
his character, upon his walk, upon his conversation, the stamp
or the mold of the world, the world will write him off as another
worldling. He will attract no one to Jesus Christ; he will have no
light to present to the world. Therefore, the apostle's command
is "Be not pressed into the mold of this world, but instead be ye
transformed by the renewing of your mind." The word *transform*
means "transfigured." At the transfiguration of Christ the glory
that was within Him shone abroad. The only light that the
child of God has is the light of the glory of Jesus Christ that has
been given him by a new birth. If the child of God conforms to
the patterns, the standards, the ethics and mores, and the habits
of the world, then he veils the light within him. We will never
attract men to Jesus Christ by becoming like worldlings. No, the
people of the world need something that they don't have already.
So Paul says to the believer, "Do not be conformed to this world."

In I John 2:15 we read a command by the apostle of love that
forbids the believer to love the world: "Love not the world,
neither the things that are in the world." Paul was dealing with
outward conduct when he forbade believers to be conformed to
the world in their standards and conduct. John, however, deals
with the heart and mind when he says, "Love not the world."
John gives three reasons why the believer is not to love the world.
First of all, one cannot love the world and the Father at the same
time. "If any man love the world, the love of the Father is not
in him." The second reason the believer is forbidden to love the
world is found in verse 16, that is, the content of the world system. All that is in the world appeals to the lust of the flesh, the
lust of the eyes, and the pride of life. Verse 17 gives the third
reason why the believer is not to love the world—because the

world is transitory, temporary, and under divine judgment. "The world passeth away and the lust thereof." Only the person who does the will of God abides forever. The Apostle James, who in James 1:27 describes the pattern of life that is to characterize the believer in the Lord Jesus Christ, concludes by saying that the believer is "to keep himself unspotted from the world."

WORLDLINESS

It is easy to make a list of things that are worldly and then conclude that one who does any one of these things is worldly and one who doesn't do these things is not worldly. But are we correct in saying that these things in themselves are worldly? Perhaps we might say rather that there are things which may be put to worldly uses. For instance, a hypodermic needle can be a most beneficial thing in the hands of a physician to administer an antibiotic but in the hands of a dope addict can be a harmful device. You could not say that the hypodermic syringe is sinful, or wicked or worldly. But it may be put to worldly uses. An automobile cannot be considered worldly when it is used to speed a doctor on his rounds of mercy. It is a blessing. But if it is appropriated by a bank robber as a getaway car, that which is good is put to a wrong usage. So it is the use to which a thing is put that determines whether it is worldly or not worldly. A radio, or a television, is not in itself a worldly instrument but may be put to worldly usages and worldly ends or it may serve to promote the purposes and the programs of Satan. Radio and television may, on the other hand, be used to proclaim the gospel of Jesus Christ and to promote that for which Jesus Christ came, namely, to bring a knowledge of God to those who are in darkness. It is impossible for us to sit down, then, and make a list of things that in themselves are worldly.

The child of God must sit in judgment upon his attitude in his use of the things that are in the world, for worldliness is not concerned principally with acts but with attitudes that control the acts. It is entirely possible that you could refrain from doing something because of your desire to be acceptable in a certain Christian community and yet wish with all your heart that you were doing that thing. The desire to be doing it constitutes you a worldling. You are conforming to the world in your thoughts. This is worldliness. In considering any matter of conduct, in questioning what is right for you as a child of God, you must go beyond the thing itself and determine your attitude toward it. Your attitude determines whether you are worldly or not worldly. It would be so easy if the board of a church could draw up a list that could be given to the congregation to determine what things are worldly. But this is impossible since worldliness is an attitude, not an act. Thus, each individual must examine his thoughts, his goals, his aims, and his ambitions in the light of the Word. The Apostle Paul makes it very clear in writing to the Corinthians that the solution to this problem is not prohibiting certain things. In I Corinthians 7:31 the words "they that use this world, as not abusing it" give Paul's principle: to use the world but not to abuse it. If I am invited to a conference in Philadelphia, or Chicago, or Los Angeles, I don't want to go there on horseback. I want to get on a jet so that I can get there in two hours, instead of two months. I want to use what is in the world, but I want to use it as unto God. Paul does not tell us to withdraw from the world. That would be the easy way, but that is not the solution. Rather, we are to use that which the world has devised for its comfort, convenience, and advancement. But we are to make certain that when we use the world we are not serving Satan's goals and ends.

God's purpose to conform us to Christ is not carried out by withdrawing into a monastery. As God conforms us to Christ He permits us to use that which the world has devised, but we are to use it in service for the Lord Jesus Christ. For instance, we believers can legitimately use the world's means of communication—radio, television, and movies—to propagate the gospel of Jesus Christ. In so doing, we are using but not abusing. If we use the world's means of transportation to speed the gospel, we are using but not abusing. We are here in the world as servants of Jesus Christ. We are here to manifest the glory of Jesus Christ, to reveal the knowledge of God. How will we do it? Not by conforming to the world, not by loving the things that are in the world, but by being conformed to Jesus Christ and by loving the Lord Jesus Christ with singleness of heart and purpose. The world has its goals and its rewards. So many of us covet the rewards that the world has to give that we are willing to compromise that set-apart position which we have been called upon to assume for the gospel's sake. We want to be like Christ, but we also want to receive what the world has to offer. With one hand we hold onto Him, and with the other hand we want to receive what the world has to give. We are like the double-minded man whom James describes as being unstable in all his ways. However, Christ has taken us out of the world and has separated us from the world in order that we might be a witness before it. May God give us the grace to examine our conduct, our ambitions, and our motives. May we desire that our every thought and word and activity shall conform to Christ instead of conforming to the standards that the world sets for worldlings. We can have a very comfortable existence by surrendering that set-apart position, but we can never have the approval of the One who has called us and separated us to Himself. Consider carefully Paul's command, "Be not conformed to the world."

CHAPTER

23

THE CHRISTIAN AND THE FLESH

Romans 8:1-13

SATAN USES both the world and the flesh to promote his program and attain his ends. Consequently the child of God must continually be on guard against both worldliness and carnality. In the previous study we saw that the child of God is continually being tempted to conform to the world and to accept its standards, ethics, morals, methods, and goals. When the child of God conforms to the world he is promoting the purposes of Satan.

In this study we shall see how Satan seeks to defeat the purpose of God in the life of the child of God by tempting him to carnality. The Apostle Paul states God's purpose for the child of God in these words in Romans 8:4: ". . . that the righteousness of the law might be fulfilled in us." The law was a revelation of the demands of a righteous God. But under law men were unable to fulfil God's righteous demands. God's purpose to have the righteousness of the law fulfilled in us is achieved by reproducing the life of Christ in the child of God by the power of the Holy Spirit.

God's purpose to reproduce Christ in the child of God is achieved as he allows himself to be controlled by the Holy Spirit. But the child of God may be controlled by the flesh. If he is controlled by the flesh, he is carnal. If he is controlled by the Holy Spirit, he is spiritual. The Apostle Paul, in Romans 8, deals with the question of carnality before he proceeds to show how the Spirit of God will reproduce the life of Christ in the child of God. The apostle first shows why the carnal believer can never live out the righteousness of Christ in his life. "To be carnally minded is death; but to be spiritually minded is life and peace" (v. 6).

DEFINITION OF CARNALITY

To be "spiritually minded" is *to be controlled by the Holy Spirit*. To be "carnally minded" means *to be controlled by the flesh*. So the apostle affirms that the flesh can never reproduce the righteousness of Christ in us because to be carnally minded, or controlled by the flesh, means a person is dead as far as the ability to produce righteousness is concerned and cannot produce fruit that is pleasing to God.

In the second place, Paul shows that the one who is carnal cannot reproduce the righteousness of Christ "because the carnal mind is enmity against God: for it is not subject to the law of God, neither indeed can be" (v. 7). Here the apostle shows that the mind of the flesh, or the carnal mind, is a rebel. It is at war with God, and will never give assent to that which God commands. The natural mind is a lawless mind and intuitively rebels against all that God reveals as His will. If one seeks to fulfil the righteousness of the law by the flesh, he will discover that the flesh turns against the commands of God, for the righteousness of God is utterly repugnant to him.

In the third place, the apostle shows that the righteousness of Christ will never be fulfilled in carnal man because "they that are in the flesh cannot please God" (v. 8). The apostle is not saying that a child of God, because he lives on the earth, can never please God. But he is saying that the one who lives under the control of the carnal mind cannot please God because the carnal mind is marked by ignorance, and by inability to reproduce the righteousness of Christ. Suppose you planted a tree in your yard from which you expected to receive fruit and later discovered that that tree had withered and died. Upon your discovery that the tree was dead you would give up all hope of any fruit because that which is dead cannot reproduce itself. And the argument of the apostle in this passage is based on this concept that the nature of man, or the flesh, or the carnal mind, is dead. Therefore, it cannot reproduce the righteousness of Christ in the experience of the believer.

The term "the flesh" is also used to describe a man's natural effort, independent of God. That which is of the flesh is that which a man does by himself, without any divine assistance, without the enablement of the Holy Spirit. The Apostle Paul emphasizes this truth in Galatians 3:3, where he asks, "Are ye so foolish? Having begun in the Spirit, are ye now made perfect by the flesh?" What Paul is saying is: "The Spirit began a work of conforming you to Christ. Has it now become your concept that, independent of the Holy Spirit, by your own efforts, you can continue to maturity, or be conformed to Christ?" Again, in Philippians 3:3, Paul says, "We are the circumcision, which worship God in the spirit and rejoice in Christ Jesus, and have no confidence in the flesh." In other words, Christians have no confidence in what they can do of themselves, independent of God, or apart from the assistance of the Holy Spirit. When Paul said that the flesh cannot please God and that the flesh cannot reproduce the righteousness of Jesus Christ, he was viewing the flesh as human nature which, as a result of the fall, is utterly incapable of conforming to the will of God, to the holiness and righteousness of God, or of reproducing the life of Jesus Christ.

The apostle shows us next that the flesh is characterized by inherent weakness. Paul says in Romans 6:19, "I speak after the manner of men because of the infirmity of your flesh." Again, in Romans 8:3, he says, "What the law could not do, in that it was weak through the flesh, . . ." In other words, the law was weak because it depended upon the flesh, that is, the old capacity, the old man, the old nature, which is inherently weak.

In Romans 7:5, Paul refers to the flesh as the sphere in which the unregenerate live. "When we were in the flesh, the motions of sins, which were by the law, did work in our members to bring forth fruit unto death." Paul there points to the flesh as the state in which the unregenerate man lives, or the state in which a saved man may live when he is controlled by his old capacity, or by the old man. He says that the man who is fleshly, or controlled by the flesh, is a vehicle through which sin operates. Paul saw this to be true of himself as he stated clearly in Romans 7:14: "We know that the law is spiritual; but I am carnal, sold under sin." Paul was speaking of his basic constitution, his constitutional makeup, when he said, "I am carnal." Paul did not mean he was living by the flesh but he meant, rather, that he possessed two capacities. We sometimes refer to these as the old nature and the new nature, or the sin nature and the new divine nature. Paul saw that he not only had the capacity to reproduce the righteousness of Christ but that he also retained the capacity which he had before he was saved, the capacity to reproduce the fruit of the sin nature which dwelt within him. We need to recognize, as Paul did, that when we believed on Christ the old sin nature was not eradicated, was not purified, was not changed; we live with this old nature within us. What Paul said of himself is true of everyone of us. In our basic, constitutional makeup we are carnal.

The terms "flesh" and "the carnal mind," as used by the Apostle Paul, refer to the vehicle through which sin operates. Some sins are physical sins. Some sins are mental sins. There are religious sins and social sins. But all sin, of whatever kind, is the product of the carnal mind or the carnal nature. Paul referred to this fact in Romans 13:14, where he exhorted the believers, "Put ye on the Lord Jesus Christ, and make not provision for the flesh, to fulfil the lusts thereof." When we give the flesh the opportunity to control our members, our actions, our words, and our thoughts, it will conceive and bring forth sin. And so the apostle faces the fact that we possess a tremendous potential for sin because we are carnal.

EXAMPLES OF CARNALITY

Perhaps no passage so clearly states the product of the flesh as does Galatians 5:19-21, where the apostle lists the works of the flesh. Just prior to specifying these works, the apostle said, "Walk in the Spirit, and ye shall not fulfil the lust of the flesh." This is the same truth he presented in Romans 8, that the child of God may be controlled either by the Holy Spirit or by the flesh. Every action, every thought, every word, every deed is under the control of either the flesh or the Holy Spirit of God. Now, if we let the flesh control, what will it produce? Paul mentions, first of all, four sensual sins: adultery, fornication, uncleanness, lasciviousness. Then he mentions two religious sins, idolatry and witchcraft, showing that the flesh is not only perverted and corrupted concerning morality but concerning God as well. Next,

Paul mentions a number of sins which reveal the basic selfishness of the flesh: hatred, variance, emulations, wrath, strife, seditions, heresies, envyings. In other words, the flesh is self-centered and selfish. Paul also mentions sins of intemperance: murders, drunkenness, revellings, and such like. Thus does Paul portray the natural heart, the flesh, the carnal mind. Carnality may manifest itself in any of these sins.

It is not difficult to find in the Word of God examples of such carnality as the apostle includes here. For instance, we read in II Samuel 11 about the adultery of David and the death of Uriah, for which David was responsible. Here we see David as a carnal man. Yielding to the lust of the flesh, and controlled by the flesh (by carnality), he committed the two sins of adultery and murder. I Samuel 28 gives the record of the carnality of Saul who, when he was set upon by the Philistines, went to the witch of Endor in order that he might make inquiry of her. He thus repudiated Samuel, the prophet of God, who was God's spokesman, the one through whom God revealed Himself to the nation.

Saul was carnal because of his witchcraft and idolatry. Saul is also an example of a carnal man's manifestation of hatred, wrath, strife, envying, and murders. If you will turn to I Samuel 18, you will see how Saul grew jealous of David. He envied David because of the praise that came to him as a result of his military prowess. Twice Saul sought to pin David to the wall with his spear. Saul's attempt to murder David grew out of envy, jealousy, and hatred. Thus Saul showed himself to be a carnal man.

The carnality of Noah is recorded in Genesis 9:20-21, where we read that Noah became drunk, so drunk that he lay naked in his tent. In his nakedness he manifested the form of carnality of which the apostle speaks when he says the works of the flesh are "drunkenness, revellings, and such like." Most of us feel quite complacent when we compare ourselves with David, Saul, or Noah.

We conclude we are not carnal because we have never murdered anybody, have never been intoxicated, have never committed adultery. But this is not necessarily so. Peter had done none of these, yet he was carnal. Peter, after hearing our Lord's warning to the disciples, "All ye shall be offended because of me this

night," said to Jesus, "Though all men should be offended because of thee, yet will I never be offended." Jesus said to him,
"Verily I say unto thee, that this night, before the cock crow, thou
shalt deny me thrice." What was Peter's reply? "Though I should
die with thee, yet will I not deny thee." The self-confidence of
Peter was carnality. Peter was trusting his own flesh to keep him
from this deed which Christ predicted would occur before the
cock would crow to announce the new day's birth.

In the third Epistle of John, John wrote concerning Diotrophes,
"I wrote unto the church: but Diotrophes, who loveth to have the
preeminence among them, receiveth us not." Diotrophes had set
himself up as a teacher, and when his teaching was contradicted
by the teaching of the Apostle John, he attempted to discredit
John as an apostle and to repudiate John's message to that assembly of believers. His pride and his love of preeminence showed
that he was a carnal man. While on the one hand carnality may
manifest itself in gross sins of the flesh, carnality may manifest
itself through sins of the mind, which can be just as destructive
to the Christian life and Christian testimony as the grossest actions recorded of any carnal man about whom we read in the
Word of God. In the pride, the self-satisfaction, the complacency,
and the indifference which characterize so many of us, we see a
manifestation of carnality which can never glorify God and
which prevents the manifestation of the righteousness of Christ
in the life of the child of God.

The believer must constantly examine his motives, ambitions,
and goals to bring them into conformity to the righteousness of
Christ, because the very things which God provides for our
physical well-being and comfort may be perverted to manifestations of carnality. God has provided food to nourish and sustain
this physical body. No one could exist long without food. Food
of itself can never be considered carnal, but many of us manifest
carnality by our use of food. When we overindulge to the point
that we have to see a tailor to let out the waistline, we are manifesting carnality. It is right and proper that we should have a
roof over our heads, and yet we need to examine our attitudes
toward the home in which we live. When we covet material things
for the position or the status that these material things can give

us, this is carnality. The car we drive, the clothing we wear, the styles we follow may be manifestations of carnality. Listing *things* that are carnal might make it quite easy for us to refrain from certain manifestations of carnality. But when carnality is defined in terms of *attitudes,* then we must examine ourselves in all we do, and bring every thought, desire, action, and motive under the Spirit's control. Things which God has provided which may be legitimately used may also be illegitimately used. Therefore, each child of God must so yield himself to the control of the Holy Spirit of God over every area of his life that the righteousness of Christ will be reproduced in his life.

What is carnality? According to the teachings of the Apostle Paul, any thought, word, or action that is generated by the flesh, motivated by the flesh, and indulged in to gratify or please the flesh, is carnality. It is not always what a man *does* that marks the difference between being carnal or spiritual, but rather *what* or *who* controls in that action. Any action of mine that is energized by the flesh is carnal; anything I do controlled by the Spirit cannot be carnal. The flesh produces carnality; the Spirit produces spirituality.

THE WHOLE ARMOR OF GOD

Ephesians 6:10-24

WHEN WE READ the last chapter of Ephesians, we find that the epistle that began in the heavenlies concludes on the battlefield. The Apostle Paul, in the first chapter, directed our attention to our glorious position in the heavenlies in Christ. In the second and third chapters, he traced the glorious union of Jew and Gentile in one body, through the work of the Holy Spirit. In the fourth and fifth chapters, he described the walk of the believers in unity. Then, as he brought the epistle to a close, he found it necessary to give a warning to those who had received these truths, for the life in unity and in love will be lived on hostile ground. The apostle desired that those who had received these truths should be prepared for battle. God's children are not only servants but soldiers. They live not only in the home but also in a citadel. They must be equipped for the life they are called upon to live, and the warfare they are called upon to fight.

Paul knew from personal experience that there were many adversaries in Ephesus. For instance, when he wrote to the Corinthians from Ephesus, he said, "I will tarry at Ephesus until Pentecost. For a great door and effectual is opened unto me, and there are many adversaries" (I Cor. 16:8-9). We read in Acts 19:23-41 the extensive account of the adversaries in Ephesus. The city of Ephesus was given over to a profligate worship of the goddess Diana. Many in that city profited by employment in the temple and in the arts and crafts associated with the worship of Diana. When Paul came into the city of Ephesus to declare that there is one true, living God and that men can only approach Him through Jesus Christ, the Ephesians rose up to throw him out of the city and to put him to death because he had belittled Diana. It was only out of fear of higher authorities that Paul and his companions were delivered from physical death in the arena in Ephesus. The adversaries of Paul were visible, human, and vulnerable. Their movements could be traced and their plans could be thwarted. But the apostle recognized that he had a greater adversary, an unseen adversary, an adversary who carries on his war in the spiritual realm. The apostle desired the Christians to whom he wrote to be equipped for this kind of a warfare. So after describing, in verses 10 to 13 of Ephesians 6, the warfare in which the child of God is engaged, in the ensuing verses the apostle described in detail the armor God has provided so that the child of God may be victorious in his conflict with the evil one.

STRENGTHENED IN THE LORD

The believer's strength is given in the tenth verse as the apostle says, "Finally, my brethren, be strong in the Lord, and in the power of his might." The word translated "be strong" does not mean you are to strengthen yourself, flex your muscles, and exercise yourself until you have made yourself into a model fighting man. Rather, the apostle uses the form that shows that these who were set apart to battle are to receive strength from someone else, and we would do well to use this translation: "Finally, my brethren, be strengthened in the Lord." The believer is not to war in his own strength but in the strength given to him by another, even the Lord Jesus Christ.

The phrase "in the Lord" shows us where this strengthening takes place. In fighting a human battle, strength is often evaluated in terms of man-power, how many men the commander can rally. Or strength is determined by military might, what weapons the commander has at his disposal. Or strength may depend upon the abilities of the commander himself. But the apostle is showing us here that as the believer enters into conflict he has no strength, no weapons, and no wisdom except in the Lord. If a soldier loses confidence in his commander, he becomes fearful of the outcome of the battle. He will not press forward in the fray if he does not believe his commander has the ability to lead him to victory. So the apostle would direct the thoughts of believers to the Lord, in whom they can have complete confidence as the One who will strengthen them for their daily conflict. We are to be strengthened in the Lord and in the power of His might.

The apostle, in praying for these believers, prayed that they might know "what is the exceeding greatness of his power to us-ward who believe, according to the working of his mighty power, which he wrought in Christ when he raised him from the dead and set him at his own right hand in the heavenly places, . . ." (Eph. 1:19-20). The apostle there expressed his desire for believers to know the greatness of the power which saved them. When God would save a man He brings into play the power that brought Jesus Christ out of physical death and raised Him up and seated Him at the right hand of the Father in glory. The power that could bring Christ out of the grave where He had gone after bearing our sins on the cross and bring Him into glory is the power that operates to bring us into glory. The power of God's might referred to in Ephesians 6:10 is the same power that operated in Jesus Christ for our salvation. That power is available to God's children to give them victory in their daily life, and the believer strengthens himself in the Lord as he counts on, and relies on, the Lord's strength.

WEARING FULL ARMOR

In the eleventh verse the apostle gives a command: "Put on the whole armour of God, that ye may be able to stand against the wiles of the devil." When Paul wrote this to the Ephesians, he was a Roman prisoner. Perhaps the soldier into whose keeping he had been committed was standing before him even as he wrote. Seeing the soldier would guide Paul as he described the armament provided for the child of God. He was not guarded by a soldier in a toga, which was worn by one who was inactive, but he was guarded by one who had put upon himself all of the military equipment provided by a Roman commander for those who served under his command. The fully equipped soldier presented an object lesson to the Apostle Paul: believers have not been called to ease; they have not been called to a leisurely life. The child of God is not to clothe himself with a toga. Instead, he is to put on the whole armor of God that he may be able to contend against the devil and his spiritual hosts of wickedness.

This phrase, "put on," in the original text means "to put on once and for all." In commanding these believers to assume this garb once and for all, the apostle is revealing to us the truth that we are to consider ourselves engaged in an unceasing warfare. We are not engaged in a brief skirmish, after which we may return to a life of ease. The apostle says we are to put on this armor and never lay it aside as long as we are in the flesh. The battle to which we are called is continuous, unceasing, and relentless because of the nature of our adversary. Neither the duration of the battle nor the wiles of the foe will permit us to lay aside armament. So he gives the command, "Put on once and for all the whole armour of God."

The phrase "the whole armour" refers to all that would be provided by a military commander for the safety and protection of his soldiers and for enabling them to fight an aggressive warfare. It was not the responsibility of the Roman soldiers to clothe themselves. If they had to clothe themselves, many would be ill-prepared to protect themselves and to forge ahead in the fray. It was the responsibility of the commander to provide for all those under his authority. When the apostle spoke of the whole armor of God, he was referring to all the equipment God has provided so that those who are in His army may be victorious and triumphant. The battle is the Lord's, and as our commander He has provided what He knows we will need. He knows what we need by way of protection so that we will not fall in battle. He knows what we need in the way of offensive weapons so that we can defeat the adversary. Our Commander is concerned not only with the protection of His soldiers so that He will have the same number in His army after the battle is over as when He led them into the conflict, but He is also concerned that His soldiers be victorious and triumphant. In His infinite wisdom and power God has provided all that His soldiers could possibly need. None of God's soldiers will ever go down in battle because their Commander has failed to provide for their need. If we go down in defeat, it will be because we have not appropriated the full armor of God. That is why, in verses

14 through 17, the apostle goes into detail concerning the equipment that has been given to the soldiers.

FACING THE ADVERSARY

In the eleventh verse the apostle also points out why God has commanded us to put on the whole armor that He has provided: "that ye may be able to stand against the wiles of the devil." God does not lead us into battle to be defeated. God is expecting victory and has equipped us that we may be able to stand against the wiles of the devil. The word here translated "wiles" is a most interesting word and means "to stalk." It suggests an animal seeking its prey. The apostle, in using that word, is revealing something about the need for this equipment, for we are not going into a battle where the adversary will use discernible tactics. This is no boxing match where the bounds of the field of conflict are marked by ropes. The boxer always knows where his adversary is and what he is up to. Our adversary will use the craft, guile, subtlety, and deceit of a predatory animal in pursuing his prey. The apostle points out to us that we are engaged in a battle with an adversary that we can't see. We do not know from which quarter he will attack. We do not know what means he will use to destroy us. But we do know that he will use subtlety, craftiness, guile, and deceit to bring about our downfall. Because of his subtlety and craft, we need to be equipped so that no matter when he attacks or from what quarter, we may be able to stand against his wiles.

In the twelfth verse the believer's adversary is clearly described. "We wrestle not against flesh and blood, but against principalities, against powers, against the rulers of the darkness of this world, against spiritual wickedness in high places." Here the apostle uses the figure of a wrestling match. The Roman wrestler had one goal in mind and that was to get his two hands around the throat of his adversary and to pin him to the ground by strangling him. The objective in the Roman wrestling match was not to pin a man to the ground by his shoulders but rather by the neck. This was a life-and-death struggle. If a man's shoulders were pinned to the mat, he could get up after the match and walk away. But if a man's neck were pinned to the ground with a strangle hold, it would be impossible physically for him to get up and to continue. The apostle is trying to show us, through the figure of the wrestling match, the seriousness of the conflict in which we are engaged. If we should fall before the adversary, we have not lost eternal life. God forbid! But the adversary is seeking to discredit our Christian testimony, to cause us to fall in such a way that we cannot rise and pursue the Christian walk again or manifest the resurrection life of Christ again. We are not engaged in a Sunday school picnic softball game that we can play in until we are tired and then sit down on the bench and leave the game to the youngsters. We are engaged in a life-and-death struggle. Our adversary is seeking to destroy us.

Paul describes the nature of our adversary when he says, "We wrestle not against flesh and blood." "Flesh and blood" is a phrase normally used to describe a human being. If we have a human adversary, he has the same strength we have, he has a mind like ours, he uses the same devices that we use, and we know how to fight him because we can figure out what he will do on the basis of what we would do in a similar situation. We can be prepared to meet an adversary of flesh and blood because we are flesh and blood. We are meeting on common terms, on common ground. But the apostle says our adversary is not an adversary of flesh and blood; we are wrestling "against principalities, against powers, against the rulers of the darkness of this world, against spiritual [hosts of] wickedness in high places."

From Ephesians 6:12 we learn that there are different ranks among these spiritual hosts of wickedness made up of fallen angels. We know from the Word of God that angels are beings which were created by God to be His ministering servants, executors of God's will. In God's governmental order, the angels were arranged in different hierarchies, each of which had different spheres of authority and responsibility. The archangels, the highest class, received their commands from the throne of God and passed them down through the ranks to subordinates who sped to execute God's will.

When Lucifer rebelled against God (see Isaiah 14 and Ezekiel 28), a great host of angels followed him in his rebellion, and Satan became their ruler. Organizing his fallen minions after the pattern of God's organization, Satan became the god of this world. He divided his demons into different classes with various responsibilities and graded authority. "Principalities" are the leaders among the demons who serve Satan. "Powers" refers to all of the angels who are under the authority of these leaders. "Rulers" refers to those who are in authority over this world. They are called the rulers of the darkness of this world. Thus Christians fight against an organized system.

When Paul says, "We wrestle against spiritual wickedness in high places," he refers to the character of the principalities, the leaders, and the powers. We are fighting against a horde of fiends who are organized by their evil leader to defeat and overthrow God's children in the battle. They are characterized by wickedness. Their nature is evil. Their methods are evil. Their work is evil. Their purpose and design is evil. Yet this evil is not in the material realm—evil that we can see and evaluate and flee from. Rather it is evil in a spiritual and, consequently, unseen realm. Paul desired that believers should get a glimpse of the enormity of the warfare in which we are engaged. The sphere of our warfare is not here on this earth but extends into the heavenlies into which we have been brought with Jesus Christ. Our battle is not in the physical or material realm; our battle is spiritual and takes place in a spiritual realm and is being fought against spiritual wickedness in high places.

STANDING IN THE BATTLE

When we grasp Paul's teaching, we can see the reason for his appeal. "Wherefore [because you do not wrestle against seen forces, but against unseen forces] take unto you the whole armour of God, that ye may be able to withstand in the evil day, and having done all, to stand." The apostle concludes almost where he began, for in verse 11 he told the believers to put on the whole armor once and for all. Now in verse 13, having shown why the armor is so necessary, he exhorts believers to take unto them the whole armor God has provided to the end that they may be able to withstand the adversary in the evil day. The evil day is not the day of judgment when the Christian's service as a soldier of the Lord Jesus Christ will be examined. The evil day is this day in which we live. It is a phrase that refers to our whole life. From the divine viewpoint, this earthly life is an evil day. It is an evil day because we are constantly set upon by evil adversaries who seek to destroy us. The apostle also emphasizes the fact that this life is a battle. The apostle has not held out a hope for the withdrawal of the adversary or the complete cessation of hostilities so we can lay our armor down. The apostle says that this battle will be constant, unrelenting, and ceaseless—for as long as we live. Even though we know that the cross of Jesus Christ was God's judgment upon Satan, and even though we know from Revelation 20 that Satan will be bound for a thousand years, we know there is for us who live today no prospect of being delivered from conflict with Satan and his hosts. We are called to be soldiers for as long as we live, and we can come through that battle victoriously, triumphantly, and unscathed. The apostle says, in verse 13, "Take unto you the whole armor of God, that ye may be able to withstand the attack of the unseen adversary who stalks us to destroy us in the evil day, and having done all, to stand." *Standing* is the opposite of *falling* in defeat. The soldier who lost his footing and fell to his knees was certain to fall before the stroke of the sword of the adversary. No soldier could hope to be victorious who was not able to stand. So the apostle assures us that Christians will be able to stand when they put on the whole armor of God. And to stand means victory!

Several things in these verses need to be emphasized. First of all, it ought to be very clear to us that every child of God is a soldier of Jesus Christ. We have been called to battle, and no child of God is exempted from this summons. We have been drafted by the King of kings and Lord of lords to serve in His army. We cannot dodge the draft; we cannot expect a deferment for any reason. We are soldiers of Jesus Christ.

The second thing we ought to observe is the nature of our adversary. We cannot see, touch, or outwit this enemy. Therefore we need protection, wisdom, and strength that is greater than our own. God offers the needed strength, for He says that we can be strengthened by the power of His might that we might be able to stand against the adversary. The protection is the responsibility of the commander who has summoned them into battle. God, who has summoned them to the conflict, has provided the whole armor of God. But it is the soldier's responsibility to put on the armor that God has provided. If you are defeated, it must be because you have not appropriated that which God has provided. If a commander provides for his men but the men through indifference or carelessness do not use the armor he has provided, the commander cannot be held responsible for their defeat. And if you refuse to clothe yourself with the armor God has given you, the only one chargeable for your defeat is you.

The hymn writer asked the question "Am I a soldier of the cross?" How pointless to ask that when God says we *are* soldiers. The only question for us to face is "What kind of soldier am I?" Are we those who recognize the adversary and avail ourselves of the whole armor that God has provided so that we might be able to stand against the wiles, crafts, and subtleties of the evil one and be undefeated in the day of battle?

THE GIRDLE OF TRUTH

John 17:13-17; Ephesians 6:14a

GOD HAS NOT CALLED US to tilt with windmills. We are not fighting against flesh and blood but against a powerful unseen adversary, Satan. Hosts of wicked angels are organized under his authority to fight his battles. His opposition is incessant and unrelenting. We never know from whence the attack will come; we never know the form in which the adversary will strike; we cannot anticipate the wiles he will employ. If God had not provided adequate armor for His children, He could be likened to a commander who would send soldiers equipped with water pistols against an adversary equipped with atomic weapons. But God has given to us armor that is adequate to enable us "to withstand in the evil day, and having done all, to stand." But we cannot obey the apostle's injunction to put on the whole armor of God so as to be able to stand in the evil day unless we understand what the armor is and how it is to be used.

A FAMILIAR FIGURE

The first piece of equipment which the apostle describes is the girdle. He says, "Stand therefore, having your loins girt about with truth." It seems strange that the apostle should begin with the girdle, for while the girdle was worn by Roman soldiers, it was not considered a piece of armor, as were the helmet, the breastplate, the shield, and the sword. The girdle was a part of the formal dress of an individual in the apostle's day. Perhaps the apostle began with the girdle, which was not usually considered a piece of armament, in order to remind these believers that the weapons of our warfare are not fleshly but are

spiritual. God does not equip His soldiers like an earthly military commander equips his; God equips us with armor that the
world would never consider protection at all. A girdle was used
by a man in Paul's time to bind his long flowing robe to his body
for the sake of modesty as well as ease in moving about. We read
in Matthew 3:4 that John the Baptist appeared wearing a coarsely
woven garment of camel's hair which was tied about the loins
with a leather girdle. A girdle of leather was worn by the poorer
classes, and a linen girdle, perhaps embroidered, was worn by
those of greater financial means. The wealthy wore girdles of
silk or of linen, embroidered with jewels or gold, with gold
buckles. Thus the girdle was an essential part of the dress of the
individual.

In Paul's day a girdle was important to the soldier who was
about to go into battle. He would pick up the lower edges of the
robe he wore and bind it about his waist. In this way the girdle
freed the man for rapid movement. If he were to engage in hand-
to-hand combat without a girdle, his long robe would trip him,
and he would be an easy mark for the adversary. So the soldier
would be equipped with a girdle.

This, perhaps, is the thought that the writer of Hebrews had
in view when he said, "Let us lay aside every weight, and the sin
which doth so easily beset us, and let us run with patience the
race that is set before us." All that would obstruct free and rapid
movement is to be laid aside. No soldier would consider going
into battle without a strong girdle to hold his robes in place.

The girdle was also used by the soldier to support his weapons.
The swordsman would fasten his girdle across his shoulder so
that he could suspend his sword from that girdle. Likewise, the
bowman would use his girdle to support the quiver which he
would take into battle. The soldier did not go into battle with a
silk or a linen girdle. It would be too light to support a heavy
sword or a quiver of arrows. The soldier's girdle was usually a
wide leather belt that would bind the clothing together and
would have in itself sufficient strength to support the offensive
weapons with which the soldier would go into battle.

In the next place, the girdle was used to display the decora-
tions that a soldier had received from his commander for distinc-

tion on the field of battle. The Roman soldier pinned these awards on his girdle. Thus the girdle became the emblem of accomplishment in battle. When a military commander had led his troops to victory it was his custom to .present special girdles to the captains who had served under him. Such girdles might be richly adorned with gold and silver and frequently were encrusted with jewels. The girdle then became the emblem of honor, of reward, and of glory. The soldier who went into battle with a plain leather girdle hoped that after the battle he would be rewarded with a girdle embellished with the signs of his valor. So, when the apostle gave command to his readers to stand, having their loins girded about with truth, he was using a figure that was familiar to them.

GIRDED WITH TRUTH

The apostle characterizes the girdle as the girdle of truth. The commonest explanation of what is meant by the girdle of truth is the revelation of truth given by God to men, the Word of God which we have received. This thought is conveyed in II Timothy 1:13-14 where the apostle commands Timothy, "Hold fast the form of sound words, which thou hast heard of me, in faith and love which is in Christ Jesus. That good thing which was committed unto thee keep by the Holy Ghost which dwelleth in us." Here the apostle is referring primarily to objective truth, the doctrine that has been revealed by God to His children. But as plausible as this seems, it is truth in a subjective sense which is to characterize the soldier. We might render it "truthfulness." The child of God who is about to go into battle must be clothed, first of all, with truthfulness, integrity of character, and sincerity. This gives him courage and confidence as he goes into battle.

The English word *sincere* comes from two Latin words *sine cerus* which mean "without wax." Because it was easy for a piece of pottery to be cracked in the firing process, the dishonest pottery vendor, to cover up such defects, would rub the cracks with beeswax. The beeswax would fill the crack and it would appear sound and whole. The honest merchant, knowing of this practice, guaranteed that his wares were without any wax—*sine cerus*. So, to be sincere meant to have no hidden flaws or defects.

The Apostle Paul refers to the need of sincerity in the life of a Christian when he prays for the Philippian believers in Philippians 1:9-10: "And this I pray, that your love may abound yet more and more in knowledge and in all judgment; that ye may approve things that are excellent; that ye may be sincere without offence till the day of Christ." The apostle desired the lives of these Christians to be without wax, that is without covered-up defects. If a Christian tolerates insincerity in his life, he gives Satan a beachhead in his life and will fall before the onslaught of the evil one.

Recently it was necessary for us to call an exterminator to our home because we had discovered termites on the back patio. After making his examination, he informed us that the termites had found a small crack between the concrete patio and the foundation. They did not need a large opening, but that small crack was all that they needed to give them entrance to a nesting place. Likewise Satan does not require a wide-open door to be able to enter the believer's life. If the smallest crack is open to Satan, he can make his way in. If the life is not sound, if it has cracks or defects that are plugged up with wax, then Satan will be able to make his way in. A life characterized by sincerity, genuineness, flawlessness, truthfulness, and soundness will prevent Satan from obtaining an entrance.

The value of a good reputation cannot be overemphasized. May we illustrate it this way. A corrupt lobbyist may be tempted to bribe a certain legislator to win his support for the bill being pushed. But because the lobbyist knows that the legislator is a man of integrity and cannot be corrupted by a bribe, the lobbyist will refrain from making an approach to the legislator. The reputation of the legislator is well known: he cannot be bought; he is incorruptible. His reputation for incorruptibility protects him from advances by a corrupt lobbyist. This is the concept that the apostle had in mind when he talked about a man being girt about with truth. Such a man is spared from the attacks of the evil one because the evil one knows of his incorruptibility. Blackmail in our country is probably a multimillion-dollar business. But unless people had flaws in character, the blackmailer could never operate. He practices extortion because the one from whom he is demanding payment is not characterized by truth. If a man were perfectly upright, the blackmailer would have no basis on which to operate. In like manner, if the child of God, by the grace of God, always chooses the way of truth and sincerity, he presents an invulnerable front before the adversary.

CHRIST THE EXAMPLE

In the first chapter of the Book of the Revelation we find a description of the glory of the resurrected Son of God. John says, in verses 12 and 13, "I saw seven golden candlesticks [or lampstands]; and in the midst of the seven candlesticks one like unto the Son of man, clothed with a garment down to the foot." And then he significantly notes, "and girt about the breast with a golden girdle." As the Lord Jesus Christ is portrayed in the glory which became His following His resurrection and ascension, He is clothed in that garment whose whiteness exceeds the shining of the sun. And that garment is bound to His person by a golden girdle. The girdle manifests the glory of the person, and one of the glories of our Lord is this: He is the truth. As our Lord sat with the disciples in the upper room he said, "I am the way, the truth and the life." "*I* am the truth." Christ's adversaries watched Him through the years of His earthly sojourn and could find no flaw in Him. Why? Because He was girded about with truth. The Pharisees hung on His every word and watched His every action so as to have a basis upon which they might accuse Him and condemn Him to death, but when they came to take Him, Christ could face His adversaries and say, "Which of you convinceth [or, convicteth] me of sin?" And they stood speechless and dumb. Why? Because Jesus Christ was girded about with truth.

When Christ Jesus went to the cross, the centurion into whose hands Christ had been committed for the execution watched Him die and said, "Truly this man was the Son of God." How could he make such a statement? Because Christ was girded about with truth. The thief who hung on the cross said, "This man has done nothing amiss." Why could he say this? Because Jesus Christ was girded about with truth. None could point to a flaw in His character. Those who sought to accuse Him of some crime found Him impervious to attack. Why? Because He was the truth. And when the character of Christ is manifested through the child of God, the child of God is girded with what Jesus Christ is—truth. Thus the child of God becomes invulnerable against the accusations of the evil one.

There is nothing like a guilty conscience to turn a man into a coward. A short time ago, a machine being used on a drainage ditch in a suburb of Miami severed a water line and disrupted water service in a large area. Within a matter of hours, over fifty people who were delinquent in payment of their water bills appeared at the water company to pay their accounts. Child of God, when the adversary attacks you, if you do not have on the girdle of truthfulness, you will be vulnerable. Your conscience will turn you into a coward and cause you to flee when you ought to stand facing the enemy. The apostle says that the first piece of equipment must be this girdle of truth which symbolizes integrity, sincerity, and an absence of duplicity before God and before men. This is one of the facets of Christ's character produced in the believer by the Holy Spirit. The child of God, thus equipped with truth, can stand against the evil one.

THE BREASTPLATE OF RIGHTEOUSNESS

II Corinthians 2:9-11; Ephesians 6:14b

IN THE ROMAN ARMY of Paul's day it was the responsibility of a military commander to see that the soldiers who went into battle under his command were adequately equipped to meet their adversaries. We who have been called as soldiers of the Lord Jesus Christ have a faithful commander, the Captain of our salvation, who has provided all the armament we need to stand against the adversary of our souls. The weapons with which we fight are not material weapons because such weapons would be useless in our warfare against the unseen hosts of spiritual darkness who war in the heavenlies.

The particular piece of armament to which we direct your attention now is the breastplate of righteousness. It is hard to distinguish the varying degrees of importance of the different pieces of armor that the Roman soldier wore, but certainly the breastplate was among the most important, for it was to cover the most vulnerable portion of the soldier's body. The breastplate frequently was made of heavy linen to which were attached overlapping pieces of horn or metal discs. More frequently, the breastplate was made of metal—woven chain, interlinked rings of metal, or solid metal, hinged in two parts so that it could be tied about the person, front and back, either with a buckle or with leather thongs. The purpose of the breastplate was to cover the vulnerable area of the chest and abdomen. No Roman soldier would have thought of venturing into any kind of battle without a breastplate for his protection, front and back. Therefore the apostle, after telling the believer that he must have his loins girt about with truth, instructs him to don the breastplate of righteousness.

THE BIBLICAL CONCEPT OF RIGHTEOUSNESS

In order to understand the meaning of the breastplate of righteousness, it is necessary for us to be clear in our thinking concerning the scriptural concept of righteousness.

First, it is to be noted that man born into the world has no righteousness that renders him acceptable to God. We read in Isaiah 64:6-7a, "We are all as an unclean thing, and all our righteousnesses are as filthy rags; and we all do fade as a leaf; and our iniquities, like the wind, have taken us away. And there is none that calleth upon thy name. . . ." Psalm 14, which asserts the same truth, is quoted by the Apostle Paul in Romans 3:10-12: "There is none righteous, no, not one: there is none that understandeth, there is none that seeketh after God. They all are gone out of the way, they are together become unprofitable; there is none that doeth good, no, not one." In verses 13-20, the apostle shows how the unrighteousness that characterizes the natural man manifests itself through every member of his body and through every part of his being. In verse 23 he summarizes God's estimate of the natural man by saying, "All have sinned, and come short of the glory of God." These are only a few of many passages which emphasize the fact that the natural man has no righteousness to render him acceptable to God. Furthermore, he has no righteousness to give him protection against the attacks of the evil one. The natural man, when he is attacked by his unseen adversary, has no armament whatsoever to protect him. Apart from God's grace, we have no ability to resist the adversary; we have no equipment with which to defeat Satan.

Second, we note that God gives or imputes the righteousness of God to those who accept Jesus Christ as personal Saviour. The Apostle Paul, after presenting the unrighteousness of the natural man in the third chapter of Romans, tells how the right eousness of God is given to the one who accepts Jesus Christ as personal Saviour. Paul, in Romans 3:22, refers to "the righteousness of God which is by faith of Jesus Christ unto all and upon all them that believe." Then he tells how God can impute this righteousness: "Being justified freely by his grace through the redemption that is in Christ Jesus: whom God hath set forth to be a propitiation through faith in his blood, to declare his righteousness for the remission of sins that are past, through the forbearance of God; to declare, I say, at this time his righteousness: that he might be just, and the justifier of him which believeth in Jesus" (vv. 24-26). Again, in Romans 5:17-19, the apostle says, "For if by one man's offence death reigned by one; much more they which receive abundance of grace and of the gift of righteousness shall reign in life by one, Jesus Christ. . . . For as by one man's disobedience many were made sinners, so by the obedience of one shall many be made righteous." The Apostle Paul is presenting in these passages the glorious fact that when one accepts Jesus Christ as personal Saviour God imputes to that one the perfection of Jesus Christ so that that sinner is clothed with the righteousness of Christ. Consequently, that one who has been born by faith into God's family is as acceptable in the sight of God as the spotless Son of God Himself. We have been given the righteousness of Christ as our portion. We have been "accepted in the beloved" (Eph. 1:6). Those who have accepted Jesus Christ by faith have the same standing before God that Jesus Christ has before God.

This righteousness is God's gift to us. It is not something we earn. This righteousness is not something that we can put off or put on, for the righteousness of Christ is our *eternal* portion given by God once and for all. So, when the apostle, in Ephesians 6, exhorts believers to put on the breastplate of righteousness, he is not speaking of this imputed righteousness of Christ. This righteousness is not something that we put off and put on.

Third, we note that the Spirit of God produces righteousness in the lives of those who have been made righteous by Jesus Christ. We often refer to this as experiential, or practical, righteousness. When the Holy Spirit is permitted to reproduce the character of Jesus Christ in our lives, He produces in us fruits of righteousness (Phil. 1:11). Now it is this practical, personal, or experiential righteousness that the apostle exhorts believers to put on as the breastplate which will protect them against the onslaught of the evil one. Unless the believer manifests personal righteousness in his daily life, he faces the foe without a breastplate. Therefore, the apostle says, it is not sufficient for the child of God to rejoice in the truth that he has been made righteous because of his position in Christ. The Spirit of God must produce the righteousness of Christ in the believer or he is incomplete—an important part is missing. It is this personal righteousness to which the apostle is referring in Romans 6:13 when he says, "Neither yield ye your members as instruments of unrighteousness unto sin: but yield yourselves unto God, as those that are alive from the dead, and your members as instruments of righteousness unto God." Again in verse 19, the apostle says, ". . . as ye have yielded [in days past] your members servants to uncleanness and to iniquity unto iniquity; even so now yield [or present] your members servants to righteousness unto holiness." Again, in Romans 8:3, the apostle says that God sent "his own Son in the likeness of sinful flesh, and for sin [and thus] condemned sin in the flesh: that the righteousness of the law might be fulfilled in us, who walk not after the flesh, but after the Spirit."

In chapters 3, 4, and 5 of Romans, the apostle teaches us that God has set down to our account the righteousness of Christ, that we have been clothed in the righteousness of His Son and stand before God accepted in the Beloved. But as the apostle moves on into chapters 6, 7, and 8, he is dealing with personal, practical righteousness and says that the child of God who has received by faith the righteousness of Christ, must present himself to the Holy Spirit as an instrument through which the Holy Spirit can work so that He may produce that which characterized the life of Christ. As this is accomplished in us, we shall have an impervious piece of armor, the breastplate of righteousness.

THE ARMOR OF PERSONAL RIGHTEOUSNESS

The breastplate was of greatest importance when the soldier was engaged in hand-to-hand combat against the enemy. Two adversaries, each with a short dagger in the right hand, would duel with their left hands joined together. In such close proximity, each would attempt to pierce through the breastplate of his adversary to kill him. The Christian believer also stands in hand-to-hand combat with an unseen adversary. The adversary is searching for any small break in our breastplate through which he may thrust his sword. If the believer's breastplate is complete and sound, he is able to stand with confidence. Can you imagine how a soldier would feel if he had neglected to care for his breastplate, or if he had gone into battle without checking on the thongs or the hinges or the clasps that held the breastplate together? When he felt the adversary take hold of his hand and saw that dagger he would then say to himself, "Oh, if only I had repaired the broken places in my breastplate! Now I am vulnerable." If sins in the life of the child of God remain unjudged and unconfessed, those sins are like a defect in the protective covering and leave an opening through which the dagger point can pierce to his destruction. A dagger does not need much of an opening in the breastplate to be able to enter and do its destructive work. If we are to have assurance of being able to withstand the enemy in hand-to-hand combat, we must be sure to have an unbroken breastplate.

One such break in the breastplate might be an unforgiving spirit. The Apostle Paul wrote in II Corinthians 2:9-11 about individuals whom he forgave "lest Satan should get an advantage of us." Another area where Satan might gain an advantage over Christians is indicated in I Timothy 5:14, where Paul, writing to the young pastor Timothy, said, "I will therefore that the younger women marry, bear children, guide the house, give none occasion to the adversary to speak reproachfully." Neglect of home responsibilities would give the enemy an occasion for slander.

Let us use another military metaphor to illustrate how Satan can gain advantage over a Christian. When a commander is about to bring his forces into an area, he sends an advance force to establish a base from which his troops can operate. From that advance base, or beachhead, his soldiers can attack and surround the forces of the opposing army. That is the way Satan works in the life of a believer. He does not need a wide-open door through some flagrant sin in the life. Any departure from the righteousness of Christ gives Satan an opportunity to gain a beachhead and to establish a base of operations from which he may fan out to bring about the defeat of the believer in battle. We may exercise great care about the big things and refrain from flagrant violations of the holy and righteous commandments of God, and yet become lax about what we call the little things, the little sins, the secret sins. But those secret sins can be as devastating in the life of the child of God as the most flagrant violations of holiness and righteousness. And such little sins can give Satan a toehold, or beachhead, that he can use as a base of operations through which to bring about defeat in the life of a child of God.

Thank God we stand clothed in the righteousness of Christ. Satan cannot rob us of our glorious position before the Father of being righteous in Christ. But how often we neglect the armor of personal righteousness! When the enemy has taken you by the left hand and has drawn his dagger, it is too late for you to try to repair any break in the breastplate of righteousness. But God has a method by which your armor can be kept ready for battle. In I John 1:9 the apostle John tells us, "If we [God's children] confess our sins [the breaks in the armor], he is faithful and just to forgive us our sins [put back all the missing plates] and to cleanse us from all unrighteousness." Unless we keep our confession of sins up to date, we leave ourselves vulnerable to the attacks of the adversary because we are not maintaining the equipment that has been provided for those who have been made righteous in Jesus Christ.

CHAPTER

27

SHOES FOR YOUR FEET

Ephesians 6:15

EMPHASIS ON FASHION has shifted attention from the utilitarian value of shoes to their decorative value—especially as part of a woman's wardrobe. Originally shoes were designed to protect the feet from thorns and stones. Those who crossed the burning sands of a desert needed shoes, for no traveler could proceed far on his journey without them. The shepherd who spent his time on the hills following the sheep required stout sandals to protect his feet.

The Apostle Paul showed he had some concept of the importance of the shoe for the soldier as well as for the traveler when he referred to the armor which has been provided by God as equipment for His soldiers. In Ephesians 6:15, after the apostle has said that our loins are to be girt about with truth, that is, truthfulness or sincerity in the inner man, and after he has stated that we are to put on the breastplate of personal righteousness as protection against the enemy, he says, "And your feet shod with the preparation of the gospel of peace." The Roman as well as the Jew normally wore lightweight sandals which consisted primarily of a leather sole tied on the feet with leather thongs. Frequently the sandals were ornamented with precious metals, or even jewels. If a Roman soldier were being sent into battle, he laid aside his lightweight sandals and donned a pair of heavy, thick-soled shoes. In the soles of these shoes hobnails were embedded in order that the soldier might have a firm and secure footing when he met the enemy in battle.

FOOTWEAR FOR BATTLE

The soldier of Jesus Christ has been called by God to lay aside that which would ornament the feet and to don the heavy, hobnailed boots that will enable him to stand against the adversary. An athlete pays particular attention to his footwear. Athletes participating in various sports wear suitable footwear adjusted to the needs of the player. For instance, the tennis player wears a particular type of footgear, a football player another, a baseball player another, and the golfer yet another. Because of the different ways in which these sports require the use of feet, the shoes are designed to give the contestant firm and secure footing. The Christian soldier also needs a firm and secure footing. His ability to stand against the adversary will depend upon the shoes which he has on his feet. It would be poor preparation for battle if he girded up his loins with truth and put on the breastplate of righteousness if he did not also wear the proper shoes. There is that in the gospel of peace that will enable a believer to stand after he has donned the other parts of the armor. This the apostle emphasizes when he says that the believer is to have his feet shod with the preparation which the gospel that brings peace provides. Since the gospel is the truth that Christ died for our sins and rose again for our justification, we may infer that the soldier of the cross of Christ is to be prepared ahead of time for the conflict by knowing this truth. It would be foolish to be fumbling around in a knapsack looking for shoes to replace the sandals after the enemy attacks. We are to put on this footwear before we come to grips with the adversary.

In the Epistle to the Ephesians the Apostle Paul indirectly refers to the feet, for the word *walk* occurs frequently. In chapter 2 the apostle asked his readers to recall the kind of life that they had once lived before they knew Jesus Christ as Saviour. He said, "In time past ye walked according to the course of this world." Their manner of life, as it was manifested through their daily walk, conformed in every respect to the standards, patterns, goals, desires, and ethics of this world, which is under the control of Satan. He reminded them that formerly they had been controlled by "the spirit that now worketh in the children of disobedience."

After the apostle pointed to the past walk of those believers, he exhorted the children of God to a new kind of walk: "This I say therefore, and testify in the Lord, that ye henceforth walk not as other Gentiles walk" (Eph. 4:17). Then he described in detail the kind of walk that characterized the Gentile. It was a vain, or empty, walk. Their understanding was darkened so they did not know the truth of God. It was a walk in deadness, for they were alienated from the life of God because of the ignorance that was in them. They gave themselves over to all kinds of immorality, working all uncleanness with greediness.

After painting this dark picture of what a person's walk was like without knowing the gospel of peace the apostle turned to the positive side and gave this exhortation concerning the new walk: "I therefore, the prisoner of the Lord, beseech you that ye walk worthy of the calling wherewith ye are called" (Eph. 4:1). Believers in Christ were called to unity; they were called with a heavenly calling; they were called as the sons of God. And their walk was to conform to this high, heavenly, and holy calling. The apostle recognized that, apart from that which the gospel provides believers, they could never walk worthy of their calling. And so the apostle said, in effect, "If you would fulfil this obligation which rests upon you as a child of God, you must prepare for this kind of walk by putting on your feet the shoes of the gospel [that which is provided in the gospel]." Again in Ephesians 5:1-2, the apostle says, "Be ye therefore followers of God, as dear children; and walk in love." The child of God has the capacity to manifest the love of God because God has first loved him, and the apostle says that if a child of God would manifest the love of God and be victorious in his Christian walk, then he must put on that which is provided by the Captain of our salvation for his feet so that he can walk in love. The apostle also pointed out, in Ephesians 5:8, "Ye were sometimes darkness, but now ye are light in the Lord: walk as children of light." The apostle referred to the fact that formerly these believers stumbled because they were in darkness. But since then the gospel had brought light to them, they had light on their pathway. But unless the believer's feet are properly equipped, he will not be able to stand against the attacks of the adversary.

A SURE FOUNDATION

The Word of God uses two significant figures to show us that Jesus Christ is the foundation upon which we must stand if we are to be victorious and triumphant in our warfare. First of all, Jesus Christ is referred to as the *rock* or the *stone*. In Matthew 16:18, after Peter's declaration, "Thou art the Christ, the Son of the living God," Jesus Christ said to him, "Thou art Peter, and upon this rock I will build my church; and the gates of hell shall not prevail against it." While there are different interpretations of the words "this rock," it seems as though the Apostle Paul identified what was in Christ's mind when He used this figure when he wrote in I Corinthians 10:4, "that Rock is Christ." Christ anticipated that the Spirit of God would join all believers into one body (the church) on the day of Pentecost. He knew they would be attacked by the evil one. All of the gates of hell would seek to overthrow them, but they had been given a Rock upon which to stand, upon which to firmly plant their feet. And when the feet of believers have been shod with that which is provided in the gospel of peace, and when their feet, thus shod, are planted on that Rock, then they can stand against the attacks of the evil one.

In Acts 4, Peter used this same figure in relation to Christ. Having preached Jesus to the people, he declared, "Be it known unto you all, and to all the people of Israel, that by the name of Jesus Christ of Nazareth, whom ye crucified, whom God raised from the dead, even by him doth this man stand here before you whole. This is the stone which was set at nought of you builders, which is become the head of the corner. Neither is there salvation in any other: for there is none other name under heaven given among men, whereby we must be saved" (vv. 10-12). The Apostle Peter, who had heard our Lord say, "Upon this rock I will build my church and the gates of hell shall *not* prevail against it," declared to those assembled before him the truth that Jesus Christ is that Rock. And one who takes his stand on that Rock has an unshakable and immovable foundation.

The figure of Christ as a rock is also used by the Apostle Paul when he speaks of the church as a building. Writing in Ephesians 2, the apostle says that believers "are built upon the foundation of the apostles and prophets, Jesus Christ himself being the chief cornerstone" (Eph. 2:20). In writing to the Corinthians, the apostle said that he as a wise masterbuilder had laid the foundation for their faith. Then he added, "But let every man take heed how he buildeth thereupon. For other foundation can no man lay than that is laid, which is Jesus Christ." Jesus Christ is the foundation upon which the whole superstructure rests.

It is always of interest to watch the preparation for the construction of a large office building. The higher the superstructure, the deeper must be the foundation. If that edifice is to stand, there must be a union between the solid rock beneath and the superstructure above. That thought is in the mind of the apostle when he says that God has laid a foundation for His church. The church will remain because Jesus Christ is our sure foundation. Believers, united to Him, are invincible because He is invincible.

SECURE FOOTING

Isaiah, writing to a rebellious and unrepentant people concerning an approaching judgment, says "We grope for the wall like the blind, and we grope as if we had no eyes: we stumble at noon day as in the night; we are in desolate places as dead men. We roar all like bears, and mourn sore like doves: we look for judgment, but there is none; for salvation, but it is far off from us." (Isa. 59:10-11). Now, how did this people come to be a stumbling, groping, blinded people? Verse 12 gives the answer: "For our transgressions are multiplied before thee, and our sins testify against us: for our transgressions are with us; and as for our iniquities, we know them; in transgressing and lying against the Lord, and departing away from our God, speaking oppression *and* revolt, conceiving and uttering from the heart words of falsehood." Israel is pictured as a nation that stumbles at noonday. For this there is no excuse. Why did they stumble in broad daylight? Because of personal sins! If a child of God falls into some sin and then tries to walk in a way that is pleasing to God—walking worthy of the calling with which he was called, walking in love and in light—he finds that he can make no progress at all because he has taken off his hobnail boots. The Prophet Isaiah made it very clear that even though God had provided that which would have enabled Israel to walk in paths of righteousness, the nation did not avail themselves of God's provision. Therefore they stumbled even at noonday.

It is not only by overt acts of sin that one casts aside what God has provided for his feet but by a certain attitude of the mind. We find an illustration of this in Psalm 73. In verse, 2, the psalmist says, "As for me, my feet were almost gone; my steps had well nigh slipped." Now what caused the psalmist to say, "My feet were almost gone; my steps had well nigh slipped"? We find the answer in verse 3, where the psalmist makes this confession to a wrong attitude of heart: "I was envious of the foolish, when I saw the prosperity of the wicked." It was a wrong attitude which removed the hobnail boots from the psalmist so that he slipped and fell in disgrace and despair.

If we were to choose where we would do battle against the adversary, we certainly would seek a terrain where there would be nothing to cause us to stumble, slip, or fall. Unfortunately we cannot always choose where we will meet the adversary. It seems as though the adversary does not attack when we are traveling on smooth ground. But when we must travel where the going is rough and where the springs make the terrain swampy, the adversary delights to attack us. He knows that we can be dispatched quickly if he can catch us in such surroundings, especially if we are without the hobnail boots provided in the gospel of our salvation. If we could choose the terrain, perhaps we would not feel the importance of preparing our feet beforehand. But because God's soldiers never know when nor from what quarter the adversary will attack, nor the terrain on which the adversary will be met, they must prepare their feet beforehand so that they will be able to stand.

Child of God, if you are slipping, perhaps you have removed the hobnail boots, that which God has provided in the gospel to enable you to stand. If a child of God walks in the old ways; follows the old pattern; conforms to the old habits, standards, and manners of life; continues his old associations, companionships, and friendships, he need not wonder why his feet slip. The child of God must by the grace of God appropriate that which God has provided in the gospel so that he will have a secure footing when the adversary attacks.

28

THE SHIELD OF FAITH

I John 5:1-5

IF THE CHILD OF GOD experiences any failure or defeat in the
Christian life, it is not because the armor God has provided for
him is in any way incomplete. The Captain of our salvation, to
enable us to stand against the onslaught of the enemy, has made
a full and complete provision. As we read the Apostle Paul's
description of the Christian's armor, we see that certain parts of
the armor were worn by the soldier—the helmet, the girdle, the
breastplate, and the shoes. As the apostle proceeds, he refers to
the movable parts of the equipment provided by the Captain for
those who serve under His command—the sword and the shield.
Paul describes the shield in Ephesians 6:16: "Above all, taking
the shield of faith, wherewith ye shall be able to quench all the
fiery darts of the wicked."

Several kinds of shields were used by different branches of the
Roman military service. The gladiator's shield was a small,
round one which he wore strapped to his left arm to parry the
dagger thrusts of his adversary while he used his right hand for
his own dagger thrusts. This small, lightweight shield allowed
the soldier great freedom of movement. But the shield to which
the Apostle Paul referred in Ephesians 6 was a shield of quite
a different kind. It was referred to as the door-shield because
of its size. It was a heavy shield approximately thirty inches wide
and forty-eight inches high, large enough for a soldier to crouch
behind it. It was primarily designed to give a soldier protection.
A Roman phalanx would overlap such shields and advance upon the enemy. When they came into close proximity to the enemy, they stood close together and formed a solid wall behind

which the phalanx hid. It is this large, protective door-shield that the apostle had in mind when he told them to take "the shield of faith, wherewith ye shall be able to quench all the fiery darts of the wicked." When the apostle used this door-shield as a figure of the shield provided by God for the soldier, he was emphasizing the fact that we have a full and complete protection. A soldier could crouch behind the door-shield, and no part of his person would be unprotected. The Christian soldier, equipped with the door-shield of faith, has the full, complete protection for the whole person provided by God the Father.

DOUBLE PROTECTION

Now the first words of this sixteenth verse have led some to a faulty idea of what the apostle was teaching. The words *above all* are sometimes interpreted to mean the piece of armor which is most important. But that was not the apostle's thought. The words might be translated "over all." The pieces of armor that the apostle had described covered the whole person. He was protected from head to toe by the equipment given by Jesus Christ. The door-shield, then, was not singled out as the most important, but it was that piece of the equipment which went in front of and protected all the other pieces of equipment. Thus the child of God is given a double protection. There is protection for his person in the helmet, the breastplate, the girdle, and the shoes for his feet, but the door-shield is for his overall protection. When he takes the door-shield of faith, his armor cannot be touched, let alone the soldier himself. In the tenth chapter of John's Gospel, our Lord spoke of the double security the child of God has. He is not only in the hand of Christ, he is also in the hand of God. In like manner, the Christian soldier has a double protection from the adversary. His person is not only covered completely by the armor provided by God but God has provided protection for his armor so that he can stand before the onslaughts of the evil one.

We see the reason why the child of God needs this protection for his armor in the sixteenth verse, where we read that this shield is given to "quench all the fiery darts of the wicked." What is meant by the fiery darts? The "fiery darts" describe missiles which were dipped in pitch, ignited, and then thrown at one's opponent. The soldier would be powerless to resist such a missile because of its weight and because it was a flaming torch. Unless the soldier had adequate protection, this flaming dart would strike his armor and the flaming pitch would be deposited on his armor and perhaps destroy him. In the spiritual warfare in which the Christian soldier is engaged he is provided with adequate protection against fiery darts of the enemy, and that protection is the shield of faith behind which he may hide. If the fiery missiles come his way, they will strike the door-shield and not the armor of the warrior himself.

These darts are said to be the fiery darts "of the wicked." This phrase "of the wicked" reveals two things. First of all, it shows the source from which the attack comes. The apostle had already told his readers, in the twelfth verse, "We wrestle not against flesh and blood, but against principalities, against powers, against the rulers of the darkness of this world, against spiritual wickedness in high places." But this phrase, "of the wicked," reveals not only the source of the missiles but the character of the missiles. What kind of missiles will they be? The missiles that are shot or thrown by the adversary have the very character of the adversary. They are devilish, diabolical, destructive. So, because of the nature of the missiles, we need in front of all the armor the door-shield of faith to protect us from them.

FAITH AS A SHIELD

The apostle describes the shield as the shield of faith. In order to understand this description, we will need to consider two different uses in the New Testament of the phrase "the faith." On occasion it refers to the whole body of divine revelation, or divine truth. For instance, Paul wrote in I Timothy 4:1, "Now the Spirit speaketh expressly, that in the latter times some shall depart from the faith." "The faith" as used by the apostle there refers to the entire body of divine revelation made through New Testament apostles and prophets which is recorded in the Word of God. And one of the characteristics of the apostasy of the days in which we live is the departure from the truth of the Word of God referred to by Paul. And that which is crucial in judging any religious system or any theological school is its attitude toward the Word of God. The apostle stresses the importance of holding fast to divinely revealed truth. But while that is of great importance, and while there can be no successful combat with the enemy apart from holding to divinely revealed truth, that is not what the apostle is referring to in Ephesians 6:16. The second usage of the phrase "the faith" refers to the faith principle. It is the faith principle which is part of the equipment given by God to His child to enable him to be victorious and triumphant in the battle. Faith is an attitude toward God in which you reckon God to be a faithful God who will perform that which He has promised. You also reckon that He who has begun a good work in you will perform it until the day of Jesus Christ. The shield of faith is not the objective body of truth, then, but rather the faith of the warrior in God's faithfulness to His promises. And this faith makes the warrior invincible.

Let us refer briefly to a number of passages where this faith principle is affirmed in the Word of God. For instance, in the second chapter of Colossians the apostle wrote to men who were in danger of being enticed away from the truth. Recognizing that false teachers had come into Colosse who were substituting human philosophy for divine revelation, he wrote, "And this I say, lest any man should beguile you with enticing [or flattering] words. For though I be absent in the flesh, yet am I with you in the spirit, joying and beholding your order, and the stedfastness of your faith in Christ" (vv. 4-5). Paul did not say, "I rejoice in the fact that you continue to hold to sound doctrine in spite of false teaching." Paul said, "I rejoice, joying and beholding your order, and the *stedfastness of your faith* in Christ." And then, in the sixth verse, he gives a charge to them in view of the fact that they are manifesting a continuing faith in Christ. "As ye have therefore received Christ Jesus the Lord, so walk ye in him."

We can make two important observations about what the apostle says in the sixth verse. First, he affirms the principle by which they came to know Jesus Christ as personal Saviour when he referred to how they had "received Christ Jesus the Lord." They had come to know Jesus Christ by faith, for by faith they had accepted the gift of God which is eternal life through Jesus Christ our Lord. They were not saved by rationalization, by good works, by joining a church, by being baptized, nor by following the philosophies of men. They were saved by the faith principle. They accepted God's word that God would save a man who came to Him by faith in Jesus Christ, and as a result they were born again. The second important observation is about the little word *so*. Just as they had received Jesus Christ the Lord by faith, they were to walk daily by faith. The apostle was emphasizing the fact that the Christian life is a faith life, that the person who is saved by faith does not live the Christian life by a different principle. He does not live the Christian life by following the philosophies of men, joining a church, or keeping the law. The principle of victory and triumph in the Christian life is the same principle that saved you, the faith principle. Anyone who trusts any principle other than the faith principle for his daily life is not using the door-shield of faith by which he will be able to quench all the fiery darts of the wicked. The apostle, writing to these to whom false teachers were making their appeal, emphasizes the fact that God has only one operating principle—the faith principle. A man is saved by faith, a Christian walks by faith, a child of God lives by faith, a soldier of God fights by faith. The Christian life is a faith life, step by step.

In I John, the Apostle John emphasized the fact that the world in which we live is a glamorous world which will make all sorts of enticing appeals to the child of God to woo him away from his position as a good soldier of Jesus Christ. Therefore, the apostle wrote, in verse 4, "Whatsoever is born of God overcometh the world; and this is the victory that overcometh the world, even our faith." *Even our faith.* Faith is the basis not only of the Christian walk but, according to I John 5:4, of victory over the enticements of the world. Now, Satan uses the world system in order to get the child of God to lay down his door-shield of faith. The Roman soldier who had been marching all day long with his large and heavy door-shield must have been tempted many times to lay it down. If a Christian soldier succumbs to Satan's persuasion to abandon the door-shield of faith, he has no protection for his armor and, consequently, no protection for his person from the attack of the adversary. Now, the Apostle John says there is only one thing that will keep a Christian from yielding to the enticements of the world, and that is faith. "Who is he that overcometh the world, but he that believeth that Jesus is the Son of God?" John agreed with what Paul wrote to the Colossians. Men are saved by faith, and the one who believes that Jesus is the Son of God is born into the family of God, and that same faith which brought him to salvation is to continue to operate as a protective shield to cover his whole person.

THE TRIUMPH OF VICTORY

In II Corinthians 2:14 the Apostle Paul employed a very graphic figure taken from the Roman military world: "Now thanks be unto God, which always causeth us to triumph in Christ, and maketh manifest the savour of his knowledge by us in every place." The marginal reading for the phrase "causeth us to triumph" is "leadeth us in a triumphal procession." The picture here is that of a conquering military commander returning home after a great victory. It was the custom for the commander to be given a great welcome. He rode at the head of a procession on a white steed, signifying that he was the victor. Behind him would march the soldiers who had fought with him in battle. Wagons would be loaded with spoils of the conquest to show the great extent of the victory. The captives taken in battle would follow in the rear. The number of captives brought back would evidence the greatness of the commander's victory. Paul pictures the Lord Jesus Christ as a returning triumphant general. Behind Him will march His soldiers bearing the spoils of battle. Believers in the Lord Jesus Christ are viewed as part of His triumphal procession. When the apostle affirms the fact that God leadeth us in triumph in Christ, he is emphasizing the fact that the battle is over, the victory has been won, and those who march with Him as His soldiers are sharing His victory. He gained a great victory over the evil one at the cross. Jesus Christ was triumphant through His death and His resurrection. Satan is a defeated foe, and yet the time of executing judgment on him is not yet at hand. Meanwhile, the Lord Jesus Christ is leading in the train of His triumph those who put faith in Him; they share His victory. Victory in the Christian life depends on the believer's appropriation by faith of the victory which Christ gained over the adversary. Then the believer by faith can follow in the train of His triumph.

These passages emphasize the great principle that the Christian life does not depend upon the strength of the Christian. The Christian life does not depend upon the child of God any more than his salvation depended upon himself. Strength in the Christian life is Jesus Christ. Power in the Christian life is Jesus Christ. We may appropriate that strength and power by faith. So the apostle tells us that God has given us all the pieces of armor to protect our person, but our armor must be protected by the door-shield of faith. As you exercise your faith, you will be invincible. Faith is not natural, it is supernatural. The desire of the Apostle Paul for those who were soldiers of Jesus Christ was that they should learn to live by this faith principle so that they should be thoroughly equipped for victory and triumph.

THE HELMET OF SALVATION

II Corinthians 10:1-7

No ROMAN SOLDIER would think of advancing into battle without a helmet to cover his head. This helmet was usually a cap made of leather to which metal plates had been fastened. Some helmets were made of solid metal cast in the form of a head-covering. Whatever the external form of the helmet, the purpose was the same—to protect the head from the blows of the broadsword. The adversary might come against a soldier armed with one of two kinds of swords. There was the short dagger-type sword which was designed to pierce the breastplate, to destroy the warrior. The soldier did not particularly need a head-covering to meet this weapon because the shield was designed to parry the thrust of the small dagger. The adversary might come against the soldier with a broadsword. Such a sword was from three to four feet long and had a long handle which the soldier would grip in both hands. He would raise the sword high over his head and bring it down with a heavy crashing blow on the head of his opponent, with the intent of killing him by splitting open his skull. Therefore, the Roman soldier expecting an attack by an adversary equipped with the broadsword would cover his head with a metal headdress.

Just as the Roman soldier was provided protection for his head, believers in Christ have been provided with the helmet of salvation. The helmet of salvation to which the apostle refers in Ephesians 6:17 is not salvation in the objective sense. Certainly one who has accepted Christ as personal Saviour is safe and secure; his destiny is settled. But he is vulnerable to attack by Satan in the sense that Satan may tempt him to doubt his salvation. It would seem that the helmet symbolizes the assurance the individual has of the forgiveness of sin, of his safety and security, also the assurance that he can stand against the onslaught of Satan because he has been judged. Such assurance is the subjective appropriation of all that is provided through the gospel for the child of God in the finished work of the Lord Jesus Christ.

Just as no Roman soldier would think of proceeding into battle without the helmet provided by the commander to protect him from the broadsword, so a child of God should not think of advancing into battle against the evil one without putting on the helmet that is provided in our salvation. The child of God needs to appropriate all that God has provided for him in his salvation in order to be invincible in the day of attack.

A SOUND MIND

Since the helmet was a head-covering, we might think of the helmet of salvation as a protection for the thought life of the child of God. The thought life determines whether he experiences victory or defeat. Solomon, writing in Proverbs 23:7, asserted the fact that as a man "thinketh in his heart, so is he." Before any commander can lead his soldiers into battle with any expectation of victory, he must build troop morale. This principle is no less true in the spiritual realm than in the physical realm. Unless the child of God is certain, because of promises of the Word of God, that he can defeat the evil one and can emerge victorious and triumphant, he is certain to go down in defeat. So when the apostle commands us to take the helmet of salvation, it is like commanding us to receive from the Word of God the promises of God concerning our position in Christ, and our victory in Christ. Only as we appropriate for ourselves these promises of victory can we expect to stand in the evil day.

There is power in positive thinking and defeat in negative thinking. We can exercise the power of positive thinking about the victory and triumph God has provided for His children; we can banish even the thought of defeat. We are to be strong in the Lord and the power of His might and take unto us the armor of God with a view to victory against the evil one. As a man thinketh in his heart, so is he. If you are a spiritual coward and afraid to face the adversary, certain that he will overwhelm you, you may fully expect to be defeated. But defeat is not necessary. If you have the helmet of salvation, this means you are assured from the Word of God that victory is certain. If you know the adversary's weapons and ammunition are inferior to your spiritual weapons, given by God, you do not fear him. This is what the apostle has in mind when he exhorts these Ephesians to put on the helmet of salvation.

In Philippians 4:13 the apostle asserts, "I can do all things through Christ." That is an unequivocal affirmation. You will notice no conditions are attached to it whatsoever. He did not say, "Sometimes I can do all things," or "I may be able to do all things." The apostle makes a positive affirmation: "I can do all things through Christ."

Now the child of God is expected to give assent to what God promises. If God has promised certain victory, then it is an act of unbelief to say that God did not mean what He said. The apostle believed that he could do all things because of God's promises of strength. The apostle could march fearlessly into the fray even against an unseen adversary because he knew the outcome beforehand. He had no questions about which way the battle would go. It never entered into his mind that he could be defeated as long as he relied on the Lord. Paul did not feel that he himself was invincible, but Paul knew he was invincible because of God's provision for him in the gospel. Paul knew nothing of a gospel which could save for eternity but was inadequate for daily life. The gospel that Paul presented was sufficient not only for the future but for daily needs. If you count on the fact that you can do all things through Christ, then the very appropriation of that fact, or the assent of your mind to that fact, means that you are putting on the helmet of salvation. When you read in the Word of God, "I can do all things through Christ," and your heart responds with an amen, your assent to that fact strengthens you for the battle. Moreover, that assent means your mind is protected with the helmet of salvation.

In John 16:11, Christ said that the Holy Spirit will convince the world of judgment, because the prince of this world is judged. If you assent with your mind that judgment has been passed upon Satan, that he is a defeated foe; then you are putting on the helmet of salvation. If you feel that your adversary is invincible, if you are convinced that the enemy who has ambushed you on the road cannot be defeated, then you *are* defeated. That defeat took place in your mind. But if you hold as truth the word of Christ that at the cross Satan was judged, that Satan is a defeated foe, and if you believe that you can walk in the train of Christ's triumph, that attitude is going to bring you victory in Jesus Christ. In James 4:7 we read, "Resist the devil, and he will flee from you." If you doubt that word, then you are well along the path of defeat. But if you count that a true word from God, then you are on your way to victory. James said, "Resist the devil," and the word *resist* means "to stand against" and is the same word which occurs in Ephesians 6:13 where we were told to withstand the evil one. James says that if you, as a child of God, firmly stand on your ground because your feet are shod with the hobnail boots provided in the gospel, and refuse to be moved before the onslaught of the adversary, the devil will turn and run. We have concluded that Satan is anything but a coward. We have been led to believe that he is absolutely fearless. That is part of the satanic deception, for Satan is anything but fearless. Satan is a coward. Satan is compelled to come against us with deception. He is compelled to use a cloak of secrecy. Because of his cowardice, he tries to overwhelm us with fright just as a lion strikes terror into a man with his mighty roar. If the child of God takes a stand against the evil one, that firm stand will cause him to turn tail and run. That is what James meant when he said, "Resist the devil, and he will flee from you."

On what grounds can the child of God withstand the evil one? The believer has no strength, no might, no power of himself. But when he accepts the fact that Satan is a coward, that Satan will flee from one who is determined to withstand him, he is clothing his mind with the helmet of salvation. Such an one is not only rendering himself invincible to Satan's attack, but is also causing the retreat of the adversary. Thus, our attitude of mind toward the truth of the Word of God is of utmost importance. Because of this, the Word has much to say about the mind. The mind, of course, is the seat of the thought processes, and plays an active part in exercising faith. Paul reminds Timothy in II Timothy 1:7, "God hath not given us the spirit of fear; but of power, and of love, and of a sound mind." Any expectation of defeat is not of God. That is what Paul means when he says God has not given us the spirit of fear. We do not advance in battle against the evil one when we expect to be defeated. That would cause fear. But God has given to us a sound mind. The sound mind means the ability to apply the promises from the Word of God to the daily battle in which we are engaged. The apostle says to Timothy, "You are going as my representative. You are to teach the Word, and ground the saints in the Word of God. In a very real sense, Timothy, you are going into battle against the evil one. As you speak the Word of God you are dispelling the darkness and bringing men to knowledge which will enable them to defeat and to overthrow the adversary. When you go into this battle, you do not have to fear, because God has given you a sound mind that can appropriate the promises and then you can respond by faith to that which you have appropriated with the mind."

Writing in Philippians, Paul has another word concerning the mind. He said in Philippians 4:6, "Be careful for nothing . . ." or, to translate this literally, "Don't worry about anything." Does this mean that even when we go into battle against Satan and all his innumerable hosts we don't have to worry? That is right! You don't have to worry. What is the antidote to worry? "In everything by prayer and supplication with thanksgiving let your requests be made known unto God." When our Commander gives the command, "Forward march," are His soldiers to advance in fear? Are they to be worried as they go forward? No, not at all. Why? Because as they march into the fray, they can, by prayer and supplication, lay hold of the promises of God and commit their way to the Lord. This trust, which manifests itself in prayer, will have the result described by Paul in verse 7, "The peace of God, which passeth all understanding, shall keep [or shall stand sentry duty over] your hearts and minds through Christ Jesus." The Christian soldier who has been summoned into battle goes with faith, confidence, and trust in

God. God stands sentry over his mind so that he is delivered from fear and discouragement, and from even the thought that he may be overthrown in battle. The one who enters the battle prayerfully, trusting the promises of God and resting upon the certainty of victory, finds that even thoughts of defeat which seek to intrude are kept out of his mind because the peace of God which passeth all understanding guards, as a sentry, his heart and mind.

THOUGHT LIFE

The Apostle Paul was deeply concerned about the thought life of the Christian in relation to the spiritual warfare in which he is engaged. We learn this from II Corinthians 10:5, where Paul wrote about "casting down imaginations, and every high thing that exalteth itself against the knowledge of God, and bringing into captivity every thought to the obedience of Christ." If one is to be victorious he must cast down imaginations and every high thing that exalteth itself against the knowledge of God. The imaginations and the high things exalted against God include the thoughts that we entertain concerning the possibility of defeat. Using the imagery of the military, if a soldier marches into battle and with every step says he is one step nearer to death or approaching defeat, he certainly will go down in defeat. As he marches into battle, he must bring such thoughts of defeat, such vain imaginations, into captivity to the obedience of Christ. Why? Because Christ has assured us of victory. The soldier who can by faith lay hold of the promises of God and advance against the adversary assured of victory in Christ, dispels the empty imaginations and the high things that exalt themselves against the knowledge God has revealed. As a result, he marches into battle with the certainty that he will walk in the train of Christ's triumph.

The thought life of a good soldier of Jesus Christ is not to be underestimated. The faculties of the mind elude description. The mind can be here one moment, and the next moment it can be hundreds of miles away. It can be occupied with one thing at one moment and completely occupied with another thing the next moment. The mind can be centered upon the Lord Jesus

Christ one moment and the next moment can be diverted to that which is displeasing to God. Unless the child of God brings every thought into subjection to the Lord Jesus Christ, he will be defeated. In effect, the apostle is saying, "Do not forget that your mind must be protected with that which salvation supplies. If you do not have the helmet of salvation, if your mind is not brought into subjection to the Lord Jesus Christ, then your mind can be the avenue of approach through which Satan can bring defeat to you." We must sit in judgment continually on our thought life, lest we open the door to defeat by not believing the promises of God or by letting our minds dwell upon that which is an abomination to God. As a man thinketh in his heart, so is he. When you are not consciously directing your attention, where does your mind wander? What are the first thoughts that flash through your mind when you're beginning to wake up in the morning, when you are too sleepy to be focusing your attention? Or what occupies your thoughts in those last moments before you drop off to sleep at night? Do you commit your mind to the Lord's keeping even during the hours of the night? May God enable us to lay hold of the promises of victory provided in the gospel so that every thought may be obedient to Christ. In this way the peace of God will garrison our hearts and minds, and we will be confident of victory in the Lord Jesus Christ.

THE SWORD OF THE SPIRIT

II Peter 1:15-21

THE HYMN WRITER asks the question, "Am I a soldier of the cross?" In the light of Scripture, there can be only one answer to this question. The answer must be in the affirmative, for the child of God has been called to war. The Apostle Paul, writing to a young minister who had been entrusted with the responsibility of guiding a flock, told him to "endure hardness as a good soldier of Jesus Christ." The Word of God knows nothing about retired officers or enlisted men whose duty is terminated. The child of God has been called to a continuous, unrelenting warfare. When the children of Israel crossed the Jordan after their wilderness experience and came into the land of promise, the land of milk and honey, they came into a new kind of life—a life of rest. But that life did not preclude continuous warfare, for there were many adversaries in the land.

As the Apostle Paul faced the problems of the believer in relationship to Satan, he did not present the idea that Satan will cease to war against the child of God. Nor did he present a concept of the Christian life as a tranquil, placid kind of existence. Rather, the apostle anticipated continuous conflict. And the more one purposes to be faithful to the Lord Jesus Christ, the greater the conflict becomes. While the prospect for the child of God is translation out of this earth into a new sphere in the heavenlies, yet, as long as he lives on this earth, he will be in the midst of conflict.

THE WORD OF AUTHORITY

In the previous studies we have examined the pieces of defensive equipment given to the child of God. We come now to the only offensive piece of equipment that the Captain of our salvation provides for us. The apostle says, "Take the sword of the Spirit, which is the word of God" (Eph. 6:17b). The girdle, the breastplate, the shoes, the shield of faith, and the helmet of salvation were all defensive. Not one of those five, in themselves, can defeat the enemy. They were for the protection of the soldier. It is significant that, of all the pieces of equipment mentioned in Ephesians 6, the sword is the only one Paul explains. We had to go to other passages of Scripture, for instance, to understand what Paul had in mind when he spoke of the girdle for the loins, the breastplate for the chest, the shoes for the feet, the shield for the person, and the helmet for the head. It seems as though the apostle considers the sword, the offensive weapon, so important that he pauses to explain this figure so that there could be no question as to what the sword is. "Take the sword of the Spirit, which is the word of God." The words "of God" describe the source from which this weapon comes. This weapon is not of human origin; this sword was not forged upon human anvils. This dagger has not been tempered in human fires. Rather, this is a weapon of divine origin, provided to give God's children a weapon which will be adequate for conflict with the kind of adversary we face. Since he is not flesh and blood, human weapons will not suffice.

As we consider "the sword of the Spirit, which is the word of God," we must remember that it is not our evaluation of the Word of God which gives it value, nor our interpretation of the origin of Scripture which makes it authoritative. It is what Scripture is intrinsically, in itself, that gives it authority, thus making it a powerful offensive weapon which can satisfactorily put to rout the adversary with whom we fight.

The Apostle Peter, coming to the close of his earthly sojourn, was concerned about the spiritual maturity and development, after his departure, of the believers to whom he wrote. For this reason he commanded the elders to tend, or feed, the flock of God. The ministry of feeding the sheep was to be not through words of men but rather through the Word of God, and he had this in mind when, anticipating his departure, he said, "I will endeavour that ye may be able after my decease to have these things always in remembrance" (II Peter 1:15). He had presented the gospel to them. He had delivered the truths which he received by divine revelation. As long as he was personally present, he could repeat what he had received from God to give to them. But he anticipated that he would not be with them much longer, so he was concerned about perpetuating the ministry of the Word of God after his departure in order that the believers might continue to grow spiritually.

Peter affirms in verse 16, "We have not followed cunningly devised fables when we made known unto you the power and coming of our Lord Jesus Christ." The apostle is reminding them of the truth that the Lord Jesus Christ will return to this earth to rule. Peter, as one of the three Christ took up to the Mount of Transfiguration, had personally witnessed Christ's majesty when He was transfigured before them. That transfiguration was an advance revelation of the glory which would be Christ's at His second advent. Peter told them that he was passing on to them that which he had seen with his own eyes and heard with his ears, also that this was truth that could be authenticated and certified by two other witnesses.

After Peter told what he had seen and heard, he made a most amazing statement: "We have also a more sure word of prophecy" (v. 19). The words "a more sure," may be translated in another way: "We have a prophecy made more certain." More certain than what? More certain than that which Peter, James, and John had seen with their own eyes and had heard with their own ears. What could be more certain than that? Then Peter tells us, in verse 21, "No prophecy of the scripture is of any private interpretation." A common but erroneous interpretation of this phrase "any private interpretation" is that no individual has the right to study and interpret the Word of God for himself, and every individual must look to the church for the proper interpretation. What Peter wrote may be rendered this way, "No prophecy of Scripture comes out of private disclosure." The apostle is dealing with the *source* from which the Scriptures came. They are not of human origin. Peter asserts that we can believe the Word of God because Scripture did not originate with men, but holy men of God spake as they were moved by the Holy Ghost. The word *moved* is a word in the original text that was used of a sailboat whose sails were filled out by the wind. When the wind filled the sails, the boat was propelled through the water by the force of the wind against the sails. So the last part of verse 21 might be rendered this way: "Holy men of God spake as they were borne along by the Holy Ghost [in the same way the wind bears along a boat]." Peter is telling us that the Word of God is trustworthy and authoritative, and it is to be believed above that which men say they have seen and heard and experienced with their own eyes and ears. Why? Because the Word of God came as the Spirit bore along, or carried along, men as the instruments through whom the Word of God was given to us. When the Apostle Paul, in Ephesians 6:17, says we are to take the sword of the Spirit, the Word of God, the phrase "of God" brings in all the truth that Peter spelled out so clearly in II Peter 1. The Word of God is sufficient because of its source.

Another familiar passage concerning the Word of God is II Timothy 3:16. In this passage the Apostle Paul anticipates the rise of false teachers. In II Timothy 3:1, Paul says, "In the last days perilous times shall come." One of the characteristics of the last days is given in verse 5. Men will have a form of godliness, but will deny the power thereof. In the verses that follow, the apostle shows the results of repudiating divine truth and speaks of the moral corruption and perversion that will characterize men. Now Timothy was being sent out as a minister of the gospel to face a world characterized by doubts, denials, deceptions, perversions of divine truth, and repudiation of the Word of God. Now what will be sufficient for Timothy's ministry in such days? The apostle points Timothy to the Word of God. He said, "Continue thou [in contrast to these evil men] in the things which thou hast learned and hast been assured of, knowing of whom thou hast learned them; and that from a child thou hast known the holy scriptures, which are able to make thee wise unto salvation through faith which is in Jesus Christ" (vv. 14-15). The apostle says that the Word of God is the only effective instrument in days such as he had outlined in the preceding portion of this chapter. Then, in the sixteenth verse, Paul tells why the Word of God is sufficient in such dark days: "All scripture is given by inspiration of God." Another way to translate these words is: "All scripture is God-breathed." The Word of God which we have in our hands is the result of the out-breathing of God. God used human instruments to bring the Scriptures to men, but they are authoritative because they are God-breathed. Because the Scripture is God-breathed, it is profitable for doctrine, that is, for teaching divine truth. It is profitable for reproof of godless men and for correcting those whose ways have been perverted by the teaching of these godless men. The Word of God is useful for instructing in righteousness those who would walk in a way pleasing to God. So when the Apostle Paul tells believers that God has put a sword in their hands, they may know that this sword is sufficient to defeat the adversary because it has come from God by the process of divine inspiration. So, when we face the adversary, we need not hesitate to move confidently against him with only one weapon because this weapon is a powerful weapon.

CHRIST USED THE WORD

The account of how Christ met Satan's temptations furnished a great example of how to use the sword of the Spirit to defeat Satan. One record of this temptation is found in Matthew, chapter 4. After John the Baptist introduced Jesus to the nation Israel as their God-given Messiah, the One who had come to redeem and to reign, Christ was led by the Spirit out into the wilderness, and there He entered into conflict with Satan and proved His moral right to be both the Redeemer and the King. Your adversary and mine is the one who came to tempt, or to test, Christ. After Christ had fasted for forty days, Satan came to tempt Him, saying, "If thou be the Son of God, command that these stones be made bread."

It is not our purpose in this study to examine the avenues of testing, nor the areas of Christ's life that were tested, but we do want to emphasize His defense against the attack of the evil one. Three times Christ said, "It is written. . . ." He repelled the first test of Satan by referring to Deuteronomy 8:3 and saying to him, literally, "It stands written." And what stood written was unalterable and unchangeable. Christ met the attack of the prince of the powers of the air by drawing the sword of the

Spirit, which is the Word of God: "It stands written, Man shall not live by bread alone, but by every word that proceedeth out of the mouth of God." You will observe that Christ, in each of the three temptations, quoted the book of Deuteronomy. While the book of Leviticus governed the worship of God's people, the book of Deuteronomy controlled their daily walk. When Satan came to divert the Lord Jesus Christ from the path of perfect obedience to the will of God, He quoted the book that governed the walk of God's child, using it as a sword to turn aside the attack of the adversary. After Christ quoted the Scripture in response to the first temptation, that testing was immediately dropped. There was no argument, no rebuttal. So Satan must attack along another avenue.

We read in verse 5 that " the devil taketh him up into the holy city, and setteth him up on a pinnacle of the temple, and said unto him, If thou be the Son of God, cast thyself down, for it stands written. . . ." You will notice that Satan adopted Christ's tactics. He said, in effect, "If you use the Word of God against me, I'll use the Word of God against you." And Satan said, "It stands written, He shall give His angels charge concerning thee: in their hands they shall bear thee up, lest at any time thou dash thy foot against a stone." But again Christ went to Deuteronomy, and He lifted out of the book that governed the walk of God's people a verse which was particularly applicable—Deuteronomy 6:16. He said, "It stands written again, Thou shalt not tempt the Lord thy God." Once again the temptation is dropped without any argument; the Word of God is irrefutable.

Satan then made a third attack. We read in verse 8, "The devil taketh him up into an exceeding high mountain, and sheweth him all the kingdoms of the world, and the glory of them; and saith unto him, All these things will I give thee, if thou wilt fall down and worship me." And once again Christ referred to the book of Deuteronomy: "Thou shalt worship the Lord thy God, and him only shalt thou serve" (6:13). And then the devil left Him. He didn't argue the case; he didn't beg; he didn't plead. He left Him! Why? Because of the efficacy of the sword of the Spirit, which is the Word of God. It was not diplomacy, argument, debate, tact, flattery, nor the offering of a truce that caused Satan to depart. It was Christ's use of the sword of the Spirit, which is the Word of God. The sword did not have to be explained, defended, or demonstrated to Satan. He knew its power, and when he saw the sword drawn, he immediately dropped the issue and turned to something else. And when Christ persisted in meeting every attack with a sword thrust from the Word of God, Satan abandoned the attack and departed.

THE CHRISTIAN'S USE OF THE WORD

Perhaps the Apostle Paul had this experience of Christ in mind when he pictured the child of God clothed in the whole armor of God and using the sword which is the Word of God. Against this sword Satan has no defense. Satan has no armor to protect him against the sword thrust of the authoritative, infallible, inspired Word of God. And when you do battle against Satan with the sword of the Spirit in your hand, he is defenseless. You stand fully clothed, fully equipped, strengthened by God, and Satan stands helpless and defenseless.

Among the several Greek words in the New Testament which are translated "word," there is one which refers to the Word of God in its entirety. We do not hesitate to say that our Bible, in its entirety, is the Word of God. I remember hearing a traveling man talk on one occasion who said that when he arrived in a city he would put his bags in a locker while he went to the telephone to make some contacts with the business people on whom he expected to call. But he said he found a cheaper way to protect his bags than using public lockers that cost him a quarter every time he used one. He said he took a Bible and he put the Bible on top of his bags while he phoned. He had been doing that for years and his bags had never once been disturbed. Now that is using the Bible in its totality to scare away a thief. But Paul is not referring to such a use of the Bible, for Satan does not run when you hold your Bible up. That is not using the Word of God as a sword.

The apostle did not use the word which refers to the Word in its totality; instead he used an interesting and significant word which refers to the Scriptures as composed of individual sayings. It is the Word in its applied sense. It is the Word which we have personally appropriated and experienced. When Paul uses this word he teaches us a very important truth concerning the Word of God as a weapon. Only that portion of the Word which has particular relevance to the temptation at hand may be considered the sword that will defeat the enemy. When Satan came to Christ with a temptation, He used a specific verse that dealt with that specific problem, and He quoted that verse as the answer to the temptation. He took from the Scripture that which was applicable to that particular temptation. You do not necessarily have a sword of the Spirit because you own a leather-bound, gilt-edged copy of the Holy Bible. You have the sword of the Spirit to use against Satan when that which is in the Bible has been transferred to your mind and heart so that when Satan comes you can apply that which you have learned to defeat him in that particular attack. The Word of God that you have appropriated is the sword of the Spirit. Your pastor's sermons are not swords for you. Your sword isn't what you can find in a concordance, or written in your notebook or in the margin of your Bible, but what you have hidden in your heart. Often people feel they are too old to learn. However, this is not true. You can learn! But it takes time and effort. Which is better? To prepare for an attack that you know is bound to come, or to fall when you are attacked because you did not prepare for it by hiding God's Word in your heart? You must study the Word and appropriate the Word, so that you may be able to stand. As a Christian soldier, you can have victory because you know the Word of God, have appropriated it, and know how to use it when you are tempted.

PART
IV

DESIGN FOR MATURITY

COMING TO MATURITY

Hebrews 5:1-14

THE WRITER of the Epistle to the Hebrews presents the Lord Jesus Christ as the preeminent One in the program by which God has revealed Himself to men. In the prologue to this epistle, found in the first three verses, the apostle shows us that Jesus Christ is superior, as a revealer, to every other form and kind of revelation which God has employed. Jesus Christ is superior to the angels, who were instruments of revelation in the Old Testament. Jesus Christ is superior to Moses, through whom the greatest of the Old Testament revelations concerning God were made. Jesus Christ is superior to Joshua, who led the children of Israel into rest in the promised land, for Christ leads into a better rest. Jesus Christ is superior to Aaron as a priest, for His ministry rests on a better covenant. Christ is superior to Aaron inasmuch as Christ ministered in a superior priestly order. To illustrate this, the writer of Hebrews takes his readers back into the book of Genesis and the book of Psalms to Melchisedek. The writer recognizes that if his readers are to follow his arguments they must be able to transfer truth. They must be able to discern what is true concerning the relationship between Melchisedek and Aaron, then transfer that truth to Christ and Aaron, and then deduce the superiority of Christ to Aaron because of the superiority of Melchisedek to Aaron. Christ is superior to Aaron because He is of a priestly order superior to Aaron's.

Before developing this argument in detail, the writer pauses to give an extended exhortation (5:11 to 6:12), for he recognizes that the truth that he is presenting is for those who have approached maturity in Christ. Apart from maturity they will not be able to make a transference of thought to see how Christ is superior to Aaron. It is not our purpose to develop the argument of Hebrews but to show you the contrast between immaturity and maturity, between babyhood and adulthood in the things of Christ. We want to base our study particularly upon Hebrews 5:11-14.

In these four verses we are brought face to face with several important contrasts. We see a contrast between the man who is a babe (v. 13) and those who are of full age (v. 14) and between those who need milk and those who subsist on strong meat (v. 12). These contrasts point up the contrast between childhood and adulthood in the Christian life, between spiritual babyhood and spiritual maturity.

MILK AND MEAT IN DEVELOPMENT

Before we proceed, it is necessary for us to understand what the writer has in mind when he speaks of milk and meat. The difference between milk and meat does not refer to the *area* of truth being considered. We might explain it this way: Some would refer to truths concerning salvation as "milk" doctrine but would refer to truth about the Christian life or prophecy or the second coming of Christ as "meat" doctrine. And they would say if you are interested only in the simple things of salvation, you are existing on milk, but if you have an interest in the deeper life, or in prophecy, or in the coming of the Lord, you have gone beyond milk to meat. According to many, the division between milk and meat is on the basis of the doctrinal areas being considered. Distinction between milk and meat refers not to the area of biblical truth but rather to the depth to which the child of God can go in any area of biblical truth. There are milk truths in the doctrine of salvation, and there are meat truths in the same doctrine. There are milk doctrines concerning future things; there are also meat doctrines concerning future things. The difference, then, is not the *area* of truth to which one gives his attention but the *depth* in that truth to which one can go. Disabuse your minds, then, of the fallacy that there are certain doctrines that, by themselves, belong to babyhood, and other doctrines that are reserved for those who are mature. The difference is in depth, not in breadth.

In physical life we expect a process of maturing. A newborn babe is just that—a newborn babe. He cannot be anything but that at that stage of his development. Normally, a newborn babe will progress from infancy to childhood to adolescence and then on to adulthood. This process follows a predictable pattern of development. An infant is marked by his lack of knowledge. Because of this lack of knowledge, in early life he soon begins to ask why. An infant is characterized by a dependence upon his parents. He looks to his parents for food, shelter, clothing, guidance, protection, everything he needs. The child is characterized by a lack of judgment. One of the great problems we face today is that our young people who have not come to maturity, physically or emotionally, are being pushed into situations where they are called upon to make mature judgments before they have the capacity to make those judgments. Some of the great sociological problems facing our country today arise because parents push their children, before they are mature, into social situations which require maturity of judgment and emotions. Our young people are suffering, and society is suffering, because it has not been recognized that emotional maturity comes only with the passage of time.

In normal physical development, we see progress from birth to infancy to childhood to adolescence and then on to adulthood. In physical growth, it is impossible for a child to be mature apart from the passage of time. But spiritual maturity may follow a slow or an accelerated time pattern. Physically, a child is bound by time in coming to maturity. The spiritual child need not be so bound by the passage of time although, as we shall see, time is a factor.

SPIRITUAL INFANCY

In considering the problem of maturity in this passage, we would like to point out, first of all, the three characterizations of babyhood that the apostle mentions. In verse 11 the writer says, "Concerning Melchisedek, we have many things to say and hard to be uttered, seeing ye are dull of hearing." The last portion of

that verse presents the first characterization of spiritual babyhood—dullness of hearing. We need to remind ourselves of the
truth presented in I Corinthians 2, where Paul states that the
natural man cannot receive any divine truth. Why is it impossible for him to understand and appropriate anything of divine
revelation? Because he is marked by a certain incapacity. He has
no capacity whatsoever to receive spiritual truths. But the apostle says that God has made known to us the things which the
natural eye, and ear, and mind, cannot appropriate or understand,
and those truths may be received as the Spirit of God teaches
the child of God the deep things of God. When a sinner believes
on Christ and is born again, he is given a new capacity—a capacity to *receive* the revelation which God has made of Himself,
to *understand* that revelation, and to *assimilate* that revelation
and make it his own truth.

How often you have heard someone say as the Word of God
was taught, "Oh, I see it now!" That child of God was witness-
ing to the work of the Spirit of God who was illuminating divine
truth for him. The apostle tells us, in I Corinthians 2:15, that
the spiritual man, that is, the man in whose life the Holy Spirit
is unhindered as a teacher, has the capacity to understand all
things. The spiritual man discerns, or understands, all things
because he has the mind of Christ. In Hebrews 5:11 the apostle
says that one of the first characterizations of spiritual immaturity,
or babyhood, is inability to receive the deep things of God. This
inability cannot be blamed on lack of clarity in the proclamation of the Word of God nor on an illogical presentation by the
teacher. For a newborn child of God this is natural, normal, and
to be expected. You do not expect a man to receive Christ as
his personal Saviour and then to understand immediately all of
the ramifications of election and predestination. There are some
things that a newborn baby is not yet ready to understand. He
needs to grow in ability to perceive the meaning of Scripture
and in understanding its truths.

When this condition exists in a newborn child of God, it is
easily understood. But, in I Corinthians 3, the Apostle Paul said
he was speaking to the Corinthian believers "as unto babes in
Christ." Here the case was reprehensible, because the failure of

these Corinthians to grow was due to their carnality. Carnality may produce in the child of God some of the same characteristics of babyhood that we see in a newborn child of God. If you have been saved but find it difficult to understand the Word of God and to accept its truths, then you must face the fact that you are in a state of spiritual babyhood. If, on the other hand, the Word of God is tedious to you, and you have no appetite for it, then you may well question whether you are carnal.

The second characteristic of babyhood is given in verse 12: "When for the time ye ought to be teachers, *ye have need* that one teach you again which be the first principles of the oracles of God." The first sign they were babies was their lack of knowledge. Second, their babyhood manifested itself in their dependence upon someone else to teach them spiritual truths. You see, the Spirit of God has been given to every child of God. The indwelling Spirit has come to assume, among other ministries, the office of teacher. The Holy Spirit in the child of God meets his need to understand divine revelation and to appropriate divine truth. But if the child of God does not depend upon the teaching ministry of the Holy Spirit of God and cannot, apart from dependence upon some other teacher, discover the truths of Scripture, then he is manifesting immaturity, or babyhood, in Christ. The fact that the Christians to whom Paul wrote needed to be taught emphasized their immaturity. It would be perfectly normal, and to be anticipated, that a newborn child of God would depend upon someone to nurture him in the truths of Scripture, just as it is natural for the newborn baby to depend upon another for his nourishment. That is why the New Testament gives abundant instruction concerning those who are pastors, or teachers, of the Word of God. They are to feed the babes. That was the commission given to Peter, "Feed my lambs . . . feed my sheep." The Word of God anticipates that need. But if one has been in the family of God for a long period of time and still must depend wholly upon someone else, and cannot, through his own study of the Word, feed his own soul, that one, regardless of how long he has been a believer, is manifesting signs of spiritual babyhood.

The third characteristic of spiritual babyhood is given in verse

13: "Every one that useth milk is unskilful in the word of right-eousness." Every one who can take only the milk level of divine truth is a babe. What does the apostle mean when he says "un-skilful"? Such people lack judgment. They lack the ability to see how a given passage of Scripture applies to a given situation, how their conduct can be guided in the light of the Word of God. If you must continually come to someone and ask if it is right for a believer to do this or that, and if you are unable to take the principles of the Word of God and determine for yourself what is right and what is wrong for a child of God, you are showing, by your lack of judgment, that you are a babe.

Summing up, this passage shows that the person in spiritual babyhood lacks the ability to stand alone, and he lacks judgment, and discernment.

It must be noted that the people addressed in Hebrews 5 were not babes because they were newborn believers. They had been Christians for some time; therefore their case is reprehensible. They bore a responsibility for their spiritual condition. First of all, the apostle says, in verse 12, "When for the time ye ought to be teachers, ye have need. . . ." I want to emphasize here the phrase "for the time." This phrase might be translatd this way: "Considering the time that has elapsed, ye ought to be teachers, but ye have need that one teach you again what be the first prin-ciples of the oracles of God [the divine revelation]." The apostle is emphasizing that these men had been saved for a sufficient length of time, and had heard enough of the Word of God to be able to teach instead of being taught. They should have been able to stand independently instead of depending upon someone else. Merely sitting under the ministry of the Word of God will not bring one to maturity, the hearer must appropriate the truth that he has been hearing. Don't get the idea that because you have been under sound teaching for a long period of time that you can be classified as a mature believer.

In the second place, the apostle shows that these who are in babyhood are to be held chargeable because their lives are marked by retrogression. They needed someone to teach them again the first principles of the oracles of God. Now notice, they were told, "Ye . . . are become such as have need of milk, and not of strong meat." In other words, you have now become something which you were not before. The people addressed had been born into God's family; they had begun to grow to maturity; they had understood and appropriated divine truth. But what had happened? They had retrogressed. Previously these believers had withdrawn from apostate, corrupt Judaism. They had taken their stand with believers in the Lord Jesus Christ. Then when they were persecuted for Christ's sake, they were tempted to go back and fellowship with Judaism again, still believing that Christ died to save them, but hoping to remove the stigma of the cross by fellowship with unbelievers in the temple. This the apostle classifies as retrogression. Dare we say that these who had grown to maturity and then reverted to babyhood had become spiritually senile?

SPIRITUAL MATURITY

In these same verses (Heb. 5:12-14), the apostle gives three characteristics of maturity. These three answer to the three deficiencies that characterized their babyhood state.

First of all, Paul says, "for the time (considering the time that has elapsed) ye ought to be teachers." The apostle is coupling knowledge with maturity. The apostle was saying, in other words, "By now you should have appropriated and assimilated sufficient truth so that you can impart that truth to others." The first sign of maturity, then, is knowledge. This knowledge is not measured by the number of sermons one has heard, the number of notes one has taken, the number of tapes of sermons one has filed away, but by the amount of truth one has appropriated so that he can teach it to someone else. One does not really know a fact until he can state that fact to someone else. Such knowledge and ability to share it answers to the deficiency described as dullness of hearing.

The second characterization of a mature man is given to us in verse 14, "Strong meat belongeth to them that are of full age [that is, those who are mature], even those who by reason of use have their senses exercised to discern both good and evil." To paraphrase the thought, the apostle is saying that the mature man is the man who can *put into use* the truth that he knows.

The mature man, instead of being dependent like a child is dependent upon his parents, is independent when it comes to the things of God. He knows how to use the Word; he is skillful in the use of the Word. When a decision confronts him, he is able to go to the Word of God and discern the will of God and the purpose of God as the truth of Scripture is applied to that problem which he faces. And the apostle says that the mature man is one who not only has the ability to teach but is able to use the Word of God effectively to settle his own problems and difficulties, and to discover the will of God for himself. This ability answers to the dependence which marks those who are in spiritual babyhood.

The third characterization of the mature man is found in the last part of verse 14: "Who by reason of use [of the Scripture] have their senses exercised to discern both good and evil." The mature man is able to judge, to discern what is right and what is wrong in his Christian experience. He does not have to run to someone he respects and say, "Do you think it is all right for me to do this?" No! Because he knows the Word and can apply the Word to that situation, he knows what is right and wrong for him as a believer, that is, he is able to discern both good and evil. This ability to discern is in direct contrast to the lack of judgment which marks those who are babes.

Now let us contrast the spiritual babe and the mature man. First, the babe is characterized by his lack of knowledge, and the mature man is characterized by his full and complete knowledge so that he can impart knowledge to someone else. Second, the babe is marked by his dependence upon someone else, and the mature man is marked by his independence. Of course, it goes without saying that the mature man is not independent of the teaching ministry of the Holy Spirit. But the mature man does not have to depend on someone else, like a child depends on a parent, for his knowledge or his spiritual discernment. Third, the baby is marked by his lack of judgment, and the mature man is marked by his judgment. He is able to discern both good and evil because of his knowledge of the Word of God. Thus the apostle, in a very practical and simple way, has put three tests before us by which you and I may determine which of two stages of spiritual development we fit into—maturity or immaturity. Is your life characterized by knowledge or lack of knowledge? Is your life characterized by independence or by dependence? Is your life characterized by ability to use the Word of God or by complete inability to apply the principles and precepts of Scripture to your daily conduct? As you and I evaluate our lives in the light of these questions, we can determine whether we fit into the category of a spiritual babe or into the category of one who is maturing in his spiritual experience.

CHAPTER

32

STEPS TO MATURITY

Hebrews 6:1-12

AFTER PRESENTING A CONTRAST between the mature Christian and the immature Christian (Heb. 5:11-14), the apostle proceeds to give instructions that will lead a man out of babyhood into spiritual maturity (Heb. 6:1-12). Notice, first of all, that the apostle, in writing to these believers, placed upon them a responsibility to progress in the Christian life. While no man comes to maturity apart from the grace of God, apart from the operation of the Holy Spirit, responsibility for growth is placed upon believers. As we have discovered in previous studies, unless the believer presents himself as a living sacrifice, unless the believer presents his members as instruments unto holiness and righteousness unto God he will not progress toward maturity. The apostle is emphasizing in Hebrews 6 the human side of going on to maturity. God places responsibility upon His child to grow out of infancy to maturity. Because of results of the fall and the effects of sin, it often is true that because of birth defects some people will never come to adulthood, or maturity. But in the family of God there are no birth defects, no congenital deformities, to prevent those born of God from coming to maturity. Everyone born into the family of God is born with the capacity to progress out of infancy into maturity in Christ. The apostle recognized that, and to those who were in danger of returning to the old things in order to escape persecution, he gave an exhortation reminding them that God had placed a responsibility upon them to go on to maturity.

PROGRESSION ESSENTIAL

When the apostle used the word that is translated "perfection" in our English text, he was not speaking about sinless perfection in the sense of an inability to sin. Rather, the word *perfection* means "maturity," or "adulthood." In these verses the apostle gave several clues to enable the child of God to progress out of infancy to maturity. The first is related to the area of knowledge. The apostle exhorted those to whom he wrote to go on to perfection. How? By "leaving the principles of the doctrine of Christ." Now what does the apostle mean? The phrase is a rather difficult one to translate. It may be paraphrased this way, "Leave the elementary teaching concerning the doctrines upon which your life has been based." The apostle is telling them to leave the milk. The first principles, or the elementary doctrines, were doctrines that Christianity had in common with Judaism. There were certain basic principles that those Jews held because they were trained in the Old Testament. But if they continued only in those things that Judaism had in common with Christianity, they would never move on to maturity.

Of the elementary principles mentioned by the apostle, the first is repentance from dead works. Because these people had accepted Christ, they had repudiated animal sacrifices as having any value before God. They had learned the fact that animal sacrifices are meaningless before God. But they had to go beyond this milk truth if they were to go on to maturity.

"Faith toward God" is also in the realm of elementary truth. We recognize that a man is related to God by faith, but if he stops after he has grasped that simple principle, he will never go on to a meat diet of the Word.

These believers were also to leave the "doctrine of baptisms," or of washings (the ceremonial cleansings that rendered something acceptable to God) and the "laying on of hands," which had in view the Jewish ordinances of identification. Other "milk" truths included "the resurrection of the dead, and of eternal judgment" as taught in the Old Testament.

We might sum up what the apostle said in this way: "If you, in your Christian experience, dwell only on those elementary teachings that you have heard from childhood out of the Old Testament, you will never progress out of babyhood." They had come to the place where they should have left those basic principles to go on to the meat of the Word.

KNOWLEDGE OF THE TRUTH

In our previous study we contrasted milk and meat. We pointed out that we cannot designate some doctrines as milk doctrines and other doctrines as meat doctrines. The difference between milk and meat is not in the area of divine truth, but in the depth of divine truth to which one can go. You might conclude that the doctrines of salvation are milk, and doctrines of prophecy are meat. That is a false classification, because there are unplumbed depths in the doctrines of salvation that no one has yet understood because man cannot go that deep into the mind and heart of God. Salvation has its milk and its meat. Every other area of doctine has both its milk and its meat.

When the apostle says that believers must go on and leave the elementary principles of the doctrine of Christ, he is indicating that maturity is inseparably united to knowledge of divine truth. It is impossible for a man to be mature who does not know the truth of the Scriptures. Apart from a knowledge of the Word, one will remain in spiritual babyhood, no matter how long he has been saved.

The Apostle Paul emphasized the importance of knowledge of the word of God in Romans 10:17, where he said, "Faith cometh by hearing, and hearing by the word of God." A man cannot believe something of which he is ignorant. A man has to have some fact to believe. The Word of God gives us facts to accept, and when we believe, we accept the facts of the Word of God because God reveals them as divine truth. Thus faith is related to knowledge. Paul, writing in II Timothy 4:1-2, gives a charge to a young pastor, "I charge thee therefore before God, . . . preach the word." Why was Timothy charged to preach the Word? Because the Word would bring these believers out of infancy to maturity in their Christian experience. Paul says, "Preach the word; be instant in season, out of season [always in the Word]; reprove, rebuke, exhort [that is, reprove with the

Word, rebuke with the Word, exhort with the Word] with all longsuffering and doctrine. For the time will come when they will not endure sound doctrine; but after their own lusts shall they heap to themselves teachers, having itching ears." And Paul warns Timothy that when he begins to set the table, there will be some who will come and look at the beefsteak that is put there, and will ask, "Where is my milk?" They don't want the meat of the Word. Nevertheless, Timothy is to keep on preaching the Word, rebuking with the Word, exhorting with the Word, because it is the Word that will bring men to maturity. It is our earnest conviction that apart from being steeped in the Word of God, a person cannot go on to maturity in the Christian life. When a Christian so saturates himself with the Word that a pertinent verse of Scripture flashes into his mind in any situation, he is in the process of growing out of infancy into maturity. Now, we do not deny that putting yourself under the teaching of the Word of God in a church and Sunday school where the Word of God is taught is an aid to maturity. But that is not the key to maturity. The key is to study the Word yourself, to digest it, to assimilate it for yourself. Then it becomes your own. Many of the best sermon-listeners and sermon-tasters you ever knew are still spiritual babies. It isn't until we get into the Scriptures ourselves, and let the Scriptures get into us that we get into the meat stage of spiritual development. If you would come to maturity in the things of Christ, you must follow some plan of systematic Bible study. The apostle's first clue to progress from spiritual babyhood to spiritual maturity is that we must leave the elementary principles of the doctrine of Christ and go into the depths of divine truth.

GOOD WORKS

In verses 9 and 10 the apostle gave a second clue to spiritual progress when he said, "Beloved, we are persuaded better things of you, and things that accompany salvation, though we thus speak. For God is not unrighteous to forget your work and labour of love, which ye have shewed toward his name, in that ye have ministered to the saints, and do minister." The apostle indicated that the good works done in the name of the Lord Jesus

Christ gave evidence that these people were saved people. The good works that believers do are not only evidences of salvation but are a means of bringing a person toward maturity. If one would go on to maturity, the Word which he has taken in must be worked out in practical living. An illustration of this is found in I John 3:17, where the Apostle John poses this question: If a Christian sees his brother in need and shuts up his bowels of compassion against helping him, how is the love of God perfected in him? John says that if you can see a brother in material need and you have the means to help him but don't help him, then the love of God is not perfected in you. You have not come to maturity in love. The Word of God received by the child of God must be translated into action. There must be an outworking of the inwrought Word. That is what the apostle has in mind when he refers, in Hebrews 6:10, to the "labour of love" which those believers showed toward Christ's name in ministering to the saints. When a child of God who has been well taught in the Word of God sees a need and responds to that need, he is manifesting growth, he is developing in maturity.

On the other hand, to see a need and not respond to it is an evidence of immaturity. For instance, if my young daughter walks through the den in our house and sees a newspaper carelessly thrown in the middle of the floor and walks over it instead of picking it up, she is showing immaturity. I wouldn't expect my wife to manifest such immaturity. If one of my daughters walks past an unmade bed without any response to that unmade bed, it is a sign of immaturity. But if she stops and makes up that bed, I may well conclude that she is making some progress toward maturity. You see, a response to a need manifests one's degree of maturity.

Maturity is also related to one's dependence or independence. If a mother has to say to a daughter, "Will you please clean up that mess?" the daughter is immature. But if, without any prompting from without, she begins to clean up the mess, this is a sign of development. Some Christians reveal that they are babes because they cannot use the Word by themselves. They have to be prompted in every action. Others can use the Word without any promptings from without. Christians will begin to make progress toward maturity as they do good to all the saints. Being able to apply the Word by responding to a need is one means of coming to maturity.

PATIENCE

In verses 11 and 12 we find another clue to spiritual maturity given by the apostle: "We desire that every one of you do shew the same diligence to the full assurance of hope unto the end: that ye be not slothful [or lazy], but followers of them who through faith and patience inherit the promises." What these two verses imply is that there can be no maturity apart from a passage of time. The apostle referred to the time element in verse 12 of chapter 5 when he said, "Ye ought to be teachers, [but] ye have need that one teach you again." In coming to maturity we need patience. For instance, in bringing up our children, we have no right to expect them to act beyond their years. What we expect of a seventeen-year-old will be quite different from what we expect from a nine-year-old, because each is in a different stage of development. Thus the apostle emphasizes the need of patience. We must not be indifferent or lazy concerning our growth, but we must be followers of them who through faith and patience inherit the promises. The promise we seek to have fulfilled in our lives is maturity, conformity to Christ. We will not be made like Him overnight. This life, this growth, this process demands constant cultivation day after day, week after week, year after year. There is no end to the process of maturing in spiritual things. The one who has been a believer fifty years has before him yet unpossessed land, just as the one who has been a believer for five years, or five months, has before him unpossessed land. What the apostle is pointing out is that we never can sit back in complacency and self-satisfaction and say, "I have arrived. I am mature." We must beware of becoming slothful. We need patience and diligence as we aim for constant growth and development in our lives.

THE DANGER OF FAILURE

This chapter contains a passage which, perhaps more than any other passage in the New Testament, has perplexed believers.

The author writes, "It is impossible for those who were once en-lightened, and have tasted of the heavenly gift, and were made partakers of the Holy Ghost, and have tasted the good word of God, and the powers of the world to come, if they shall fall away, to renew them again unto repentance; seeing they crucify to themselves the Son of God afresh, and put him to an open shame." Is the apostle teaching that if a man has been saved and then commits a sin he loses his salvation and can never be saved again? God forbid! That denies the whole divine revelation. What is the apostle saying? These verses which contain the most sober warning to the child of God found anywhere in the Word of God, have to do with the danger of not progressing to ma-turity. The apostle is showing us, from the divine viewpoint, how serious it is for a man not to heed the exhortation, "Let us go on unto perfection." How serious it is for a man to continue as a milk-fed baby when he should be going on to maturity! God de-sires not only to save us but also to bring us to the position of adult sons in His family. It is a most serious thing not to fulfil God's purposes for us, and for this reason the apostle warns those who have been saved but who have not progressed to maturity or are retrogressing. He says, to summarize his argument, it is impossible to erase the record of failure and immaturity by losing our salvation and being saved all over again. If we could lose our salvation, being saved a second time would erase all previous failure. But this we cannot do. Suppose I live my Christian life for twenty-five years as a spiritual babe—in slothfulness, indiffer-ence, carelessness—on a milk diet. At the end of that time I realize that my record is one of prolonged infancy, and I want to erase that record. How can I do it? If I could lose my salva-tion and then get saved over again, all that record of failure and continued infancy would be blotted out. That would be a con-venient way to eliminate it, wouldn't it? The apostle says that such is impossible. A person, by falling away, cannot erase the record of his failure. His record must stand, and he must face it at the judgment seat of Christ. We must exercise care over our spiritual diet, over our spiritual growth, for it is impossible, by any means, to remove the record of failure. God has made us responsible for growth, and at the judgment seat of Christ we will be examined in reference to our growth.

The last words that Peter penned to those who would read his epistles were the words, "Grow in grace, and in the knowledge of our Lord and Saviour, Jesus Christ." Grow in grace! That is your responsibility, child of God. The means are provided, but you will never grow unless you diligently appropriate what God has provided. Are you growing? Are you any stronger today than you were yesterday? Do you know more of your Lord today than you knew yesterday? If not, you need to heed these words: "Let us . . . go on to maturity."

SCRIPTURE INDEX